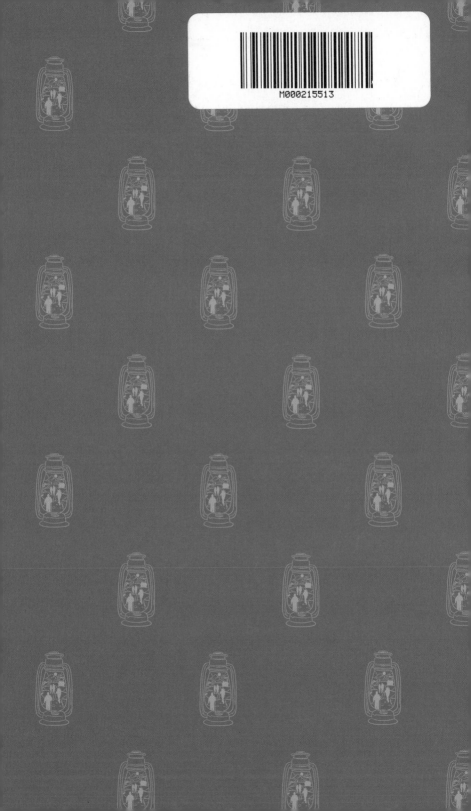

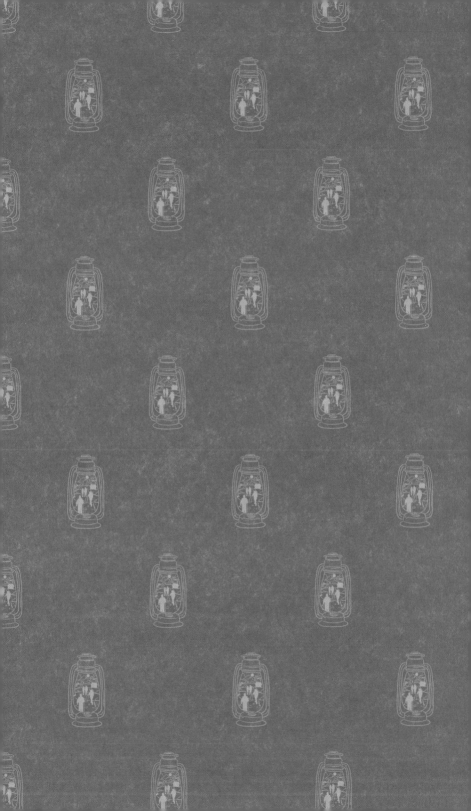

PRAISE FOR

# PATHFINDERS

"Few people have bridged the gap between spreadsheet and the real world like JL Collins—this book is full of real stories from real people seeking the greatest gift money can provide: independence."

**—Morgan Housel,**
**Author of *Same as Ever* and the**
**#1 international bestseller *The Psychology of Money***

"Most people believe that achieving FIRE is impossible. JL Collins' brilliant new book proves otherwise. It's packed with stories of ordinary people who mastered their finances and now live extraordinary lives, and proves that reaching FIRE is achievable no matter your current circumstances. It's also filled with the wit and wisdom JL has become famous for. Highly recommended."

**—Brian Feroldi,**
**Author of *Why Does the Stock Market Go Up?***

"*Pathfinders* proves that the path to financial independence is simple, achievable, and doesn't require a degree in finance … These stories will make you feel less alone in your struggles and find solace in knowing that no matter how bad your situation is, there is a way out."

**—Kristy Shen and Bryce Leung,**
**Authors of *Quit Like a Millionaire***

"Prepared to be inspired, motivated, and humbled by the array of successes discussed in this must-read."

**—Scott Trench,**
**CEO + President, BiggerPockets**

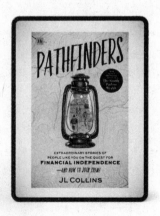

# PATHFINDERS

EXTRAORDINARY STORIES OF
PEOPLE LIKE YOU ON THE QUEST FOR
**FINANCIAL INDEPENDENCE**
*—AND HOW TO JOIN THEM*

## JL COLLINS

Harriman
House

HARRIMAN HOUSE LTD
3 Viceroy Court
Bedford Road
Petersfield
Hampshire
GU32 3LJ
GREAT BRITAIN
Tel: +44 (0)1730 233870

Email: enquiries@harriman-house.com
Website: harriman.house

First published in 2023.
Copyright © JL Collins

The right of JL Collins to be identified as the Author has been asserted in accordance with the Copyright, Design and Patents Act 1988.

Hardback ISBN: 978-1-80409-000-8
Paperback ISBN: 978-1-80409-001-5
eBook ISBN: 978-1-80409-002-2

British Library Cataloguing in Publication Data
A CIP catalogue record for this book can be obtained from the British Library.

Icon illustrations by Nikolett Meresz. Lantern illustration by Tata Wijana.

*To those whose inspiring stories appear in these pages, and to all the others who have found and are following* The Simple Path to Wealth.

*To the little girl who wouldn't listen, forcing me to write this all down.*

*And to my wife, Jane, who assured me through the years that little girl was absorbing more than I knew. She was right.*

# CONTENTS

# FOREWORD

## BY HASAN MINHAJ

**G**ROWING UP, FINANCIAL literacy is something we never discussed as a family.

If you talk about money, you're labeled as being obsessed with it, or you're blaming a loved one for not having it. Money was always too scary, too touchy, and too real to talk about in our household. Especially the stock market. It was framed as something that only Wall Street bigwigs could figure out, or it was an outright rigged system that turned the layman into a sucker. So I stayed away from it. I spent years in school learning about Mesopotamia and mitosis, but didn't know the difference between a W-2 and a W-9. I figured I'd stack my bread like a drug dealer and tuck it away in a mattress. That would be my protection.

But it wasn't. It was a defense mechanism to avoid dealing with the painful truth of adulthood: You need money to take care of yourself, your loved ones, and ensure a financially stable future.

Money doesn't solve all your problems, but it sure as hell solves your money problems.

When I first heard about JL Collins' new book, I knew I had to read it. I'd been a long-time fan of his first book, *The Simple Path to Wealth*. In fact, it was *The Simple Path* and his savage Google Talk that helped start my FI journey. (By "savage" I mean JL had the guts to tell Google employees to not hold individual Google stock while he was speaking at Google. In that moment, I knew that either JL was the truth, or he was completely out of his mind.)

After quickly applying these principles I started being all about that VTSAX life and forgetting the rest. That's not to say there wasn't uncertainty, doubt, or days where my VTSAX position tanked. But I was unbothered because I had bought into the "set it and forget it" long-hold strategy. I was holding my financial plank for 30 years. I was committed to my path.

And that's exactly what *Pathfinders* is. A collection of **real** stories of people on their path to financial independence. After reading *Pathfinders* I realized something: this book is not just about investing. It's about so much more. Sure it's about empowerment. Of course it's about taking control of your financial future. **But most importantly, it's a set of principles to help you manage the financial fear and uncertainty of adult life.**

And that's why I'm so excited to write this foreword. Because, as someone who ran away from learning about money, I know how daunting it can be to navigate the world of investing. But JL and the *Pathfinders* contributors make it feel real, practical, and accessible. The Path may be bumpy, but rest assured there are many on it with you. And the best feeling of all? Your future self won't regret you making these decisions now. Good luck with your Path. I'm still on mine.

HASAN MINHAJ
*New York, 2023*

# PREFACE

## A MAP OF THE BOOK

### WHY

Ever since *The Simple Path to Wealth (SPW)* was published in 2016, readers have reached out to me with stories of how they have taken the principles in the book and applied them to their unique situations. These tales from the road are endlessly fascinating and highly instructive. They provide not only ideas and guidance as to how following The Path can be done, but proof—given the extraordinarily wide swath of people from all over the world who have done it—it can also be done by *you*. For years I have wanted to pull together and share these stories as a sequel to *SPW*, and now you hold it in your hands (or your earbuds).

### WHO

*Pathfinders* is for anyone who wants to achieve financial

independence (FI), or at least consider the possibility. Becoming FI is the process of buying your freedom—the freedom to own your life and spend your time as you choose. Whether you are just starting to consider this as an option, are already on The Path and interested in what your fellow travelers have to say, or are fully FI and looking back on your journey with an interest in how it is unfolding for others, this book is for you.

# WHAT

In these pages are around a hundred of the most compelling of these tales from people of all imaginable backgrounds, at all stages of life and wealth, and from all over the world. I have found them enlightening, inspiring, entertaining, and educational. Perhaps you will too.

You'll also find some of my thoughts in the introductions to each section of the book, along with a transcribed interview between me and my daughter—the "little girl who wouldn't listen" and thus inspired (forced?) me to first articulate, define, and finally to write *The Simple Path to Wealth*.

But the heart of the book is the collection of these real-life stories from people just like you who have decided to follow The Simple Path—the powerful, simple, low-cost, low-risk, tried-and-tested route to financial freedom that I slowly pieced together over my own decades of wandering in the wilderness.

If you have read *The Simple Path to Wealth* you'll likely enjoy reading how these travelers have applied its principles. But it isn't necessary to have read *SPW* in order to enjoy and benefit from this one. It is fine to read *Pathfinders* first and then pick up *SPW* if you feel inspired to do so.

Regardless of the order in which you read them, The Path itself is simple, robust, and has worked for tens of thousands of people around the world at every level of income. It will work for you, if you choose to walk it.

## HOW

Where *The Simple Path to Wealth* lays out this approach to achieving financial independence, *Pathfinders* shows you how others are following it. The "how" of their stories can help guide you if:

- you've heard of FI but wonder if it is too good to be true
- you're wondering if reaching FI is possible for normal people with average resources (spoiler alert: It is. Even with less-than-average resources)
- you're already on The Path but struggling a bit
- you're on The Path and are wondering if there are other approaches or techniques to consider
- you're on The Path and looking for ways to make it more applicable to your unique situation
- you're just curious about this whole business of becoming FI
- you're wondering what it takes, and if it is worth the effort
- you're wondering just how powerful this Path really is
- you're almost there and are wondering what crossing the finish line looks and feels like.

## PURSUIT

Maybe you've never really thought about FI at all but are ready to be more intentional about your path in life.

Perhaps you are looking for a better work/life balance. Or you might be considering the possibility of a life change: a new career, living in a new part of the world, travel, or simply a different path than the one you've been walking.

FI unlocks all these options and more. But here, as these stories show, is the coolest thing: So does its pursuit.

From the moment you step on The Simple Path you are a bit stronger, a bit freer, and able to be a bit bolder in the choices you make. The further along you go, the more pronounced those advantages become.

Sure, you might give up some material things to start buying your freedom, but this is not about donning a hair shirt and being miserable for a decade, so that you can sit around in a hair shirt without a job for a few more decades after that.

This is about creating a rich, free life. It is about opening up a whole new world of options and becoming a more robust and independent you.

## USE

This book is organized by theme, in a logical order—starting with getting our final destination in view, then moving through the steps it takes to get there and dealing with the obstacles you might encounter along the way.

You can comfortably read it from cover to cover. But you don't have to. You can just as easily dip in and out as the spirit moves you. As you'll see, many of these stories could sit in multiple parts of the book, and each can stand alone.

By opening this book you are stepping into a kind of wayside tavern set in some exotic locale along The Simple Path to Wealth. A place where travelers from all over the world and of every level of experience are pausing for refreshment on their quest for financial independence. The fire is roaring, the drinks are flowing, and there is the intoxicating aroma of something mouth-watering simmering in the huge cast-iron pot resting over the flames.

At each table small groups of pathfinders are laughing, crying, and sharing their tales…

- of struggles overcome and the rewards that followed
- of enterprising solutions to unexpected problems
- of sacrifices made and the kindness of strangers
- of the amazing places a few simple steps can take you
- of unexpected adventures and friendships.

They are waving you over to join them. You are free to sit wherever you choose and move on to the next table as you please. It is all waiting for you just over the page. Enjoy the journey!

JL COLLINS

# SOME KEY TERMS

Technical terms are usually explained or easily inferred by context, but if you're dipping in and out and new to FI you might find this brief glossary useful.

## THE SIMPLE PATH

Spend less than you earn. Avoid debt. Invest the difference in broad-based, low-cost index funds. Hold them forever. The result will be financial independence and the real, permanent freedom it brings.

## 4% RULE

This is a concept developed in the 1990s. Basically it says that from a portfolio of at least 50% stocks and the balance in bonds, you can withdraw 4% per year, adjusting for inflation each year. The research indicates that by doing so your money will last at least 30 years 96% of the time. Most times, it will last much longer and in fact grow much larger than your original stake.

Of course, no one should set a 4% withdrawal rate and forget it. You'll want to monitor it and adjust to what is happening in the real world. Not just to avoid running out of money, but to be able to fully enjoy your money as it grows.

Lots of ink has been spilt debating whether 4% is the right number. Some say, "Too high!" Some say, "Too low!" I say it is a terrible "rule" but a great guideline.

## FINANCIAL INDEPENDENCE (FI)

FI is when your money makes enough money to fund your lifestyle forever.

Here's the formula using the 4% Rule: Net worth × 4% = annual spending. Also: 25× annual spending = net worth required.

Example: You need/want $40,000 to spend each year.

- $1,000,000 × 4% = $40,000.
- $40,000 × 25 = $1,000,000.

## FIRE

Financially Independent Retire Early.

## RETIRE

This term generates a surprising amount of angst in the FIRE community, at least among its detractors. Most people who achieve FI, quit their job, and "retire," typically go on to do interesting and productive things. This is kind of the point. Often these activities earn them money.

For some reason this draws the ire of those who have been dubbed "The Internet Retirement Police" and who loudly complain that if you are earning money you are not "retired."

Who cares?

FI is about having options. Retirement, however you define it, is just one of those.

## LEAN FIRE

The money your money earns is enough to fund a very simple lifestyle. Often more than enough, given you will probably earn at least some money in your "retirement"—and especially useful in escaping a soul-crushing job situation.

## FAT FIRE

The money your money earns is enough to fund a very lavish lifestyle.

## COAST FIRE

The money your money earns is enough to reach FIRE at a point in the future without the addition of new investment cash. This is the power of compounding at work.

By calculating this future date and matching it to the time you want to retire, you can stop saving and begin spending all of your current income. Your already invested money will take you to FI by itself.

## VTSAX

The Vanguard Total Stock Market Index Fund. This is an example of a low-cost, broad-based total stock market index fund, and it is the one I personally hold. With it you own a piece of virtually every publicly traded company in the United States, ~4,000 stocks.

Equally, you can hold a low-cost, broad-based total stock market index fund from investment firms other than Vanguard.

## VTI

This is the ETF (exchange-traded fund) version of VTSAX. They both hold the same portfolio and you can use either. There are some differences, but none that matter to us.

## VFIAX AND VOO

These are Vanguard's S&P 500 Index Fund and ETF. These own and track the 500 largest publicly traded companies in the United States. While I slightly prefer the broader total stock market options above, these are fine choices as well. As are the equivalents from other investment firms.

## 401(K)*

A personal retirement savings account offered by many US employers with certain tax advantages.

## 403(B)*

Same as a 401(k) but offered by nonprofit and government employers.

## IRA*

An Individual Retirement Account available in the US. You contribute pre-tax dollars which provides a current tax deduction. Once in the IRA, this money grows tax-free. Upon reaching a certain age, you can withdraw the money penalty free. These withdrawals are then taxed as ordinary income.

## ROTH IRA*

An Individual Retirement Account available in the US. You contribute after-tax dollars, so there is no current tax deduction. Once in the Roth IRA, this money grows tax-free. Upon reaching a certain age, you can withdraw the money penalty free. These withdrawals are also tax-free.

*There are lots of regulations, such as contribution and income thresholds, that can apply to these. They are covered in more depth in *The Simple Path to Wealth*. Similar types of accounts are also available in many other countries.

# INTRODUCTION

## WALKING
## THE SIMPLE PATH
## TO WEALTH

## WELCOME, TRAVELER!

**C**OME ON IN out of the cold and sleet, pull up a chair here by the fire and let's have a chat—you, me, and a hundred other people who have come this way before and who will share something here of their journeys on The Simple Path to Wealth.

That, of course, is the title of my first book and perhaps you are here because you've read it. *Pathfinders* is a sequel of sorts after all.

Or maybe you have just picked up *Pathfinders* and are now wondering if you should go out and read *The Simple Path to Wealth* (*SPW*) first. No need. For now, just enjoy these tales. Then, if they resonate, there will be plenty of time to read *SPW*.

Either way, my hope is that when we are done with this chat

you will go out and embark (or continue) on your own journey to a rich, free life. What we around here call The Simple Path.

## ORIGIN STORY

These days my now-adult daughter likes to tease me.

"You know, Dad," she'll say, "if I had listened to you when I was a child there would be no jlcollinsnh.com blog, no Chautauqua retreats, no books, no interviews. No one would be calling you 'The Godfather of FI.' There would be no international following."

She is right, of course. This has all grown out of my efforts to persuade her that money is important and learning how to master it would make her life easier, freer, and filled with more options.

We all want our kids to have a better life than ours. We want them to benefit from the hard lessons we learned, to help them avoid the traps and blind alleys into which we blundered.

But, in my eagerness, I pushed these concepts of investing and financial freedom too hard and too early. I managed to turn her off to all things financial as a result. Who knew a four-year-old wouldn't want to go through *The Wall Street Journal* with you?

I kept trying, of course, and my wife would tell me she was absorbing more than she was willing to let on (which turned out to be true). But to me it felt like I was pouring it all into a black hole.

When my daughter started college, it occurred to me I'd better get some of this stuff down on paper so it would be there for her even if I no longer was.

Against the day she might be ready, I began to write her a series of letters setting out all she needed to do to ensure that money would always be her servant rather than—as it is for most people—her master. My goal was to map out a financial path that was smoother, more direct and filled with fewer stones, detours and ditches than my own had been.

I shared these letters with a colleague and he said, "This is pretty interesting stuff. You should put it on a blog to share with your family and friends."

I figured my family and friends wouldn't be much interested (they weren't) but a blog seemed like a great way to archive the information. In June of 2011, jlcollinsnh.com was born.

Then, slowly at first, an amazing thing happened. Readers began to find it, and it resonated with many of them. I had no idea the blog would go on to be such a success, drawing an international audience of nearly 20 million readers. (I'd have picked a cleverer name for a start.)

It led to my creation of Chautauqua, an annual retreat. The first was held in Ecuador in 2013 and we've since taken it to the UK, Greece, Portugal and Colombia. Our mantra: Cool places, cool people, cool conversations.

In 2016 *The Simple Path to Wealth* was published based on the blog and especially the sequence of articles known as the Stock Series (jlcollinsnh.com/stock-series).

And now, in 2023, the book you hold in your hand: *Pathfinders*.

I owe it all to the little girl who wouldn't listen.

## SOME SECRETS

Want to know a secret?

*The Simple Path to Wealth* was just the working title I came up with while writing the book, and I never liked it all that much. I always figured, at some point in the process, something cleverer would come to mind. Nothing ever did.

That turned out to be a blessing. That title describes exactly this proven and remarkably straightforward process of becoming financially free—forever.

Here's another secret:

It really is simple...

- spend less than you earn
- avoid debt
- invest the difference.

Secret #3: The investing part is simple, too, not that you'd know it listening to Wall Street and the financial news.

Think of it this way: Imagine you have before you an immense banquet table groaning under the weight of every exotic dish imaginable. Each infinitely complex to prepare or even understand. On one small corner of this table are the simple foods your body really needs to be strong and healthy. You can put your arm on that table and sweep all but those off and onto the floor.

So too with all the endless, and endlessly complex, investments the financial community loves to sell. Once you've swept those to the floor (as you should), what you'll see left on that corner of the table are the simple, low-cost, broad-based index funds. These are all you need for peak financial health.

Here's our final and maybe most shocking secret, #4: If you really don't care about all this money financial investing stuff, this will be your superpower.

That likely bears some explaining.

## YOUR SUPERPOWER

One day, when my daughter came home from college, I started in on all this stuff. (Again!) It is just so critical and can make such a difference in a person's life.

She stopped me and said, "Dad, I get it. Money is important. I just don't want to have to think about it all the time."

For me, this was an epiphany. I, and people like me, are the odd ones out. Normal people, like my daughter, have better things to do than to obsess about investing, money and financial independence. They have bridges to build, diseases to cure, fires to fight, children to raise, breakthroughs to make. In writing to my daughter about this stuff, by extension these are the people to whom I am speaking.

All she, and they (and maybe you) need is to understand a few basic principles, set your investments up on autopilot and get on with your more important life activities. That is your superpower. Here's why:

Investing is one of those rare (maybe the only) areas in life where once you get those basics set, *the less you do the better your results*. The more you tinker with them, as those of us interested in this stuff are prone to do, the worse your results will likely be.

Of course, I have readers who are into this stuff. They are easy to recognize. They are endlessly suggesting ways to tinker with The Simple Path. But I'll wager this: Twenty years from now, my daughter—and you with your superpower—will have outperformed them.

## DO YOU WANT TO BE FREE?

Money is the single most powerful tool we have to navigate this complex modern world we've created. As you'll see in the stories that follow, it is a wonderful servant, but a tyrannical master.

For most, money is ever elusive. They live in a world where there is more month than paycheck. Where money is a never-ending concern. Where retiring is a dream and losing the ability to work a disaster.

It doesn't have to be. With a little thought and planning, your money will work for you. You'll come to no longer depend on your ability to earn it. Your assets can generate income—handy if you'd rather not trade your time for it, essential when the time comes you are no longer able to.

# GATHERING THE TALES

During my Google Talk in 2018, Rachel the interviewer asked me why other financial writers didn't offer the kind of specific advice found in *The Simple Path to Wealth*. I replied that while I couldn't speak for those folks, the advice in my book is specific because it is exactly what I have told my daughter. It is exactly what I recommend she do financially to unlock a rich, free life.

At the time she was in college and at the beginning of her journey, and she is an American. Not surprisingly, the book reflects this starting point, and it is very US-centric.

What is truly remarkable is how readers from all walks of life, at every stage of the journey and from all over the world have taken the principles in it and adapted them to their own unique circumstances. It doesn't matter where you are, when you start, or what mistakes you must unravel on the way. Understanding these few simple principles can unlock a wonderful life free from financial worries and filled with the options money can buy.

Over the years, the stories readers have shared with me have been humbling and awe-inspiring. This is the wellspring behind *Pathfinders*. Its goal is to collect, preserve and share the priceless lessons that others have learned in their own time and place on The Simple Path to Wealth.

In early 2022 I put the call out to my readers. I wanted to gather their most valuable insights from pursuing financial independence and share them with the rest of the world. A kind of compilation of travelers' tales, offering practical encouragement and real-life inspiration—proof that it's possible, roadside advice to make it easier.

The results exceeded expectations. I received stories from nearly every continent (still waiting on you, Antarctica), and every stage of The Path, peppered with wisdom and wit, abundant with practicality—from people of all ages, backgrounds and walks of life.

I guess I shouldn't have been surprised. Pursuing FI is simple—but intentional. It forces you to think about what really matters to you, and what you're really doing with the most valuable resource you have: your time.

This book collects around a hundred of the very best of these tales to help you find your way and keep going. You might not have taken a single step towards financial independence. You might have stumbled many miles through inhospitable terrain to catch your first glimpse of a better route. Or maybe you've made considerable progress, then taken what seemed a picturesque shortcut only to run into a dead end—and you don't know where to turn. If you're unsure how to adapt The Simple Path in your own life, you will find countless examples—some perhaps identical to your own situation—in these pages.

Even if you're finally in view of the finishing line, this book can help. It's not always easy to take that last step. Here you'll see exactly how others have done it.

## YOU GET TO DECIDE

Above all, the book's message is one of hope. It shows that life is messy—but The Simple Path really is simple, and adaptable. The philosophers say that the only things you should worry about in life are the things you can control. And it turns out on this Path you can control all the things that make a difference.

You can avoid going into debt, and you can get out of it if you're there. You can arrange your life so that you're not spending every dime you get. You can take that surplus and invest it for the long term. This book shows you how, in a startling variety of ways.

What you do today is either going to leave you broke in the future or it's going to leave you financially free. You get to decide.

The Path awaits. And you don't have to walk it alone...

JL COLLINS

"MONEY FREES YOU FROM DOING THINGS YOU DISLIKE. SINCE I DISLIKE DOING NEARLY EVERYTHING, MONEY IS HANDY."

—GROUCHO MARX

# PART ONE:

# FREEDOM

# JL'S VIEW

## YOUR NEXT BREATH

I GET A LITTLE impatient with people who dismiss the importance of money. It seems to me that comes from a very privileged point of view.

Jim Dahle, author of *The White Coat Investor*, says money is like oxygen. As long as you have enough, it's not important. You don't think about it. But the moment you don't have enough, nothing matters other than your next breath.

Money is the same. It is unimportant as long as you have plenty of it. But if you only have barely enough for your needs, it will prey on your mind. The moment you don't have enough, it suddenly becomes extraordinarily important. At that point, few things matter more.

When people say, "Money is not important, other things are more important in life," what I hear is, "I am in a wonderfully comfortable position and don't really appreciate it." Maybe that's understandable, even good in its way. Most of us don't walk around appreciating oxygen.

Then again, for the most part oxygen is freely available. For most of us, money is something we have to actively bring into our lives. And, if we are smart, we'll keep some of it around to work for us.

So this opening part of the book is all about taking a few moments to appreciate what oxygen gets you: Life. And what money can give that life: freedom and options. Which is what financial independence (FI) and The Simple Path are ultimately all about. On this journey, as with any other, it's always helpful to keep in view our ultimate destination.

## MY FIRST STEPS

I learned young that we live in a very financially precarious world.

My father was a successful guy and we enjoyed a comfortable upper-middle-class life. But he was also a cigarette smoker.

> Unlike you, once your money starts working it never grows tired, never gets bored, never sleeps, never stops.

The thing about smokers is not just that they tend to die young. It is that cigarettes slowly, relentlessly debilitate them along the way. As my father's health failed, so did his ability to work. And as his income slipped away, our comfortable life slipped away with it.

I was an adult before I realized it didn't have to be this way. But once I knew, I resolved that I would never depend exclusively upon my own ability to work for income.

The ability to trade your time and labor is only one way to bring money into your life. The other better and much more secure way is to take some of what you earn and, rather than spend it, put it to work making more money for you.

Better because, unlike you, once your money starts working it never grows tired, never gets bored, never sleeps, never stops. It keeps working 24/7/365. You can deploy it across many tasks so that even as some fail, others prosper. It will keep working for you as long as you live. And after you die, it will keep right on working for whomever or whatever you have told it to.

The amount of money working for you grows as you add new money to your investments. But it also grows as the money it earns, in turn, earns more money itself. This is called *compounding*, and it is why your money can ultimately earn more money than you.

I call this **buying your freedom**.

The desire for this freedom from fear and want drove me to seek out a financial buffer and led to my first steps on what became The Simple Path, long before I thought of it in those terms.

## THE POWER OF FREEDOM

But, as I was to learn, following this Path has other benefits as well. Like shifting the power in the employee-employer relationship.

When your only source of income is your labor, you are effectively shackled to your job. The employer holds the keys. But when you have money by your side, the power shifts a bit; and it can take surprisingly little.

Back in 1976 I was in Chicago, in my mid-20s and two years into my first professional job. I loved it, and it had taken me two long years after graduating college to get it. Times were tough. The economy was wracked by high inflation and stagnant growth in what would come to be known as "stagflation."

Earning $10,000 a year, I had amassed the princely sum of $5,000, and in those days this was more than enough money to go and backpack around Europe for a year. Which I decided I wanted to do.

I didn't really want to quit but I also didn't want to pass up the opportunity to travel.

One day I stumbled on a dirt-cheap airfare to Luxembourg. It required you leave on a certain day in the Spring and return four months later on a certain day in the Fall. It wasn't the year I'd dreamed of, but it seemed a reasonable compromise that might allow me to keep the job. I went to my boss Carl and asked if I could take a sabbatical for a few months.

He said, "No."

Carl was an older gentleman who had been through the Great Depression and World War II. People just didn't do that in those days—not if they had a job. He probably wondered about my sanity.

It never occurred to me this might be negotiable. It probably never occurred to him either.

I thanked him and left his office to ponder my dilemma. Keep the job I loved and worked so hard to get, or quit and head to Europe?

A week later I went back to Carl and resigned. He was shocked. "Why?" he said.

"I want to go backpack through Europe for a year."

He sat back in his chair and looked at me a bit, convinced more than ever (I'm sure) that I was nuts. Finally, he said: "Don't do anything hasty. Let me talk to the owner of the company."

I was dumbfounded and, to my utter amazement, a few days later he called me back into his office and said, "Well, if you can promise you'll be back on that date in four months we'll hold your job for you."

I spent some of the five grand on traveling around Europe. But the first thing it bought never actually cost me a penny, despite being priceless. It bought me freedom.

## A DIFFERENT WAY
## OF SPENDING

At most every Chautauqua, the financial retreat I created back in 2012, we have what we've come to call "dragged-along spouses." These are the partners of attendees who come in support, but who are not really all that interested in this financial freedom business.

Cathy was one of these, and during one of our conversations

she said, "FI sounds great, but in the family I grew up in, spending money is what we did. The idea of saving just feels like depravation."

Sometimes, out of nowhere, inspiration strikes and in that moment I had an epiphany. I said to Cathy something I had never said or even thought before.

"Cathy," I said, "I'm going to tell you a little secret. The truth is, I have personally spent every dime I've ever gotten and, for the most part, I've spent them as soon as I got them."

"Really?" she said, clearly not quite believing what she was hearing.

"Absolutely, and I've spent at least half of them on the single thing I value most. The thing that gives me the most joy and satisfaction of anything I own. I've spent them buying my freedom."

The other half of those dimes have bought many wonderful and essential things, but nothing else comes close.

But that's just me.

Most people don't even consider that this is possible, and even when they do they still choose to buy the luxury car, fancier house or remodel of their kitchen. And that's fine. It is their money.

But you, like me, might be different.

## RULES FOR THE ROAD

- Money, like oxygen, is only unimportant if you already have more than enough of it.

- Your money can buy your freedom. For my money, nothing is more valuable.

- The Simple Path first brings you the freedom of security—of not being at the mercy of your ability to earn a paycheck.

- Then it brings you a wider and even more intoxicating freedom—to use your time as you see fit.

Now you know: Buying your freedom is an option for your dimes too.

## "IF YOU FIGURE OUT MONEY, LIFE IS INCREDIBLY EASY. IF YOU DON'T, LIFE IS INSANELY HARD."

**—KRISTY AND BRYCE,
AUTHORS OF
*QUIT LIKE A MILLIONAIRE***

# THE STORIES

## THE SUPERPOWER OF TIME

### UNCLE MIKE

*Pacific Northwest, USA*

*tinyurl.com/unclemikeYT*

**W**HAT IS YOUR time worth?

There was a time when I knew the answer to that question. It was around ten years ago and I was making $40 an hour as an aerospace tooling engineer. If I worked overtime it was $60. I loved that job.

I was paid an obscene amount of money to play with some of the coolest toys on the planet, and if I ever somehow found that wanting, I was called upon to invent even cooler toys to supersede those that had somehow disappointed me.

My name is Uncle Mike, and I retired early three years ago. As I mentioned, I was an engineer, in the sense that I did engineering work and was paid handsomely for it. I am still an engineer, in the sense that I continue to be home to a host of proclivities and neuroses consistent with that occupation. I just don't get paid any more.

But I used to, and therein I found the answer to my question: My time was worth $40 an hour, or perhaps $60 an hour on the weekends.

Optimization is a thing that engineers are driven to. We can't help it. So, ten years ago, the naïve version of me that knew what his time was worth began to optimize his life around that fact.

If his car broke down and a mechanic quoted him $500 to fix it, young Uncle Mike could just do some simple math. He could pop into the office and earn $500 in less than nine hours, so if fixing the car himself would take any longer than that, he'd be better off hiring the professionals. Easy math.

Or if he wanted his bathroom remodeled, it was the same calculation. He could spend his free weekends remodeling it himself, or he could spend his weekends at the office to earn the money to pay a contractor to do the work.

At this point in his career, young Uncle Mike's time was becoming so valuable that many tasks were beginning to appear beneath him. Why should he mow his own lawn? Or tune-up his motorcycle? Or cook his own food? If he could make $60 per hour doing a job he loves, he should simply hire people to handle all of his other chores, provided their time could be had for less money. Right?

And what of recreation, then? A good eBook is $10 on the high end. But the hours spent reading it would cost him a fortune! Would you pay thousands of dollars just to read a book? How much is a lively poker night with his friends worth? There's a $5 buy-in, just for fun; plus $300 lost in hours he could have been paid for.

These were the questions rattling around in young, naïve Uncle Mike's head ten years ago. Because ten years ago, back when that was me, back when I knew the answer to the very important question that began this story, I wasn't happy.

I don't think it's exactly that I'd answered the question wrong, per se. But how I applied that answer was not resulting in a life well lived.

When I first stumbled upon the strange and wonderful FI movement, I followed what I believe to be a fairly standard trajectory. I doubted, I marveled, I devoured.

I doubted such a thing was possible. If you were allowed to retire early, everyone would be doing it! My high-school guidance counselor never even mentioned the option to me.

I marveled at the incredible lives of those who went before me, taking on vast artistic projects and traveling the world unencumbered by the shackles of regular employment.

I devoured the content, seeking bloggers and podcasters telling their stories, authors detailing the techniques of success and the pitfalls to avoid, and financial gurus preaching a reliable route to wealth.

I remember being surprised during the "devour'" phase at how often financial independence writers become philosophical. I sought the wisdom of frugal lifestyle-building, asset allocation, and Trinity Study application. Why was I repeatedly finding articles on Stoicism, explanations of hedonic adaptation, and reflections on optimism, gratitude, and wings and roots intermixed with financial advice?

During the process of achieving financial independence myself it became clear. When you don't have enough money, acquisition of more is always a high priority. But once you do have enough, you are faced with the most wonderful problem: choosing what replaces that priority.

What do you do with yourself when earning money is no longer important? What drives you when the motivator of wealth suddenly evaporates? What makes you happy? See? Philosophy.

Before I even knew that early retirement was a thing, I discovered that trading my time for money wasn't as simple a calculation as it seemed on the surface. Now that I am retired, my life reflects the philosophies I developed following that discovery.

Fixing things makes me happy. Building things makes me

happy. Learning new skills makes me happy. Connecting with old friends makes me happy.

I can easily afford to pay a mechanic to fix my car, but I'd rather do it myself. Every time something new breaks I learn a little bit more about how cars work.

I could eat at fancy restaurants all the time, but the food my wife and I cook together is faster, healthier, and tastes better. Over the years, of all the myriad of skills I have collected and things I have learned to make, cooking is quite possibly the most rewarding.

I could have hired architects and contractors to design and build my house, but I am taking that on myself as my first grand retirement project. If I'd hired it out I'd probably be done already, living comfortably in luxury. Instead we live in a travel trailer as I work my way through the seemingly-infinite project list leading up to the start of construction. I'm hoarding all of the fun for myself and the project creeps along at a glacial pace.

But I smile every day, and learn more every week. The point of the project is not to have a house. I could just buy a house. The point of the project is the project itself.

But where does that leave me? What is my time worth now?

As my career went on, my days of earning $40 an hour were left behind. At the peak I was paid just over $100 per hour counting benefits. It stands to reason that in those days I valued my own time at slightly less than $100 per hour, as I was willing to exchange it at that rate. It also stands to reason that following my retirement the value of each of my hours increased even further, as I was no longer willing to make the same exchange.

There are many things to love about retired life, that make it worth walking away from a lucrative job for. Perhaps my favorite, though, is having the time available to seize the opportunities that were always there. When I worked, I still made time for the things that made me happy. I fixed things. I made things. I spent time with the people I love.

But when a neighbor needed a hand putting on a new roof, I didn't have time to help out. When some coworkers took a week off to go sailing, I had other obligations. When a friend needed his transmission rebuilt, I was just too busy.

Now that I am retired I am blessed with the superpower of time. When my neighbor's woodshed began to fall in on itself, I happily took two days to rebuild it stronger than ever. I enlisted the help of a friend who had been wanting to learn about wood-frame construction. Now my neighbor's shed is shipshape, my friend got a hands-on education, and I got an enjoyable two days of outdoor physical labor. Everybody won and it was a great experience all-around. If I'd still had a full-time job, I surely would have missed out on the opportunity.

Two of my best friends in the world just had their first baby. I wanted to do something extravagant for them, but I don't know the first thing about babies. But I do know that they've been wanting a back porch for a while and are suddenly far too busy to take on the project themselves. Because I have the superpower of time, I'm going to build it for them. I'm milling the lumber myself from a cedar tree from my property. I'm getting the fun of a nice-sized construction project, an education about chainsaws, and a new lumber-milling skill to add to my toolkit. They're getting a deck that they can enjoy for decades and a nice boost in their home's value. Again, everybody is winning and I'd never have had the time for such an undertaking when I still had a job.

> Now that I am retired I am blessed with the superpower of time.

But I no longer consider the hourly cost of such work. If I kept track of my time milling lumber and compared it to my old engineering salary, I could easily have purchased the materials and hired skilled contractors to perform the work.

But that's a recipe for a life spent chained to a computer working for someone else, earning ever more money for your bank account but no experiences for yourself. And while more money is nice, I have enough now. I'd rather have the experiences and the skills acquired thereby instead, thank you.

So to answer the question: For me, my time is worth more

than $100 per hour, and one of the greatest results of my financial independence is that I am wealthy enough to give of it freely.

What is your time worth?

## THE FREEDOM TO CHOOSE

### PAUL M.

*Cologne, USA*

THE YEAR WAS 2008. I was working for a very successful financial planner. Two years previously I had sold my business in order to pay for a divorce, and bought a townhouse for my daughter and me to live in.

There are three things to point out here. One, purchasing a townhouse during the 2006 real estate bubble didn't work out too well. Two, you might think you're selling a business for a good amount of money—but once you pay remaining debt, taxes, and cut everything in half in a divorce settlement, there isn't a lot left. Three, fielding panicked calls from clients for a financial planner during a market crash is one miserable job.

I was 44 years old, debt-free (other than a mortgage that would soon be underwater)—but also investment and savings free. I had been in the workforce for 25 years and was starting over.

It was then that I met and started dating Amanda. Little did I know at the time that she was amazing with money. Every penny of hers was spent with a focus on *value*—and there was no greater value than investing for the future. I just thought she was cute.

While I instinctively possess some FI characteristics—avoiding debt, an entrepreneurial spirit, no need to keep up with the

Joneses—other aspects of FI had to be learned. Amanda is inherently FI through and through.

Two of the best decisions I've ever made were: one, marrying her; two, following along with her and her FI ways.

Somewhere around 2015 I had moved to a new job, but we still had our investments with my former boss, a financial planner. It was then that Amanda and I started discovering others pursuing FI—and The Simple Path they were walking to Wealth.

After many blogs and podcasts and meetups, we pursued The Path in earnest.

We moved every penny of our retirement accounts from my former boss to Vanguard. Our savings rates got to 70% or better. Whenever the market dips, we invest more. I have even written more than a hundred letters to my young adult daughter explaining it all.

Early in 2022, I notified my boss that I was going to scale back my job responsibilities and take a fitting cut in pay to do so. My wife had done something similar a couple years previously. Fewer than 15 years from having to start over in life, when I have to make a decision between money and time I now have the freedom to choose time.

## I DIDN'T WANT MORE MONEY, I WANTED FREEDOM

### GEORGE CHOY

*Tenterden, UK*

*mycastleproperty.co.uk*

I WAS IN A corporate job in the United Kingdom, with a decent salary, working with global brands and traveling all over the world. From the outside, it might have appeared as though I'd made it…

The reality was very different.

I was in the office during the week so much that I barely saw my wife or two small children. On Saturdays I was so exhausted that I often fell asleep in the middle of the day while sitting up. On Sundays, I frequently had to travel to the airport in the afternoon ahead of a meeting early Monday morning.

I traveled alone, slept in hotels alone, ate my dinner alone, and only had contact with people during meetings.

I remember I stopped looking up. Everywhere I went, I stared at the floor. Life had lost its meaning. I was so exhausted, lonely, depressed. I withdrew, barely talking to my family. But I had to go on—my family was relying on me to pay the bills.

One weekend, my wife Sarah and I were sitting having coffee at a soft-play center, while our two little kids played in a ball pit. She knew something was wrong. Finally, she managed to get me talking. I spilled out all my feelings—and she gave me permission to quit my job.

I handed in my resignation letter the next day.

I didn't know how we would survive without my income, but Sarah—ever the optimist—felt we would find a way. We owned four rental properties, but we didn't have enough income to cover our expenses. There were times when we could barely afford to eat.

We set ourselves a goal to become financially free within six months. But we didn't know where to start. So I started researching everyone I could find who was financially free. There weren't many. I quickly discovered there were a lot of people promoting how to make money, but they didn't have *freedom*. I wanted the freedom to never have a boss and never have to work again.

That was when I found JL's Simple Path.

Sarah and I decided to increase our wealth through property investing, rather than the stock market. We liked the fact that they were tangible assets and paid us income every month. Our house had substantially increased in value in a very short time, so we added many more rental properties. We also found innovative ways to reduce our personal expenses, including geoarbitrage—we moved to a cheaper area and rented. We also became substantially more tax-efficient, so we could keep more of what we earned.

I was focused on a clear goal to get to financial freedom as fast as possible. I remember that day so well. Sarah and I were looking over the numbers and were shocked—we'd achieved it at last. She was only 39 at the time. Our original plan for FI was six months, but it took two years in the end. I know we could have done it much faster with hindsight and I wish we'd started in our 20s.

Since then, we've carried on adding more and more residential and commercial properties, to make sure we are resilient under any economic circumstances. Every day we get moments where we appreciate that we have our time freedom, and can focus on what is most important to us: our family, our health, and helping other people.

## THE TWO KINDS OF WEALTH

### TIFFANY S.

*Vermont, USA*

WHEN PEOPLE HEAR of our adventures over the years—gorilla trekking, photographing pit vipers, diving with sharks, renting a car and driving all around South African parks on our own—they often remark how adventurous we are, how they could never take such risks.

I always respond that we have only engaged in activities we felt matched our abilities. We never sought to take uncalculated risks. We made decisions based on our skills and stage of life, such as when we geared up to do an 11-day trek around a remote island in New Zealand.

At some point we realized we could apply this mindset to our finances.

They don't need to be scary or mysterious. Deciding what to do with our retirement savings is really no different to deciding if we were fit and able to safely go off trekking on our own in the mountains of Nepal or Chile.

Fortunately, we had always been good savers before we discovered FI. In our 30s, we realized we could go for years and not work if we didn't want to.

In the decade since we have worked seasonal jobs, usually taking months off to go on adventures and travel. We drove around Australia for two years in an '89 Mitsubishi van and took a year off to travel around Southeast Asia.

> I grew up thinking that if someone had a flushing toilet in their house, they were well off. If they had two toilets, they were rich.

Along the way we have grown our savings, increased our investments, and had some of the best youthful and healthy years of our lives to go off trekking into jungles or bounce around on chicken buses all over South America.

Working seasonally, reducing our expenses, and being consistent savers and investors has put us on track to surpass seven figures before the standard retirement age of 65. We have built both financial wealth and experiential wealth.

There is no one way to financial independence. We each get to choose how we construct and walk on The Simple Path to Wealth. I always remember asking my dad what he thought was great life advice and he said, "Do the things you will most regret not doing." I have followed that, and there is no other path I would rather have taken.

For a long time, it never occurred to me I could become a millionaire. I grew up thinking that if someone had a flushing toilet in their house, they were well off. If they had two toilets, they were rich. I am glad to have been proven wrong, in style.

## THE FREEDOM OF
## FUTURE GENERATIONS

J. GONZALEZ

*Washington, USA*

I AM A FORMER child migrant worker. At the age of eight, I began working in the fields alongside my parents and siblings. I continued there until the age of 16. I grew up near a reservation, my community was poverty stricken, and child agricultural workers were common.

My family lived paycheck to paycheck and my parents never even had a bank account. As you can imagine, "generational wealth" was not part of our vocabulary, and it was assumed that none of the kids would receive any monetary assistance from our parents. As soon as we reached our teenage years, we were expected to provide for ourselves, and that is in fact what I did.

When I turned 18, I moved to the nearest city to attend college, the first in my family to do so. I had a strong work ethic from working at such a young age and knew that I would have to figure out life. I understood that I was truly on my own.

I was in a city with a high cost of living and the majority of my paycheck was going to rent, food, and transportation. I felt hopeless but reassured myself that if I was not homeless, I was doing OK and should be grateful.

A few years later, at the age of 25, I finally discovered FI and JL's Simple Path with the help of a coworker, after I mentioned that I didn't have any retirement accounts and knew nothing about investing.

I immediately opened a Roth IRA and began contributing

to my 401(k), something I had neglected for the past three years despite my employer's 3% match. Ouch!

When I discovered FI, I also discovered the idea of generational wealth. This was a thing? Great-grandparents, grandparents, and parents leave their children assets? It felt incredibly foreign and at the same time hurtful. My grandparents and parents were never able to leave their children anything. Could I do that for the next generation? Could I possibly leave them assets? I felt a strong desire to be the first person in my family to change this.

So, I did.

At age 31, I have an approximate net worth of $300,000 in both tax-advantaged and taxable accounts. While I do not have any children, I do have six nephews and nieces. They are all beneficiaries to my investments. Upon my passing, the funds will enter a trust that will only allow them to use the funds as follows: (1) educational purposes (including student loan repayment), (2) down payment on a home, and (3) to start a new business.

The beginning of generational wealth—and with it, true freedom.

## BUYING FREEDOM

### ERIC REINHOLDT

*Mount Desert Island, Maine, USA*

*twosidesoffi.com*

"**Y**OU'RE RETIRING?" I said. "At 46?"
"I am, yes."
I couldn't believe it. My childhood friend of 34 years seemed hesitant to say more.

"But, *how*?" I pressed. "I need details."

He seemed surprised. "You're not going to ask me what I'm going to do with all my 'free time,' or tell me how bored I'll be? You really want to know?"

"Yes, of course!"

So began a years-long conversation that continues to this day. It was the first time I heard the term "FI." And, although I was elated to discover it, I was sorry I hadn't learned of it sooner. Financial independence was the very thing I'd been seeking for years—the retiring early part an unexpected, positive side effect. The important thing was freedom.

At the time I was a 46-year-old self-employed architect and part-time YouTuber, designing homes, making videos, and sharing my process with a growing audience. Happily married, with two teenage boys, our family had settled on a little island just off the coast of Maine. At this point in our lives we had found our financial footing, no longer living paycheck to paycheck, but we had a mortgage, student loan debt and very little saved for our two sons' college expenses (fast approaching).

We had retirement accounts, but retirement was at least two decades away, and we didn't have any specific savings goal we were working toward. Having just graduated from the messy middle of our 30s—raising young kids, acquiring a home, and squeezing in a vacation here and there—we were living for the now. We had only just loosened the purse strings and started to spend more freely. Retirement wasn't an option that excited us, mostly because it was an abstract distant goal far on the horizon. Something for our 65-year-old selves.

Learning about FI changed that. I was all-in.

But, I had questions. So I cajoled my soon-to-be retired friend into a scheduled weekly phone call to chat all things FI. In the interim, I consumed everything I could on the subject. The more I learned, the more it became clear: I needed a plan.

My friend helped walk us through the early stages of calculating a FI number, tabulating our assets, setting a savings rate and an aggressive asset allocation. We continued documenting our weekly FI conversations as he reached his FI date and we gave our project a name: *Two Sides of FI.* He on one, I on the other.

In early 2020, two weeks before the global pandemic forced the world into isolation, we began to implement our plan. We would max out our pre-tax contributions to our retirement accounts for the year and use our idle cash position to pay off the last remaining student loan and the balance of our mortgage. The following week, free of debt, we opened our first taxable brokerage account, set our FI number and a projected date to reach it: 48 months in the future, June of 2024.

> With our goal quantified we could be more purposeful in our spending. We were buying our freedom and the savings goals forced us to be disciplined and intentional.

As we reviewed our calculations, we were surprised to learn that we were much closer to financial independence than we had expected. To reach it, our plan assigned every dollar of income a job. Seven out of ten of them went toward purchasing low-cost index funds. We started saving for our boys' education, opening two 529 accounts, and we now had monthly FI meetings to track our progress and course correct. With our goal quantified we could be more purposeful in our spending. We were buying our freedom and the savings goals forced us to be disciplined and intentional.

Along the way we revised our FI target number up a few times and watched our portfolio rise and fall with the market as we continued to invest through the ups and downs. We've sharpened our vision of the actual costs required to live the life we want in the location we want. As our FI date draws near, we've tempered our asset allocation away from all equities to a slightly more conservative 75/25 position and we're making more nuanced, careful calculations for withdrawal rates (3.3%) based on current market valuations.

For years my wife and I were working heads-down in parallel toward an abstract and undefined "retirement." Our path to FI has brought us closer as we've designed and work toward a shared vision of a future together that no longer requires trading our time for dollars. Our plan leverages our most valuable resource to be spent by us rather than selling it to others.

In the two years since discovering FI and drafting our plan, we've maximized our pre-tax savings, paid off our debts, opened Roth accounts for backdoor conversions, saved for college expenses, purchased umbrella insurance to cover our net worth, moved to low-cost index funds and increased our savings rate. But it's the vision for what FI buys us—the freedom to do as we choose each day—and a commitment to maintaining strong relationships with friends and family that's been the most liberating and life-changing.

Sharing our journey publicly on YouTube has reconnected me with an old friend and allowed me to build a network of like-minded FI friends. It's also proving to be an off-ramp and glide path for me into my new life on the other side of FI.

## FROM SURVIVAL TO COMFORT TO FREEDOM

### PENNY PRICE

*Minnesota, USA*

WHEN I WAS about 21, I recall reading somewhere that a poor person struggles to survive, a middle-class person struggles to be comfortable, and a wealthy person struggles for freedom.

Ten years later, that idea continues to stand out to me.

First came survival. I began my adulthood struggling to both eat and pay the rent. I quickly determined that a combination of working more (three jobs at once, before kids came along) and spending less on certain things could lift me out of that bind. And it did.

The issue, back then, was that my skills had a low ROI. Nevertheless, I was able to put a lot of sweat equity into a crummy house, *and* pay off the mortgage.

Then came comfort. I sought out a nearly-new car. And regular trips to the hair salon. And purses. And traveling.

*Sigh.*

Now, as my cup runneth over with parenting and all that goes with it—well, I am understanding the draw of freedom. Freedom from all debt and from being owned. Dreams of F-You Money.

I continue to experiment with ways that my family and I can do more for ourselves, in part to avoid having to pay someone to do it for us. Mending clothes. Cooking. Growing food. Bartering. Repairing. You get the idea. It feels good to know that I have control over my future. And I love that I can model this for my daughters. Here's hoping one of them soaks it in, at any rate.

Actually, as I type this, I sound like some sort of Prodigal Son. And maybe that's not too far off, either. But the fact remains that I put in the work, made amends, and grew up. Becoming responsible and self-reliant feels amazing. I can't recommend it enough!

## MINIMUM WAGE BUT
## MAXIMUM FREEDOM

OUTOFTHEBOXTRAVELER

*Canada*

I AM A SERVER at a restaurant in a busy high-end ski resort in North America on track to reach FI in the next few years, despite working an unskilled minimum wage job.

Ski resorts in North America have a high cost of living but

I quickly learned how to live it up and have a great time while maintaining a budget. As Tim Ferriss puts it in *The Four-Hour Work Week*: "People don't want to be millionaires— they want to experience what they believe only millions can buy." And I've been able to do that. Living in this town I can afford a luxurious lifestyle for very little money. It's put me on the way to freedom—and it's an enjoyable taste of freedom already. But most people here struggle to survive. Here's how I do it while working towards FI:

> People without college degrees might be interested to know that three months of work in the winter is often enough to fund my entire year's expenses.

- I like living with lots of people, so I lease a six-bedroom house and rent the other bedrooms out. My housemates pay me, I pay the bills and the landlord. I get a big discount for making sure rooms are full, and everyone's respectful, clean and keeps the place in good condition, and the rent is paid on time.
- Socially it's an expensive town to go out in, but I've tracked everything I spend since 2010. The drinking costs do add up a bit (I swear I don't have a problem, I just love to meet people—plus I'm single). If or when I have a partner, my socializing costs will go down—especially if I have kids.
- My commuting costs are zero: I have a three-minute cycle ride in summer, a ten-minute walk in winter. We get free food while at work. Our uniforms are cleaned and provided for us. Ski passes are mainly subsidized. And there are many benefits such as a really good extra health care package.

So, all in all, I can live comfortably on Can$24,000 a year.

But I actually earn quite a bit more than that, despite working a minimum wage job. People without college degrees might be interested to know that three months of work in the winter is often enough to fund my entire year's expenses.

I have had years with a take-home pay of $91,000 after taxes, and years with as low as $65,000. Most years I take at least six or seven weeks off twice a year to travel.

The secret is a bit of geekiness on my part. For nearly a decade I kept track of all the tips and sales on my shifts, as well as the time and day of the shifts and the sections of the restaurants I worked in. It showed me how to get the best overall pay. Tips can be significant if you're good at your job, not just in North America—I once worked a year in Norway, where people are very generous tippers.

In all, I average $90,000 take-home per year, with a max of $30,000 spending money so as to save $60,000.

I know my lifestyle will change over time, and I would like a partner and family at some point. Paying more rent in the future is likely too. (Though when I settle down, I'll socialize and travel less, so that will even things out a bit.)

My original goal was $1,000,000 to fund a $40,000 lifestyle per year with family. But I assume when I eventually meet a partner she will have a job or even (hopefully) be looking for a similar FI lifestyle to me. So lately I've been thinking $750,000 might do it. That should net me $30,000 a year.

I only need a few more years to get there. And I used to think I'd keep working as a server till then. But Covid has changed things. A lot of guests have become rude and difficult. It's tough, especially since we were one of the few places in the world to open safely throughout the pandemic. And lots of my colleagues have left as a result. I'm also ready for a break—and the freedom of not working for a little while is, for now, probably more important than arriving at the date I never have to work again.

But I know I'll get there before long too.

## THE KILLER QUESTION

GREGORY EDWARD BRENNER

*Houston, Texas, USA*

**A**FTER 18 YEARS of hard work, countless sacrifices and many job transfers, all with the same company, I found myself working in Louisiana. Anyone that's not from there can attest that it's a whole different planet. I found myself under a mountain of pressure in a difficult environment.

I recall completing interviews for new employees and trying to juggle phone calls, text messages, and emails from my vice presidents. The demands of the job were enormous.

The stress began to show in my body: One of my eyes would twitch uncontrollably, and my right hand would start shaking out of nowhere. I often wondered if the applicant I was interviewing could see what my eye and hand were doing.

A few short weeks later, after a questionable performance report, I was on the receiving end of some unwelcome criticism. I was discussing the situation with a close out-of-state friend. This friend had a simple question: "Why aren't you pursuing financial independence?"

I had never heard that term before. He told me he would send me some links to bloggers I needed to follow. A few hours later I received an email. I dove right in and started digesting what FI meant. I did this for week after week. It was all I did after I finished work. I became obsessed!

Fortunately for me, I was gathering all of this knowledge the year before my stock options came fully vested and huge decisions would have to be made. Most executives at my level chose to spend spend spend, and raise their lifestyle. Many had already spent the money before it hit their brokerage account.

With all this newfound knowledge, I knew I had to go to a zero-debt policy, downsize, then diversify while minimizing taxes. I did the math over and over again. I finally came to the conclusion that I could achieve FI on my 44th birthday, just under three years after learning about what FI entailed. I made that my obsession and started a countdown.

Saving, investing, budgeting and watching the countdown while my portfolio grew became my top priority. I also began to teach others about FI.

Well, in 2019, I hit the number I planned to hit—and my FI goal was achieved. Work stress went out the window. I could walk away from the golden handcuffs whenever I wanted.

## THE FREEDOM OF SIMPLICITY

### DEREK SINGER

*UK*

*www.fireintheuk.com*

THE OLDER I get, the more I value freedom.

Perhaps this is for negative reasons, such as becoming jaded with the way the world works, or growing tired of the repetitious, monotonous workday. The shriek of the alarm clock, the commute, being chained to a desk, office politics. Feeling like someone else is in control of my life.

Perhaps it's for more optimistic, hopeful reasons. There's another path. A Simple Path. A better way. The epiphany that I don't have to live the standard life. That by doing things differently, I can break the shackles and live life on my terms. Do what I want, when I want. Permission is not required.

There are many scammers and financial advisors out there (some would say they're one and the same), wanting to part you from your money. There are many, many books, podcasts, and social media platforms with conflicting advice and differing strategies. How do you pick the right one? How do you cut through the noise? It all seemed so complex.

Finding The Simple Path changes that. And it really is simple. I spend less than I earn. My only debt is my mortgage. I live in a modest two-bedroom bungalow. I drive a used car. I manage my own money since no one will ever care about it more than I will. I've embraced minimalism.

Following these principles and avoiding lifestyle inflation left me with surplus money each month. How to invest it? I'm in the UK and if you mention a Roth IRA or a 401(k) here, all you will get is a blank look. They don't exist. We don't have VTSAX. I needed to find their British equivalents.

But now I had the knowledge I needed, and I knew what I was looking for: low fees, avoiding tax where legally possible, and a broad-based index fund.

I now have a simple and highly effective setup. I automatically invest every month with Vanguard in the FTSE Global All Cap accumulation fund. It's highly diversified, it's passively managed, and the fees are low. My investments are within a stocks and shares individual savings account (ISA), which is a tax-free wrapper. All the gains and dividends are completely exempt from tax.

So, I was confident I had the right strategy, was consistently investing in the right fund, and had done so in a way to minimize tax. All I had to do was stick with the plan until I reached financial independence.

But what about those stock market drops? During the pandemic, my portfolio dropped in value by nearly £20,000, which at the time was around a 25% drop. The panic was palpable. People on the news and social media proclaimed it a "once-in-a-lifetime" event, so you better sell all your investments while you still have something to sell. And, of course, that classic: "This time it's different."

But, as those on JL's Simple Path know, the market always recovers. Instead of panic selling, I invested all the spare cash I had. I saw "BUYING OPPORTUNITY" in great big neon letters and I went for it. Not that I'm an advocate of timing the market, of course—JL's Simple Path has taught me too well for that. The market did indeed recover, and far faster than anyone thought possible.

Since then, there have been a number of drops. That's OK— they're part of the process. I just continue down my path. It's a simple one. And freedom lies at the end.

# PART TWO:
# DEBT

# JL'S VIEW

## SPENDING MONEY
## YOU DON'T HAVE

Y OU CAN'T BECOME wealthy if you spend all the money that
comes into your possession. So it should be no surprise that
you can't become wealthy if you're also spending money you don't
have. Borrowing to spend is like saying, "Oh, you want $xx for
this? I'd rather pay much, much more." That should sound nuts to
your ears. It certainly sounds nuts to mine.

Debt is deadly. In *The Simple Path to Wealth* I call it the
"unacceptable burden." After reading some of these next stories,
you might agree.

Debt is the next part of *Pathfinders* because it's the opposite of
freedom. It's something from which you must break free on your
Simple Path to Wealth. It's hard to ease on down the road shackled
to the starting post. But you don't have to be resigned to that fate.
Debt is no more inescapable than it is inevitable. Regardless of
what the marketers have told you.

Don't listen to their siren song.

Of course, breaking free is not easy. These chains are stout. There is a constant drumbeat in our modern economies encouraging you to borrow and spend. It's been going on so long, carrying debt feels normal. Car finance, credit cards, payday loans… In recent years, online shopping has been overtaken by it. You can't purchase a pair of slippers without a button appearing at checkout offering you financing to spread the costs. In 2022, one firm even offered installment plans to pay for Domino's pizza. Yikes!

It may feel normal, and maybe these days it actually is. But you'll never be financially free if you accept this new normal. In the old days we knew, as my father would say, that if you can't pay cash you can't afford it. That advice is as sound today as then.

## THE DAMAGE OF DEBT

Debt is extraordinarily damaging. It swallows your income with interest payments, enslaving you to that source of income. Money becomes your master.

This creates a deeply negative mindset and a real burden of guilt and stress—sometimes driving people to relieve it with, you guessed it, more shopping and more debt.

The people who sell you debt are doing you no favor. It is simply a way to shift your money to their pockets. You're lured into spending money you don't have for stuff you don't need. And when people can buy things on credit, they are willing to pay more for those things and the price goes up. If you plot the cost of anything and the availability of debt to pay for it on a chart, the lines move in lockstep.

And all the money you're spending servicing your debt is money that isn't working for you. You're missing out on investment returns—and the returns on those returns. Instead, your debts are incurring debts on those debts.

Viewed in those terms, you can clearly see debt for what it

is. Great for the lenders and merchants. Deeply corrosive to your wealth.

Does occasionally borrowing money serve a useful purpose? Sure, occasionally. Borrowing money to launch or operate a business can be a useful tool, for instance. But you should think long and hard before you take on that burden. Explore more creative options. Rather than err on the side of borrowing money, err on the side of *not* borrowing money.

Debt, like many dangerous things, frequently has a veneer of attractiveness. But it is an enemy on your path to FI. You should avoid it. I have.

> All the money you're spending servicing your debt is money that isn't working for you. You're missing out on investment returns— and the returns on those returns. Instead, your debts are incurring debts on those debts.

Other than mortgages, I have never carried any debt. Not even a car payment. My father taught me well.

## THE HOUSING TRAP

You can't talk about debt without talking about housing.

I have a reputation as being anti-homeownership. When you write posts like "Why Your House is a Terrible Investment" (my blog's all-time most popular) that tends to happen. The truth is, I have owned houses for most of my adult life. So how do we square these seemly conflicting things? Simple.

I am anti the relentless housing industry drumbeat that housing is always, or even commonly, a great investment. It is not. It is a place to live, and most often an expensive indulgence at that.

To be clear, there is nothing wrong with expensive indulgences— I've enjoyed my share—so long as you can easily afford them and they don't interfere with your greater goals. Goals such as achieving financial freedom.

Now this will vary from country to country and place to place, and there are exceptions to what I am about to say. But generally speaking, renting is cheaper than buying. When you rent you are more likely to be paying for only the space you need, rather than what you might need in some imagined future. If you rent, should your needs change, it is easy to move to more space. Or less.

With renting you are not going to be lured into expensive renovations, and there will be no expensive surprises. For the duration of your lease you know exactly what your housing cost will be.

In considering the rent vs buy issue, most people never bother to run the numbers. You should. Not all decisions need be based on financial considerations, but you should always be aware of the financial implications—especially with a purchase this large.

Don't fall into the all-too-common trap of simply comparing your pending mortgage payment to your rent. This, of course, overlooks all the extra costs owning a home entails: taxes, maintenance, remodeling, repairs, furnishings, appliances, landscaping. You'll also need to keep a significant emergency fund. Unexpected expenses are just part of owning a house.

If you decide to buy, be aware that the industry has a vested interest in seeing you buy the most house possible. Mortgage companies will urge you to take the largest loan they'll allow. Agents will urge you to buy the grandest house that loan will permit. Remodeling, furnishing, appliances must all be at the level of this grand home to insure its resale value. This is a trap that benefits everyone, except you.

Finally, let me say: Buying a house is no guarantee of future appreciation. It entails risk. Sure, the media is full of stories of those people who bought in San Francisco and saw the value of their house explode on the upside. Less is said about those folks who bought in Detroit, a once vibrant city, and watched their equity implode. And before you say, "Well, I'll just buy in the good areas bound to go up," consider this: Who's to say San Francisco won't suffer the fate of Detroit? Or that Detroit might not be tomorrow's dynamic turnaround story?

Many people disagree with me on this, and if your heart is set on a house nothing I say here will likely deter you. But if your goal is to be financially independent, keep your eyes wide open. You'll be best served buying the most modest home that meets your needs.

## BREAKING THE CHAINS

If you're in debt, don't despair. Millions have escaped and flourished financially. You can too.

There are many articles and books out there focused on getting out of debt, but there is no magic bullet. You are simply going to have to stop spending and start using that money to pay it down. Don't overthink this, or fall prey to some expensive scheme.

The best way to get rid of debt is to start. Here's what I suggest:

- compile a list of all your debts
- cut out all non-essential spending to free up cash
- order your list of debts by interest rate
- pay the minimum required on all debts each month, and pour the rest of the cash at the debt with the highest interest rate
- when that one's gone, aim the cash at the second highest
- repeat till done.

Now here is the good news, and it is *really* good news. In going through this process you have also:

- brought your spending under control
- developed the habit of investing—initially in eradicating the debt, next for building your wealth.

Now, with the debt gone it will be easy to shift those payments to buying investments, and with them your financial freedom.

# RULES FOR THE ROAD

- If you can't become wealthy spending everything you earn (and you can't), you certainly can't if you're spending money you haven't yet earned.

- Debt = danger. It is a ball and chain, and almost always a trap.

- Having debt makes your money your master.

- Money spent servicing debt is money not working for you.

- Debt makes for poor decision-making—it's sold as "free" money and people tend to spend it more recklessly than cold hard cash.

- Debt allows firms to charge more for their products.

- Think long and hard before buying a house.

- Paying off your debt is hard, but when you are done you will have formed an extraordinarily useful habit that will serve you well in building your wealth.

- Debt is a dumpster fire. There is no financial freedom until you put it out. Don't overthink this. Start today.

## "TOO MANY PEOPLE SPEND MONEY THEY HAVEN'T EARNED, TO BUY THINGS THEY DON'T WANT, TO IMPRESS PEOPLE THEY DON'T LIKE."

**—WILL ROGERS**

# *THE STORIES*

## THE PATH TO A BIG MISTAKE

TRAVIS DAIGLE

*USA*

*TravisDaigle.com*

**I** COULD TELL YOU dozens of stories about my relationship with cars. From prom-night pressures, to car-town college envy, to working in Motor City itself—I have always had a thing for the automobile and the freedom it brings. But it also brings other things, if you're not careful.

All the stories of my love affair with cars ultimately show one thing: the path to a big mistake.

Outcomes are about small decisions made over large amounts of time. We have to learn to be intentional with every moment of every day. Patterns of thought over long periods of time influence our most pivotal decision-making.

Though I always had a lot of desire for a nice car, I had little understanding of money or cars. I just knew I always wanted a nice one. The reality is, cars are a luxury, whether they are new or beat up. They require money to own and operate. They decrease in value. They break. They Break. THEY BREAK. You need money to fix them!

These were huge gaps in my understanding of what it means to own a car. I only saw the status symbol. I didn't see the liability. I had formed a poor story about car ownership that centered on image rather than practicality. These critical flaws had been in place my entire life. Eventually, these weak points got exposed.

The 2005 Atlantic Hurricane Season was record-breaking. Three weeks after Hurricane Katrina had displaced so many people from Louisiana into Texas, Hurricane Rita was forcing everyone to evacuate Houston. Many people drove towards Dallas. The freeways were like parking lots from all the traffic. I chose to drive east, home to Birmingham. It was towards where the hurricane would land but I calculated that we had enough time to get through the hot zone before the storm hit. The freeway would be wide open because everyone else was going the opposite direction.

> The process of paying off debt totally reoriented the way I thought about money, time, and energy. Material things beyond necessity have almost no significance to me. I refuse to be dominated by things.

During the trip, the power steering in my Acura started to fail. Obviously, this was not what we needed while running from a hurricane and going in the wrong direction. I say *we* because my best friend at the time, my sister, and my three-year-old nephew were riding with me. My sister, God rest her soul, could be incredibly challenging. She was insistent about stopping at a Walmart to get some clothes for the baby (we left in a rush so she didn't have much). I told her that she could do that when we got to Birmingham because the car was being funny and we were running from a *hurricane*.

The combination of the hurricane and what it might do, the car acting funny, and the dynamic of arguing with my sister about something I felt was utterly unreasonable, had me on edge.

When I got to Birmingham, I took the car to get looked at.

It needed some significant work. I had just started working as an engineer and I didn't quite have the money to pay for it. I was tired of the lack of reliability in the cars I had. I was frustrated at the fact that I had spent so much time working hard and sacrificing in school and yet I couldn't rely on my car to evacuate a potential disaster area. "Screw it! I'm getting a new car!" When I got back to Houston I began looking, and two weeks later I was driving a 2005 Subaru Legacy with a five-year $28,000 loan.

When I got the new car, I went from $22,000 in debt from student loans to $50,000 dollars of debt, in the span of a few hours.

I knew when I started working as an engineer that I probably wasn't going to like it but I had no idea how bad it would eventually get. Three months after I financed the car I began to realize that I was driving the very thing that was forcing me to keep a job I couldn't stand.

As I became more depressed about the job I began to resent the car more and more. The car meant that I didn't have freedom of movement. Ironically, the thing that represented freedom when I was a kid was now clearly my oppressor. But I chose it.

When I ultimately quit my engineering job I had two choices:

1. Let the depression play itself out and hope that I didn't commit suicide or have a heart attack.
2. Let my credit go to crap as I turned the car in for voluntary repossession.

I chose the latter.

Paradoxically, the ensuing years of paying off debt gave me a sense of what real freedom is. Freedom, in this sense, is the ability to have a high level of control over what you do with your time and energy. Because of the loan for the car I had to make money right away. There's no room in that equation for experimenting with work or any other area of life for that matter. The car dictated what I did with my time and energy. Even after I didn't have it anymore. That sucked! It's one thing to go to work for shelter, food, clothing. Those are basic necessities. It's another thing to go to work to have *stuff*.

Worse, to go to work you hate, for stuff. I want to own my things. I don't want my things to own me.

I tried being a personal trainer for about six months after quitting engineering. I was making virtually no money. I wanted to keep going but I had the debt monkey on my back and I had to get out from under it. When I left the personal training job it became very apparent to me that controlling my material cravings was a direct correlate to how much control I would have over the work I chose to do. Eventually, I would learn that precise budgeting with money helped to limit anxiety and helped me deal with sudden financial emergencies with much more ease than when I had no budget. This discipline with my financial resources has given me the freedom to experiment with work over the last eight years. As former Navy SEAL Jocko Willink would say, *"Discipline Equals Freedom!"*

The process of paying off debt totally reoriented the way I thought about money, time, and energy. Material things beyond necessity have almost no significance to me. I refuse to be dominated by things. Having the money for a nice car and having the money to take care of a nice car are two different things. I still like cars but I don't love them.

## THE DOLLAR BILL IN THE ROAD

### MICHAEL D. SUTHERLIN

*Madison, Wisconsin, USA*

THE YEAR WAS 1975 and times were bad. I was six years old. My mother was divorced, laid off from her factory job, and working whatever odd job she could find to make ends meet. We were doing our weekly grocery shopping and I was begging her for some ice cream. She looked at me and said: "We don't have money for that this time."

While I was disappointed, I knew all too well that no amount of sobbing would change the circumstances. When we left the grocery store and headed back to our apartment, we passed the Dairy Castle, yet another reminder of the ice cream I so longed for. And right at that moment, my mother spotted something in the middle of the road.

It looked like money.

She turned the car around, stopped, opened the car door and picked up a dollar bill. We were both stunned at our good fortune. She headed straight for the Dairy Castle and bought me a chocolate ice-cream cone. She saved the change. I was a happy boy that day.

Through the 1980s and beyond, life improved for us. I went to college and earned an engineering degree. The first in our family.

As I started my career and my own family, I wanted to live better than my parents, so I took on debt—something my mother avoided like the plague. As I entered my mid-40s, I grew tired of the debt struggle and feeling like I could never get ahead. After some deep thought and researching my options, I went back to my roots and began living on a tight self-inflicted budget.

> Just living week to week was all we were trying to do back then. No one taught us how to get rich. I wish I had known of JL's Simple Path at that time. I might have told mom to forgo the ice cream and buy VTSAX.

I gave up credit cards, using only cash to make discretionary purchases. I went to the bank, got out $200, and determined to make that last for the month. I got to the end of the month and discovered I still had about $150. I was amazed at how fast the habits I had grown up with out of necessity came back to me.

In less than three years, I was out of debt. Also, during this time my wife and I put our two daughters through college without debt. That was tough. But, as each daughter graduated, it was like getting a raise. Our savings rate began to grow, reaching over 50%. I was fortunate enough to have been saving and investing since I started my career in 1992, but not always consistently.

To our surprise, we achieved financial independence and retired in our early 50s.

What about my mom? She and my stepfather always lived well within their means, avoided debt and achieved financial independence in their 50s as well—and retired in their early 60s. They didn't have college degrees or high-paying jobs. And yet they still achieved a very comfortable lifestyle. Being debt-free and frugal was the key for them.

While what she did with the dollar bill in the road showed a mother's love for her son, the real lesson my mother gave me was the discipline of living within your means even when the outcome of a high net worth was nowhere in sight.

Just living week to week was all we were trying to do back then. No one taught us how to get rich. I wish I had known of JL's Simple Path at that time. I might have told mom to forgo the ice cream and buy VTSAX.

## THE WORST POSSIBLE LESSON

### GROWINGINFIRE1

*Fishers, Indiana, USA*

I STARTED ACQUIRING DEBT through credit cards when I was in college. When I was a kid, my parents had always been quick with a credit card to pay for whatever they wanted. It didn't seem like a poor choice; they could always pay the bills. Then my parents divorced. My dad was diagnosed with cancer and was no longer working, and no longer paying child support. My mom became more creative with the bills. She would pay the minimum, bridging gaps by using other cards. I learned that as long as you could pay the minimum, you could use credit cards as a sort of emergency fund.

> While paying down my debts, I was limited in the jobs I could accept as I needed a high-enough-paying job to cover my credit cards and car loans.

This was, of course, one of the worst possible lessons to learn. It was a mindset that took years to overcome.

Getting out of credit card debt was hard. By the time I got out of college I had built up over $10,000 in debt. Something that began to help was using any additional leftover cash I had from working two jobs to pay down more than the minimum on the cards. Back in the day—before you could pay cards online—you could pay Discover at any Sears store. So I would go in and put $10 or $20 every week on the cards. The minimum I had to pay every month slowly went down.

While paying down my debts, I was limited in the jobs I could accept as I needed a high-enough-paying job to cover my credit cards and car loans. I moved to Indiana for a new position, and soon my credit card debt had grown again—to $45,000. I got angry. I was determined to get this under control. By working hard (day job and side hustle), I chipped steadily away at it, putting *everything* extra towards it.

I finally got debt-free in 2006.

After that, I was able to build an emergency fund and contribute to a 401(k), as well as securing short and long-term disability insurance. This proved a life saver: Inside of two years I had surgery, got married, and had a daughter. I weathered all these major life events without going into debt, while still working on paying my house off early. Yay, me.

After that came more debt paydowns for my husband's credit

card debt, paying off our mortgages (long story short, we kept his house too), and investing for our retirement. More expenses came along—especially with a move to a nicer neighborhood for raising our child—but with hard work, we've been able to get ahead. We kept working throughout the pandemic and were able to significantly cut our costs by working from home. We were saving, investing, learning new cooking skills and having more family time.

When the big push for folks to return to the office came in 2022, our family had grown our emergency fund to a year's worth of expenses and some sinking funds for upcoming expenses. I was able to push back on my boss's request for people to come back into the office. The tables were turned.

## LEARNING WHAT NOT TO DO

ANTHONY

*Olathe, Kansas, USA*

INVESTING WASN'T SOMETHING ever discussed during my childhood. If I learned anything it was what *not* to do with money. Debt, overspending, payday loans, pawn shops and vehicle repossessions were all I saw through high school.

It wasn't until college that I learned what a stock was, through a business finance class. I began investing once I started work, but I made all the dumb moves of buying individual stocks based on news, tips from friends, or what some TV "expert" recommended.

When my eyes were finally opened about index funds and ignoring the noise, I simplified my investments and upped my contributions. I'm on a much better path now. I can focus on life while Mr. Market yo-yos up the mountain; I'm just along for the ride.

## WHEN DEBT RULES YOUR LIFE

### JENNIFER C

*Chicago, Illinois, USA*

TO GET DEBT-FREE, I've had to unlearn all the bad financial habits I acquired when growing up. Things like paying bills late, only making minimum payments on credit cards, taking on enormous debt for things like luxury cars (for the sole purpose of impressing others).

I used to think that budgeting meant you were poor. Rich people, after all, spend as they please. Now I know it's all about having a plan—a guiding framework, not merely something that inhibits you.

And I realized that if I wanted to achieve true happiness in life, debt was going to inhibit me much more than a budget. Homeownership and other goals would remain forever out of reach. My options were truly limited as long as debt ruled my life.

My first step to freedom was making an inventory of all my debt. It consisted of student loans and credit cards.

I then did everything I could to pay off my credit cards in full within three months. I also made sure that any future spending on credit cards would be automatically paid in full at the end of each month, so no new debt could accumulate.

Credit cards are not inherently evil if used responsibly, in my opinion. I continue to use them to protect myself and my purchases from fraud. And the reward points are worthwhile too.

Next came student loans. This took a bit of finessing. I found that no loan servicers really told me how my loan debt was actually structured. I discovered:

- Rates were set as of 1 July every year.
- Your rate was contingent on when the loan payment was dispersed. If it was dispersed before 1 July, it was different to if the loan was dispersed after 1 July.
- So, for the four years of student loan debt I took out, each loan was at a different rate and had a different combination of subsidized vs unsubsidized.

I dug up all my paperwork, separated the loan amounts by year, interest and type—with subsidized loans meaning the interest was deferred if I was still in school, while unsubsidized meant that the interest accumulated the moment the loan was disbursed.

I called the servicer up to confirm the interest rate for each year and type of loan. Then I ranked the loans from highest to lowest interest rate, and by type (subsidized vs unsubsidized). I continued to make my monthly payments—but also threw large payments whenever I could at the unsubsidized loans with high interest rates.

> Sometimes life gives you lemons and that means you're drinking lemonade instead of the tequila sunrise you had originally planned—but tequila can still come to those who are patient.

I quickly saw my student loan balance drop. Nothing was more satisfactory than when that final payment was made.

If your student loans are astronomically high, I know even this method might not be enough—but it is a good way to drive down the balance.

Progress is progress.

Once I paid off my debt, I found there was huge freedom with knowing I had options again. I was no longer weighed down by my debt obligations.

Obviously, paying off debt is one thing—*staying* out of debt takes a lot of discipline. But I think it also requires being flexible. Life happens, priorities change. Just because a goal is slightly delayed does not mean the goal isn't achievable. Sometimes life gives you lemons and that means you're drinking lemonade instead of the tequila sunrise you had originally planned—but tequila can still come to those who are patient.

## OPTIMIZING THE DEBT-REDUCTION PROCESS

### STEVEN

*Waconia, Minnesota, USA*

**M**Y WIFE AND I officially retired at the end of 2020. Unlike many in FI, we only retired a bit earlier than the established full retirement age. I was introduced to FI by my child who had recently graduated college. We had been saving in 401(k) and even earlier plans, so our starting point was not zero, but discovering JL's Simple Path focused us on the savings side of the equation considerably.

The flip side of saving funds for retirement is eliminating debt and cost control on expenditures. Since my wife is an accountant and I am a project manager, we applied our respective talents to work our way out of a debt situation that had gotten out of control. Based on what we learned, we really weren't in an unrecoverable position.

There are many reasons we were in the precise position we

found ourselves, but mainly it was an accumulation of lots of smaller decisions. This is probably the most difficult thing to impress upon people; wise decisions require understanding an entire budget, not just a single item under consideration.

We started our process by understanding where our income was going. Each month we answered, in excruciating and spreadsheet-logged detail, the following questions:

1. Where is our monthly income being spent?
2. How much debt do we have?
3. How large is the monthly debt service?
4. Is there any unallocated money left each month?
5. Where can we reduce spending?

The answer to question one was fairly straightforward. We simply started logging each payment, including amounts invested in 401(k) accounts. These items were the natural targets for consideration in question five.

Question two was equally easy, but much more painful. While we remained current on credit cards, we had a mortgage on our house with a three-acre slice of the countryside, a couple of zero interest loans for home improvements and some other loans. Understanding the debt—question three—led to a rapid discussion of how large a slice of our income was going to pay off these lines of debt.

The answer to question four was a resounding no, but mainly because anything extra was already being applied against the debt service. It seems we were already on the right path, but reading sharpened our focus.

We had to determine how to rid ourselves of the debt. We had always held that retirement was a non-starter until we had paid for the house. We quickly realized that the mortgage would require the most time to complete.

A major point in our decision-making was that simply looking at the interest rate or size of the loans would not provide the optimum plan for reducing our debt. The mortgage remained the largest debt, as well as the highest interest debt, while simultaneously providing some income tax relief to make it a bit more palatable. The item that we became concerned with was monthly debt service. We decided to look at each loan and see which could hurt us in the event that we lost income for any reason. We had managed to lose my income a couple times in the last 20 years, so it remained a possibility to plan around.

We looked at each loan in turn and evaluated. It turned out that the zero interest loans were the first to be addressed. These loans are commonly used by home improvement contractors and appliance dealers, who want the sale without the prospect leaving the store to research and/or save more. Very attractive offers, no interest if paid off by a specified date—but, in each of our loans, if the loan was not paid off by that date, all the accumulated interest would flood back onto the loan. We had not quite understood that when we signed the loans.

We focused on paying off each at least a month early, so that we could make sure that they were fully paid. Imagine our surprise when we discovered that we still technically owed all the accumulated interest! Several phone calls, one of which included the contractor and the loan company, and this was corrected. It turned out that the loan was set up incorrectly. However, if we had not focused on each item, we would have had a much larger bill to pay.

> Wise decisions require understanding an entire budget, not just a single item under consideration.

Each time we reduced the minimum debt service amount, we applied as much as available to the next loan on the list. This did two things: a) in the event one or both of us lost our job(s), a smaller amount of money would be required to keep going during the job search; and b) the next loan was completed sooner. When we finally completed the mortgage, the last item, it was amazing how quickly the savings account grew. Within a year, we had a full year's worth of reserve funds available, not counting the 401(k) accounts which had continued receiving payroll deductions.

While the debt reduction process was underway, we started challenging each of the monthly utilities and every other monthly expenditure looking for areas to reduce. The following examples are highlights where we managed larger savings. We added a warehouse club membership which reduced our costs on certain items that we consumed regularly, in some cases by more than half. We had been adding cell phones for each family member, especially as the children headed off to university. That led us to challenging our landline bill. For a while, we negotiated a lowered fee. When the phone company changed their methods, we discontinued the landline *except* for the internet connection. This minimized the communications bill. It also helped that switching to Republic and eventually having children earning and paying their own cell phone bills also reduced our phone bill to the absolute minimum. Most recently, we switched garbage haulers, saving nearly 50%.

As a result, we retired a bit earlier than we ever expected. We are of an age where we qualify to receive social security, but are waiting to take benefits until closer to full retirement age. Likewise with the rather smallish pension I qualified for with my first employer. In both instances, it is a matter of matching income to spending. Careful consideration is the key.

## THE DIFFERENCE DEBT MAKES

ANDREW

*Montana, USA*

**T**WO THINGS GROWING up made me interested in money and life and how to get them right. I credit them with making me interested in FI, and therefore for making the investments and savings that eventually got me to a million-dollar net worth before my 32nd birthday.

As a kid, I remember seeing friends and family chase the American dream of keeping up with the Joneses. When times were good, everything was great. When times became tough, it was shocking how bad they got—homes falling into disrepair or foreclosure, cars repossessed, and worse.

I couldn't work out how adults could work for years—decades even—and then find their world crumbling around them when they went just a few months without a job.

Secondly, I remember also meeting a few (seemingly normal) individuals who retired early, around age 50. And I remember the jealous comments of those less fortunate—*particularly* those with higher incomes.

The biggest difference, of course, was debt. When you can't service it, everything falls apart.

These strange paradoxes made me do everything I could to get it right. I got into real estate and house-hacking, turning around neglected duplexes, using the money to eliminate my mortgage and car loans and pay off my student debt as quickly as possible. And I spent a decade investing my savings and profits into low-cost index funds. My only blip along the way was a $3,000 "education fee" I had to pay—for attempting individual stock picking.

# PART THREE:

# SAVING

# JL'S VIEW

## ESSENTIAL AND
## PERFECTLY DOABLE

THE OLD SAYING goes, "It's not how much you make, it's how much you keep."

There are lots of variations on that saying. Things like, "Pay yourself first." But all point to just how critical a robust savings rate is to your financial well-being. If you intend to achieve financial independence in a reasonably short time, you are going to have to get aggressive on this front. The greater your savings rate, the shorter that journey will be. The more modest your savings rate, the longer it will be.

An old high-school buddy of mine never made more than $40,000 a year. And yet he became financially independent at a relatively young age because he organized his life and his spending in such a fashion as to free up money to invest. In the essay opening the next part of this book, I'll introduce you to Ken, whose $800,000 annual bonus was not enough to make ends meet.

Personally, I've always been a saver. I'm not sure from where this instinct comes. Maybe it was my mother encouraging me with tales of the red convertible I could buy when I turned 16. Of course, by then, my father's health had failed and along with it our financial situation. My savings went to pay for college. Convertibles came later. Or perhaps it is simply hardwired into my genetic code. Either way, this affinity for saving has served me well. It can serve you, too.

Even if it doesn't come easily or naturally for you, you can do it, as the stories in this part of *Pathfinders* will show. Saving follows debt because it is the key mechanism by which we not only escape debt (if we've been unlucky enough to fall into it), but build wealth. It makes everything else possible.

Saving is what powers this journey.

## 50%? INCONCEIVABLE!

With all due respect to Vizzini, it's not.

In *The Simple Path to Wealth* I suggest, now a bit infamously, readers save 50% of their income. Exactly what I have told my daughter and what I myself have done.

Spending every dime—and borrowing more—is so ingrained in the public imagination that this idea was stunning to some. They dismissed it as simply not possible. But, of course, it *is* possible. I've done it. Many other people have done it. Indeed most everyone on The Simple Path is doing it.

The irony for me is, while some are loudly complaining I have recommended the inconceivable, others are chiding me for setting the bar far too low. These people routinely save 60, 70, 80, even 90% of their income.

When people say it's not possible, that's nonsense. It's *absolutely* possible. It is simply a matter of setting your priorities and organizing your life accordingly.

But is it easy? No. Though, as you read the stories that follow, you might be pleasantly surprised by some of the techniques that can reduce the difficulty.

So, is 50% too aggressive? Or is it too wimpy? That's for you to decide. But if reaching financial independence is important to you, the following table will give you a good idea as to what any given rate can do for you.

| Savings Rate | Years to Retire |
|:---:|:---:|
| 10% | 38.3 |
| 15% | 32.7 |
| 20% | 28.6 |
| 25% | 25.3 |
| 30% | 22.6 |
| 35% | 20.2 |
| 40% | 18.1 |
| 45% | 16.1 |
| 50% | 14.3 |
| 55% | 12.6 |
| 60% | 11.1 |
| 65% | 9.5 |
| 70% | 8.1 |
| 75% | 6.7 |
| 80% | 5.3 |

The numbers in the preceding table assume an 8% annual investment return and that you'll live on the classic 4% withdrawal rate, which implies assets of 25 times your annual needs. So, this is not a gospel, but a guideline.

The table is taken from my pal Darrow's book, *Can I Retire Yet?*

The table assumes you are starting at zero. Should you have debt to unwind, it is going to take longer. If you already have some savings and assets, you are further along.

How the stock market is doing while you're going through

this journey is, surprisingly, much less important. Your savings rate absolutely trumps the performance of stocks. Certainly, if stocks are rising and you have the wind at your back, it'll shorten the time. But even if they're down, you're acquiring them more cheaply—which will serve you well in the long run.

If you have dismissed a 50%+ savings rate out of hand, take a look at the results of the lower rates. At least then you'll know what you're signing up for with yours.

## WHAT DOES SAVING 50% LOOK LIKE?

In the early 1970s when I graduated college and entered the workforce, there was little information out there on financial independence. I was wandering in the wilderness. I picked 50% kind of randomly. Somehow, it just felt right.

In my first professional job, I was making $10,000 a year (~$70,000 in 2023). I knew there were people living on $5,000 a year and there was no reason I couldn't do the same. And that would free up $5,000 to buy, through investments, the most valuable thing I could imagine: my financial freedom. So that's what I did.

It never felt like deprivation to me. Early on I avoided the big financial drains others take on way too easily: houses and cars. It was a great life. Maybe some of my peers were taking expensive vacations while I was backpacking or bicycle touring, but I probably had the better of that. Then, as my income rose, so did my investing and my lifestyle. When I was making $20,000 I had $10,000 to invest and $10,000 to spend. At $100,000: $50,000 and $50,000. With each passing year I grew fiscally stronger and lived larger. It's a simple approach, and really rather effective.

Of course, as the table earlier shows, you can get to financial freedom without saving 50% of your income. It'll just take longer.

And you can get there more quickly with more aggressive rates. It's your call. For me, 50% has always felt like the sweet spot.

# STARTING EARLY VS STARTING LATE

If you are young and reading this at the beginning of your journey, financial freedom might look impossibly far in the distance. But no time is better, and you have some distinct advantages. You are less likely to have gotten enmeshed in a lifestyle you must now unwind (more on that in the next section) and your invested money will have more time to compound. Compounding is one of the wonders of the world and time is its lifeblood.

It is common for people to tell me they wish they discovered The Simple Path when they were younger. The 70-year-olds say, if only I'd found this at 60. The 60-year-olds say, if only I'd found this at 50. The 50-year-olds say, if only I'd found this at 40. The 40-year-olds say, if only I'd found this at 30. The 30-year-olds say, if only I'd found this at 20. The 20-year-olds say, if only I'd found this when I was 10. The 10-year-olds say, if only my parents had introduced me to this while I was in the womb.

Me too. I didn't figure out the investing part of this (which we'll talk about later in the book) until I was 50 myself. Of course, I had been accumulating assets so that gave me a head start on the chart. If you are older, perhaps you have too. You also probably have the maturity to have learned that spending money isn't the key to happiness and, while market crashes are scary, they are no reason to panic and sell.

Young or old, if you make achieving financial freedom a major goal, you are looking at about a 10–15 year journey. Shorter if you already have some assets, longer if you have debt to unload.

With every step you take you have a little more freedom.

# HOW IMPORTANT IS
# YOUR FREEDOM?

It is important to understand this is a process, not a light switch. From the first small step, you are that much more fiscally strong. Even if you never reach the technical definition for being financially independent, you will be increasingly freer, more secure and blessed with more options than if you had never begun.

Faced with the tantalizing prospect of financial freedom, most people say "Sign me up!" But as they get a clearer look at The Path and what it will take to walk it, they start to say, "That's not possible." But the stories that follow show it *is* possible.

Many with established lifestyles say, "I'd love to do this but I must have the house, the cars, the private schools, the exotic travel." That's certainly what my friend Ken would have said. And that's fine. It is your money, your life, and your decision.

However, I call this "The Tyranny of the Must Haves." The more of them you have in your life, the more remote your odds of becoming financially independent. Indeed, unless becoming FI is your primary "must have" you are unlikely to get there. And that's OK. This is not a path for everybody and the truth is very few will follow it.

I have only ever tried to persuade one person to head down it: my daughter, and I am grateful to have succeeded. For everyone else, it is your call. But now you know it is possible and, should you decide to take it up, those of us already on it are here to welcome you.

## RULES FOR THE ROAD

- If you aspire to financial freedom a high savings rate is critical.

- For me, 50% has always felt like the sweet spot. Others have done far more.

- The idea that such high savings rates are impossible is nonsense.

- Thousands have gone before you and many were earning less than you.

- Young or old, this is about a 10–15 year journey.

- But it is a journey, not a light switch. With every step you are that much stronger.

- Beware of "The Tyranny of the Must Haves."

- Whether to start on this Path or not is entirely your call, but at least now you know it exists and you, too, have the option.

## "IF YOU WOULD BE WEALTHY, THINK OF SAVING AS WELL AS GETTING."

## —BEN FRANKLIN

# THE STORIES

## WORKING HARD NOW
## TO BE LAZY LATER

JOE OLSON

*Seattle, Washington, USA*

**M**Y FINAL YEAR of college I began the application process for MBA programs. I was going to make money, lots of money.

Then I got drawn in by a pitch from Teach for America, an Americorps program that places high-performing college students in low-income areas as teachers to try and help close the achievement gap.

"I can do two years of that before starting my real career," I thought. I was accepted and placed in Las Vegas. Little did I know I would fall in love with teaching. My spouse became a teacher, too, and my dreams of being a millionaire by age 30 were shot.

Or were they?

My first year out of college I earned $31,000 and my wife Ali earned $17,000 as a substitute teacher. Hardly something to write home about.

We kept living like broke college students, though, and our expenses were low. A $339-a-month mortgage on our 400 sq ft condo was the biggest monthly expense, and overall while living there we spent about $18,000–20,000 per year.

As the years passed, our salaries grew. Ali became a full-time teacher, and while the Great Recession froze our salaries for a few years, we both got pay raises from obtaining our master's degrees, and then the annual raises started again. By our final year teaching, we were earning a base salary of $44,000 each. Under six figures combined still isn't amazing, but we didn't stop there.

We did every teaching-related side gig we could; we taught Saturday school, tutored after school, taught summer school, graded high-school proficiency exams, taught clubs, did paid after-school committees, and as many other similar things as we could.

Our motto became: "Work hard now so we can be lazy later."

These activities added tens of thousands of dollars to our savings each year, and by pushing up our income but keeping our expenses low we began to save 40, 50, 60 thousand dollars a year, and more.

> When people ask how it's possible that two public school teachers—a notoriously underpaid profession—retired so early, the answer is simple, because The Path is simple.

Nevada having no state income tax and teachers there not paying into social security kept our taxes low, leaving us with lots to invest; over $80,000 in our final year alone. And investing tens of thousands of dollars every year for eight years of working saw us investing over $650,000 total during our working career, which had grown to over a million by the time we were ready to quit just before age 30.

When people ask how it's possible that two public school teachers—a notoriously underpaid profession—retired so early, the answer is simple, because The Path is simple. Increase income, decrease expenses, save and invest the surplus.

Doing that consistently, year in and year out, will get you there. It may not always be easy, but it is simple.

# PASSING $1M

### JEN

### *Portland, Oregon, USA*

I T TOOK ME some time to figure out why I embraced frugality and financial independence like a religious zealot. I've realized that much of my obsession is rooted in my relationship with my dad.

My dad passed away in the Spring of 2000. He was 47 years old and I had just graduated college. His death continues to weigh heavily on me. To this day I still categorize every event in my life as happening before or after his death.

Growing up, my dad made a good salary working as an independent actuary. But we lived in a working-class neighborhood in Portland and drove unassuming cars. My dad was the only dad in my friends group who wore a suit to work.

He tackled wealth accumulation on all fronts. He bought rental homes throughout the Portland area and invested heavily in the stock market. On weekends, he would take me and my four younger siblings to the public library and research stocks while we roamed the shelves for books. He moonlighted as a high-school basketball referee.

His frugality was legendary. He was always on the hunt for free wood to feed our wood-burning stove. My siblings and I feared nothing more than the sound of the trailer being pulled out of the garage on a Saturday morning because it meant we were about to spend the day gathering and splitting cords.

In 2013, my husband and I moved our two young children back to the Pacific Northwest after 11 years away. We married in Portland, but after a year of subpar salaries, plates of Pasta Roni, and dollar theater dates, we were eager for opportunity and landed in post-9/11 New York City.

NYC salaries helped us quickly pay off our student loans and rocket-launched our net worth. We witnessed a lot of money being thrown around this colossal city and we knew that wasn't our style. We wanted to be good stewards of our money. But we lacked financial focus and continued to save aimlessly and haphazardly through our years on the East Coast.

Around the time of our move to Seattle, I discovered financial blogs and quickly became obsessed with increasing our savings rate. I had finally found a clear financial goal. I wanted to be financially independent and I could not wait to start! And even more importantly, I had found a way to stay connected to my dad.

In urban Seattle, we ditched our car and navigated the city by bike and city bus. My neighborhood Goodwill replaced my Target runs. When I found my Buy Nothing neighborhood group, I was hooked. Free stuff from neighbors! I loved the giving economy and community within the group. I learned to be a smarter grocery shopper and to cook healthy, often meatless meals my family enjoyed, mostly thanks to Budget Bytes. I was gifted a nice tent on Buy Nothing and my family started camping in the Olympic Peninsula and San Juan Islands. I found a program that provided my eldest son high-quality autism therapies at a nearby university for much less money than we had been paying to private providers. This had been a significant expense for us since his autism diagnosis at the age of two.

The unrelenting economic growth engine of Seattle opened up many opportunities. Housing was in short supply throughout the city, so I created an additional income stream by renting out the lower third of our townhome to international students and summer interns. I started a lucrative side hustle providing STEM after-school classes to local elementary schools. Most of my students were kids of Amazon software programmers and these parents were not price-sensitive. This allowed me to charge premium prices while providing ample scholarships to students who weren't lucky enough to be born into the tech economy.

How did my husband and kids adjust to our new hardcore frugal lifestyle? My kids were still fairly young and oblivious. They didn't care if their clothes were new or used. They still don't, honestly. They enjoyed helping me with my DIY projects—everything from making their own Halloween costumes to creating homemade birthday cards for friends and family. My now-17-year-old still says his favorite birthday was the year I made homemade cinnamon rolls and created a treasure hunt for him and his friends around our neighborhood lake. I don't think I spent more than $20 for the entire party. Frugality breeds creativity—which can make for fun, intimate memories.

My husband went along with my conversion to frugality reluctantly. He had been so focused on his journalism career, I think he felt obligated to support me. He obediently packed a brown-bag lunch to work and even taught an adjunct college journalism course for his own side hustle.

One day in early 2016, I casually looked up from my laptop and announced that I had just checked our Vanguard accounts and we had passed the $1m mark in our financial (non-real estate) accounts. I finally had my husband's attention. He stared at my spreadsheet for a solid hour in disbelief.

A million dollars isn't what it used to be, but for a kid who had grown up a poor immigrant in East Los Angeles, whose dad often took advances on his pay as a garbage collector in order to buy groceries, it was beyond his wildest imagination that he could ever attain such wealth.

Today, we live back in Portland. We are financially independent on paper. We haven't retired, but we've adapted our paid work to fit around our chosen life. When Covid hit, I went part time to help my eldest son with special needs navigate distance learning. I regularly turn down side jobs in favor of focused time with my teenagers or volunteer work. Sometimes I wonder if my dad would be proud of the financial life we've built. I think he would.

These are just a few of the gifts our high savings rate has afforded us. I can't wait to open the rest.

## A FATEFUL QUESTION

MARK E

*Mountain View, California, USA*

HAD BEEN WORKING as a paper boy for a few years when it happened. I was 11 and had saved up about $5,000. My father was an English teacher, my mother a stay-at-home mom. They'd struggled financially since getting married in 1969. One day my father came to me. He asked me a simple question: *Could he borrow everything I had to keep up with their bills?*

He offered to pay me 13% interest, the going rate at the time. I really had no choice. And I was interested in earning interest.

So I said yes.

In the end, he paid me back every dime on schedule. But it taught me a memorable lesson at a young age: I was on my own financially.

This created a drive in me, which helped when I finally found JL's Simple Path.

I would *always* save.

After college I moved to the San Francisco Bay area. Along with my wife, I went to work at a technology company. I realized that if I could minimize or eliminate my housing costs, I could save even more than we had been.

We started with a townhouse that we lived in for two years and refinanced six times as rates declined. By the time my son was about to be born we moved to another home and kept our townhouse as a rental. After ten years in that new home, we had accumulated $1m in our checking account.

I had no idea what to do with the money other than real estate. The stock market was a casino to me. So we bought another house in 2014—our current home.

Then, in 2020, I was laid off.

Fortunately, since 2016, I had not only been saving—but following the FI path in full. I even convinced my wife to increase our savings rate to 85% of our income (an option because of our level in the company). We put 15% in the Total Bond Market Index and 85% in the Total US Stock Market Index.

When the day came, I was pretty sure that we were financially independent.

Looking back at our savings rate, I estimate that we saved about 40% on average over our careers. I retired sooner than I thought, at the age of 48. My net worth is two thirds in real estate, one third in stocks and bonds. It has been a wonderful transition.

We still have children at home. We travel extensively. And I have started to help others with personal finance for free.

## SAVING LIKE CHUCK BERRY

### CL ROBINSON

*North Carolina, USA*

**W**HEN I WAS in college, I happened to read a magazine interview with famous musician Chuck Berry. He said that he saved 80% of his earnings, and had done so throughout his life, even when he worked as a carpenter before he became famous.

I thought that was amazing. I had never heard of anyone saving so much. But being a college student at the time, I didn't have any excess money to spend, let alone save. So, I just tucked the idea into the back of my mind.

Once I finished college and started working as an engineer, I was able to save about 8% of my gross income each month. At the time, I had student loans, a car loan, and some credit card debt, on top of my other living expenses. There was not a lot of room in my budget, so saving 8% was the best I could do. But after working for a couple of years, I had paid off the credit cards and the car loan, and was able to increase my savings rate to nearly 20%.

Then I recalled that interview with Chuck Berry. Although I was making progress financially, I thought that saving 80% was unreachable. Still, I kept thinking about it. If other people could save 80% of their earnings, I should be able to save a lot more than 20%. Eventually I decided on a 50% rate as my goal. I didn't have a specific purpose for those dollars, but I liked the idea of saving as much as I could. And 50% seemed like a nice round number to aim for. It felt achievable, even though I wasn't sure how I would achieve it.

Around the same time, I got a 3% pay raise at my job. In talking with my coworkers who had worked there for a while, I learned that every year I could expect an increase of about 3%—sometimes a bit more, but usually not less. That's when I came to an important realization: If I could just hold my expenses constant, and increase my saving rate by three (or slightly more) percentage points a year, I could get from a 20% saving rate to a 50% saving rate within (roughly) ten years. (3% per year exactly it would take 17 years, but some years it was going to be slightly more than that, which would add up.)

In other words, I could reach my goal in a decade just by

funneling my modest annual raises into savings rather than spending them to inflate my lifestyle.

With this realization, I had a plan. I just had to hold my expenses constant for a decade. I wasn't sure how to do this, so I looked for opportunities. I moved out of my rented apartment and bought a small, inexpensive condo. Since the mortgage payment was a fixed amount, and the condo didn't require much maintenance, it allowed me to hold my housing costs constant.

When I replaced my car, instead of buying new, I bought one that was four years old, which kept my transportation costs low. It also helped that my condo was a five-minute drive from my workplace, so I didn't spend much money on commuting. (In retrospect, I should have bicycled to work during this period, at least during the summer.)

> I happened to read a magazine interview with famous musician Chuck Berry. He said that he saved 80% of his earnings, and had done so throughout his life, even when he worked as a carpenter before he became famous.

Finally, it helped that I had cheap hobbies and inexpensive tastes. I enjoyed bicycling, reading, and playing the guitar, all of which can be done very cheaply. And I didn't care much for wearing fashionable clothes or eating at fancy restaurants or going on lavish vacations. Somehow those things just didn't appeal to me.

I just worked at my job and directed my annual pay raises toward my savings and retirement accounts (401(k) and Roth IRA). And as it turned out, my annual pay raises were occasionally more than 3%, so I was able to reach a 50% saving rate in about eight years rather than ten.

It's been a few years since I reached that 50% goal. And once I got there, I did allow myself a bit of lifestyle inflation (buying a house and a three-year-old car). Currently, my saving rate is about 64% of my gross income. I could try to get to 80%, but I don't think it's necessary. Those early years of holding down my expenses and saving aggressively gave my finances all the momentum they needed on my journey toward FI.

## CONTROLLING COSTS AS A STUDENT

### FROOGAL STOODENT

*Ohio, USA*

*froogalstoodent.blogspot.com*

**W**HEN YOU WALK to work every day—even through eight-degree weather and bitter winter winds—people raise their eyebrows. When you have no cell phone at all for four years of college, people *really* raise their eyebrows.

And when you're living debt-free on a salary of $12,500 per year, people are incredulous!

You can do it, though—and you don't have to be an extreme couponer to make it happen. You just have to set your priorities straight, and establish habits that don't undermine your financial goals.

When I was accepted to a PhD program, I knew I wasn't going to be making much. I would have to keep my expenses as low as I possibly could.

First up was rent. I found one of the cheapest apartments in town. Actually, I had my choice of three. I picked the one I liked the most, which also happened to be the least expensive. It was small and poorly insulated, but it held me and all my stuff, and was in pretty decent shape.

It was an efficiency apartment (also called a "studio apartment") in which the living room, bedroom, and kitchen are all part of the same space (13 foot by 13), along with a narrow walk-in closet and an 8-by-6.5-foot bathroom (including storage cabinets).

My apartment came furnished with a bed, refrigerator, stove, kitchen table and chairs, as well as a window air conditioner for the summers. My monthly rent was $365, later raised to $385.

Most of my friends and colleagues had nicer apartments, but I wanted to keep my rent as low as possible. I needed a place to live—I did not need a big place.

Granted, these rents were in a semi-rural college town with a low overall cost of living. Rent in a big city like New York, Boston, Atlanta, or Los Angeles would have cost at least three times as much! But if you live in a big city, I sure hope you earn more than I did...

Next came my phone. I had never had a cell phone before moving out of state to my graduate program. People were endlessly astonished at how I got along without one—but, never having had one, I hadn't missed it. However, for my PhD, I wanted (not *needed*) to get a cell phone to stay in contact with friends and family more easily. I picked a $35 per month no-contract plan and a smartphone. I found this to be a reasonable cost for unlimited text and data, with 300 minutes of talk. I got to do the same stuff on my phone that other people did on much more expensive contracts.

When it came to groceries, there was an Aldi in town, as well as a Big Lots and a dollar store. Between these three, I got almost all of the food I needed for low prices, including fruit, vegetables, pasta, granola bars, bread, cereal, milk, and lunch meat. I also shopped at Kroger sometimes, especially when I needed something I couldn't find at Aldi. My grocery bill was $25 to $35 a week.

Again, the cost of living was low in my area, but you can follow the same principle, even if costs are higher in yours. Instead of paying more for name brands, I got the food I needed at the lowest prices I could find. The flavors were almost always the same as the more expensive name brands.

Being a student in a small apartment, I obviously didn't have a washing machine or dryer—but I still needed to do my laundry. At $1.50 per load of wash, and $0.25 for 7.5 minutes in the dryer (yes, they time it to 7.5 minutes), I went through about $10 per month in laundry money.

Due to my low income, I was eligible for a vastly reduced rate on my health insurance. I had a very high-deductible plan, but that was OK because I maintained enough savings to cover my deductible.

I paid less than $20 per month for my health insurance. Given that I was a healthy individual in my 20s, with virtually no family history of early-onset disease, there was an extremely low risk that the insurance company would have to pay out a dime for me (as it turns out, they never did). So I used a high-deductible plan to keep my monthly bill as low as it could go.

Let's count up the predictable expenses: rent at $365 per month, phone bill at $35 per month, groceries at about $120 per month (estimating on the high side), $20 per month for health insurance, and $10 per month for laundry. I also had to pay several hundred dollars in student fees every semester; these averaged out to around $100 per month.

My total expenses: around $750 per month. This worked out at $9,000 per year.

Yep. I lived on a grad student salary of $12,500 a year. And I did it debt-free.

## YOU CAN STILL SPEND

### TINA PLUMLEY

*Meridian, Idaho, USA*

**W**HEN I FIRST began tracking my spending with a goal to retire early, my focus was obviously on finding where I could reduce it. So I kept things I considered "extras" (entertainment, eating out, alcohol, wellness, and crap I want but rarely actually need) separate from what I considered more essential spending.

This allowed me to easily notice when unnecessary spending was creeping up. However, I found that there were times I felt great about spending money on extras—so focusing only on reducing or eliminating the total wasn't the right answer.

> The more I get myself to think in terms of how I will feel about the money spent, the more my overall spending decreases.

To help, I added a separate tab to assign value to such purchases.

In creating this tab, I began to pay closer attention to the thoughts and feelings I experienced when spending. I translated that into a value assignment:

1 = Shouldn't have
2 = Obligatory
3 = Intentional
4 = Relational
5 = Wellness
9 = New experiences
10 = YES!!!

My main focus was decreasing the percentage of dollars spent in 1 and 2, and removing guilt about dollars spent in 9 and 10.

I value adventure and new experiences and I'm willing to pay for them. On the other hand, I struggle with spending out of obligation. Perhaps it's a birthday gift I'm "supposed" to buy, or feeling like I need to cover lunch for someone who bought it for me previously. I'm only doing these things because I feel like I need to, not because I truly want to. Paying attention to these feelings and purchases in category 2 helps me address this struggle.

The biggest hurdle for me is making sure I thoroughly consider anything in categories 3, 4 and 5. Learning to think ahead about how I will track the spending has helped me determine how to approach activities.

I still spend money that I shouldn't, or based on obligation, but the more I get myself to think in terms of how I will feel about the money spent, the more my overall spending decreases. Since I first began tracking my expenses, my extra spending has been cut by about 60%.

## FIND YOUR BUDGET'S RUBBER BAND

### MICHAEL HE

*Los Angeles, California, USA*

*michaelhe.me*

**W**HEN I GRADUATED high school, I had a long conversation with my mother. She'd worked hard for years to support my education up to that point, and drained her life's savings. I couldn't let her pay for my college education by selling everything she had. Instead, I chose the college with the best scholarship and financial aid offer. Then I maxed out my work-study to cover my after-grant tuition.

Doing that for four years (especially during the pandemic, when I had multiple part-time jobs) taught me four valuable lessons.

**One**, it's never too early to save. Even for someone young like me, I regretted not opening a Roth IRA right after getting my first paycheck. The key is to make it a painless amount and automate it.

**Two**, true austerity hurts. Very few people can actually live like a monk for their FI goals, and I know I am not one. I've spent so much money on (used) books, K-pop albums (beautiful collectibles), and treating people to nice food, I would be frowned upon by the super-frugal crowd.

But these things make me feel happy and rewarded for the hard work I put in. You just have to be deliberate and honest with yourself on what brings you the kind of joy that lasts longer than the fleeting thrill of clicking a buy button. This lets you set a relative "rubber band" for your budget, which shouldn't change dramatically even as you gradually earn more income from promotions.

**Three**, make time your friend by compounding.

**Four**, and lastly, do not let credit cards trick you into overspending. If you can't budget life with hard cash, you can't handle credit.

## SUPERCHARGING SAVINGS OVERSEAS

### JOANA AND TONY CAROLA (MEETCAROLAS)

*Portugal*

*www.youtube.com/meetcarolas*

**W**E ARE A Portuguese couple who met at university. Even though we have quite different personalities, we have always shared a passion for saving money and the thrill of scoring good deals.

After university we decided to be adventurous and get jobs abroad. This took us to Belgium, where we continued to live below our means—saving around 60% of our income.

Belgium, back in the day, had a lovely labor law. After five years, you were allowed to request a sabbatical year with your employer—no questions asked, *plus* an allowance of $700 dollars a month.

When we found out about this rule, we thought we had hit the jackpot. It was perfect for us—never mind a honeymoon, this could be a honey*year*. And the sweetest element of this labor law was that your employer couldn't fire you after you came back. Your job waited for you.

So we packed our bags and went backpacking for 365 days across Southeast Asia, New Zealand and South America. Without even knowing it, we had what is now called a "mini-retirement."

Friends and family asked us if we weren't falling off our career train in our 30s. We told them we were taking the bullet train in our career! And we were absolutely right.

Towards the end of our trip we decided to finish our journey in San Jose in the States. Our employer had offices there, so we went in and networked like crazy.

We had always dreamed of living and working in the US, rubbing shoulders with American go-getters and entrepreneurs. This was our opportunity.

When one of us got a job offer and L1 visa sponsorship, the other automatically qualified for an L2 visa because we were married. With both of us employed in the US, our income increased 50% above what we made in Belgium. We didn't cave in to consumerism and kept our superpower of saving—now at 70% of our income.

Fast-forward five years, we had bought a home, paid it off in full, were still saving 70% of our paycheck… but we had a massive blind spot.

Other than our home, we were terrible investors.

Our flaws were a mixture of extreme conservatism and short-termism. It was frustrating. We were doing so well at saving—but terrible at making our money grow for us.

Around this time we started hearing about the FI movement. We dove in head first, researching and reading everything we could find.

We found our way fully onto JL's Simple Path at last—having accidentally made good progress on a parallel route.

We were able to catch up on our 401(k) contributions through a mega IRA backdoor that was available in our company. We went from only putting in 4% a year to get the company match, to putting in around $100,000 combined, investing it in simple low-cost ETFs.

Meanwhile, after having kids and going through Covid without family in the USA, we decided it was time to return to Portugal— and once again take advantage of geoarbitrage.

As soon as we reach our FI number, we will be back, living in a low-cost area where our money goes further and we have the quality of life and slow pace we need for raising kiddos.

## SWAPPING STATES TO MAKE IT ALL POSSIBLE

### BRAYDON AND LAURA LARSON

*Kingman, Arizona, USA*

**W**E GOT MARRIED in 2014. Braydon was a year and a half away from pharmacy school graduation and I was a wedding photographer in Las Vegas. As graduation drew closer, $244,000 of student loans was at the forefront of our minds. Then Braydon was approached by a drug company with an offer.

It was lower than we had anticipated, but it kept us in Las Vegas, close to family and comfortable. He accepted. Days later, the same company posted an opportunity in a small, dusty Arizona town (population 30,000 with as many tumbleweeds).

It came with a $30,000 sign-on bonus and a salary $26,000 higher per year. We seized the opportunity—sold our home, left family, and switched breadwinning roles. I became a stay-at-home mom while my husband went full time as a pharmacy manager.

We wanted financial freedom. And this sacrifice immediately began to make our FI aspirations possible. We paid off $100,000 of the school loan after selling our Vegas house. Then we refinanced from a ~7% interest rate to a ~3% rate. The loan was then paid off in April 2018.

Around this time, we discovered JL's Simple Path. The stock market finally became crystal clear. We quickly dumped a lump sum in our new Vanguard account, and continue to make automatic monthly purchases there.

> We are done growing our family—but, if we decided to have more, it would not affect our FI journey in the slightest.

Many years earlier, I remember a friend of mine suggesting I invest in the stock market. He took the time to explain it and was very thorough—but I just couldn't grasp it. And because I didn't understand it, I didn't invest. Of course, now I wish I had gotten a head start. I just didn't know what I didn't know.

A few months after opening our Vanguard account, we purchased our first home together in the same town for less than our annual salary. Our family of six lives comfortably in under 1,400 sq ft. We have found great joy in living well below our means in an already low-cost-of-living town.

Now, after maxing out our 401(k) and hefty regular VTSAX contributions (just three short years of following The Path), we are completely debt-free and have enough F-You Money that we are planning on taking a sabbatical so we can buy more time with our kids while they are still under our roof.

This was all possible while starting a family and having as many kids as we wanted. Our kids were born in 2015, 2016, 2019, and 2020. We are done growing our family—but, if we decided to have more, it would not affect our FI journey in the slightest.

## FLEXIBILITY IS OF THE ESSENCE

### BRUNO BONTEMPI

*Italy*

ALL DRESSED IN white and covered by orchids, Ganesh was lying at the other end of the large hall. I had never seen him alive.

Our wives were proud members of the Italian Moms Club, and our daughters had spent some time together at the park. The club organized social events on public holidays and a few birthdays, but he was exclusively focused on his business activities, so I hardly knew of his existence.

As a respected software development executive, Ganesh was an incarnation of the Silicon Valley dream, an American dream on steroids. His purpose was not just social affirmation or financial security for himself and his family. What really motivated him was the quest for a unique market-changing idea, to be developed into a wildly popular application thanks to a close-knit team of people he had successfully worked with in the past.

As the chanting grew louder and he was carried out of the hall, I bid Ganesh farewell. At age 37, I was ready to leave Silicon Valley and its broken dreams. I wanted to spend more time with my family, tighten the knot with my wife, watch my kids grow, and smell with them a rose or two.

And most importantly, I wanted to save my life, when I still had time to do it.

I was later told about Ganesh's last request, as he was fighting a heart attack on the way to the emergency room. He begged doctors and nurses to keep him alive. "I cannot go, my daughters have just started school," he said.

Spring in Italy was unbearably dull, after the mind-blowing experience of six springs in California. There were no tulips to be seen, the poppies were a uniform red, and the streets were covered by white fluff falling from the trees. Most of all I missed the community, the coming together of people from so many different places and cultures.

The challenges, however, were interesting. As a full-time volunteer—that would be my job title, going forward—I was in charge of taking a half-abandoned house in the hills near Bologna, and turning it into a foster home for up to six children. The work required daily interaction with the local social services, and frequent consultation with a whole team of psychologists and educators.

As a software developer I had always been an individual contributor, at the very bottom of the org chart, but now I had a cost center to my name. I was proud of myself, though my family was mostly disparaging. I would earn no income, but household expenses would be covered, if properly accounted and justified.

> I wanted to spend more time with my family, tighten the knot with my wife, watch my kids grow, and smell with them a rose or two.

Most of my excitement depended on the newly rediscovered importance of the human factor. I would be dealing with people all the time, serving their needs. What could be better?

And they were indeed a rewarding ten years, helping about 20 children recover from trauma, and contributing to the growth of the organization I had joined. It was much more and much better than working from home. It was work, real work, *for* my home.

I had been an avid consumer of FI materials since the turn of the century. In the beginning it was mostly bulletin boards; in time, popular websites would emerge. The main approach proposed was to track family expenses, and calculate the minimum net worth required for financial independence. After that, it was a matter of saving as much income as possible, and investing most of those savings.

I never followed that. I was educated in Italy, where higher education was affordable, and accrued most of my assets in the United States, where salaries and the cost of living were much higher. In short, I had been engaged in geoarbitrage long before the word was coined. Likewise, as I was envisioning my early retirement, I expected to move to a country with a low cost of living.

On the other hand, I had saved and invested no more than 30% of my income—a dismal percentage by FI standards. So I periodically reviewed my net worth, and sought out where in the world I could afford to retire. After a handful of years in a high-tech Silicon Valley job, and two handfuls of years at zero income, zero expenses, and reinvested dividends (or "coasting," a term I would learn later), I found I could comfortably retire in the Philippines.

So that's what I did. If my net worth strongly increases, I might move back to a European country. If it permanently decreases, I am more than ready to lower my current living standards. I keep my withdrawal rate much lower than the canonical 4%, so that an optimistic scenario is more likely to unfold.

As is often the case in life, flexibility is of the essence. We cannot control the sea, but we can keep a hand on the rudder.

## THE EXPRESS LANE TO WEALTH

NOMADICC

*Mexico*

INHERITED MY FINANCIAL operating system from my mom: Never carry a balance on a credit card. Make sure you never owe more than you own. Always try to maximize the fun you can get from the money you earn.

That worked early on in my career, but when I lost my job my wife and I had to learn to cut our expenses dramatically— and use geoarbitrage to get them even lower. Then we upskilled and got better jobs and that meant moving back to somewhere expensive. While searching for ways to keep living expenses down (difficult in Silicon Valley), we discovered FI at last.

> Most of her start-up peers spent the money buying houses or investing in lumber. We decided to "VTSAX and chill."

I would say that VTSAX is a simple path, and geoarbitrage turns it into an express lane.

We used it again, moving to Austin. Our savings and budgeting left us well prepared for the pandemic, and allowed us to look after our parents when they lost their jobs due to a combination of health issues and lockdowns.

My wife then sold her start-up for the equivalent of two years' salary, and a high-paying job at the acquiring company. If she doesn't lift her foot from the accelerator, I think she'll be the CEO of a Fortune 500 company in 20 years.

Most of her start-up peers spent the money buying houses or investing in lumber. We decided to "VTSAX and chill."

I no longer dream of labor. When my last stock bonus vests, I will consider retiring at 33. Our nest egg is enough to cover the 4% rule in our hometown and many amazing Latin American cities. If we have a kid, I will be the main caretaker. Whenever my wife wants to join me in retirement, we can move back home; or we can choose a retirement destination and sprint to the finish line together.

## PULLING THE FINISH LINE CLOSER

### JOHN AND SARA GRAFTON

*Dayton, Ohio, USA*

Living in Silicon Valley put us on the path to wealth, and avoiding lifestyle inflation kept us making progress. But ultimately geoarbitrage got us to the finish line.

We are native midwesterners, and Silicon Valley in 2012 was the first time we had lived somewhere with a truly high cost of living. Home ownership was particularly expensive, so we rented—first, an apartment, then a small house.

It was hard to find a rental with two dogs, but we weren't tempted to buy a house (or a condo). Not least because we had discovered FI and JL's Simple Path.

Late in 2014, we learned that our beloved rental was going to be renovated and sold. We had the option to buy it. We passed. With the improvements, it was going to be larger and more expensive. Instead, we found another rental nearby.

It was stressful to have to find a new house roughly every two years, but it paid off in the long run. Whenever we got frustrated, Sara researched the real estate options around Dayton, Ohio, where we both grew up and still went to see our families each year.

We lived in Silicon Valley for John's tech job while Sara worked in education. Tech jobs came with stock drops and bonuses, but educators felt the pressure of rising housing costs. It gave us two views of California. John came home each fall with stories of colleagues' new cars and boats after the bonuses arrived. It was a lucrative time to work for a large tech company, but we strove to avoid lifestyle inflation. We invested money in VTSAX instead.

We didn't feel deprived. We still enjoyed exploring the Bay Area and trying new restaurants. John bought an electric bicycle to improve his daily commute instead of an electric car. Bicycling improved our health and saved us some headaches from traffic and parking in congested areas. We rented a slightly larger house in our favorite neighborhood when our second child arrived in 2017.

Like most people, our lives changed with the pandemic in March of 2020. We quickly shifted to working, and attending school, from home. Our youngest was only two years old at the time, and her daycare closed. We juggled two remote, full-time jobs while caring for a small child and making sure our older son participated in his online school. Our biggest struggle was living so far from family during this challenging time. We knew that we were fortunate to have built up wealth and flexibility during our years in California—if not FI.

That came with the move back to Ohio.

We closed on a house near Dayton at the end of May 2020. The significantly lower housing costs finally allowed us to reach financial independence, while also living close to family.

We've gone back to California to visit friends since, but we know we made the right decision. You can't beat flexibility and freedom. Geoarbitrage finally unlocked that fully for us.

# PART FOUR:

# *LIFESTYLE INFLATION*

# JL'S VIEW

## BANDIT!

**B**Y NOW ON The Simple Path you're debt-free, and you're saving—when out of the forest emerges a bandit intent on permanently interrupting your journey. Or perhaps this bandit has gotten ahold of you before you even came across The Path and is doing everything possible to keep you from it. Under that bandit mask is the face of lifestyle inflation.

## LIVING DIFFERENTLY

When I began walking this Path myself, I'm sure there were others doing so too. But in those days there was no way to connect with them. In my daily life, no one I knew thought this way. Nobody knew I was saving and investing 50% of my income. I didn't talk about it. I knew it was too far outside the realm of everybody else's experience. But they sometimes noticed I lived a bit differently.

I spent the first ten years after college in Chicago, and I lived in an unfashionable neighborhood. My friends who were living in the more fashionable parts of the city would occasionally tease me about it. "When are you gonna move over here?"

But their apartments were expensive and mine was cheap—and, unfashionable though it might have been, my neighborhood had its charms.

It is not that my lifestyle didn't inflate, but rather I only allowed it to do so in a controlled fashion. As my income and the amount I had to spend on buying investments grew, so did the remaining 50% I spent on my lifestyle.

My wife was on board from the beginning. Once married, and as our careers progressed, we moved first to Ohio and then to New Hampshire. We bought houses and cars along the way, but unlike our peers we never felt the need to buy the biggest or the fanciest. We had a much more attractive thing to buy with our money: **Financial Freedom**.

## STRUGGLING TO MAKE ENDS MEET ON ONLY $800,000 PER YEAR

One year just before Christmas back in the early 1990s, my pal Ken and I had lunch together in Chicago. He was in the financial business. In that business your annual bonus is a big part of your income, and Ken had just gotten his. It was $800,000. In the early 90s, this was real money.

Want to know what we talked about at lunch? We talked about how you can't make ends meet on $800,000 a year.

I'm sure that sounds absurd to virtually everybody reading this. You're thinking, "Pay me $800,000 for a year or two and I'm done." Me too.

But listening to Ken talk about the lifestyle he'd put together—

the multiple homes, the luxury cars, the private schools, exotic travel—you realized that he was absolutely right. Eight-hundred-thousand dollars was not enough. So, unless he changed his ways, Ken—for all his huge income—would never be financially independent. He'd built a gilded cage.

Whereas my high-school buddy we met at the beginning of the last part of the book—who never made more than $40,000 a year—got there. A big income helps, but it is what you keep that matters.

## THE BIGGEST CHALLENGE

This lifestyle inflation is relatively easy to avoid if you are aware of (and control) it from the start. But for those who come to The Simple Path later in life this can be the single biggest challenge. Often they have followed, like Ken, the "normal" path of buying the most extravagant lifestyle their income can provide and then borrowing still more to expand it further. Frequently they have a spouse and children accustomed to this life they may now realize makes no sense. Unravelling what they have created—setting down those burdens to walk more freely along The Path—isn't easy.

I am deeply grateful I never had to deal with this, and I deeply respect those who have successfully done so. In this part you'll hear some of their stories. If you are in this situation, perhaps you'll find the hope and inspiration you need to slip past this forest bandit who has held you up.

# RULES FOR THE ROAD

- People may notice if you don't live like them. That's OK.

- You have to decide if status symbols and other people's opinions matter to you more than freedom.

- If you desire a different life, you must expect that life and the path to it will be different from that of your peers.

- Lifestyle inflation is an insidious foe—you are best served never letting it take hold.

- If it has you must resolve to unwind it.

- However much you make, it's all about how much you keep.

- If your spending expands to meet—or, even worse, exceed—your income, you will never be free.

## "IF YOU OBEY ALL THE RULES, YOU MISS ALL THE FUN."

## —KATHARINE HEPBURN

# THE STORIES

## THE HAPPINESS QUEST

### JSD (JUST SOME DUDE)

### *USA*

*escapingavalon.com*

**A**RMY TRAINING WAS not only one of the happiest moments of my life, it also represents the cheapest my cost of living has ever been. Though the Army provided me with everything I needed, if I were to replicate such a lifestyle using backpacking gear and living in public forests, I could live in relative comfort for less than $8,000 a year.

Hell, I could sleep more and eat triple what I was given, plus I wouldn't be dragging a bunch of weaponry around; my pack would be under 40 pounds.

In comparison to the life I lived for months in the mountains while training, that sounds like pure luxury.

Of course, my lifestyle has inflated since then, almost in

lockstep with the other happiest moments of my life—marriage and the birth of my kids.

After the Army I became a cop, and my standard of living shot up. At first I was amazed at the abundance my career provided, and enjoyed no longer training or being deployed for months. I fell into the standard pattern of most young professionals—eating out regularly, going for drinks a few times a week, generally not paying attention to money.

A few years later I met my future wife. Shortly thereafter I got on the SWAT team and became a detective. Both roles increased my spending considerably. As a street cop I patrolled an inner-city neighborhood and wasn't allowed to drive outside its confines during my eight-hour shift. That restricted my restaurant choices to McDonald's or an inferior local barbecue joint. I brought lunch most days.

When I became a detective, I was allowed to go to any restaurant I wanted; we investigated crimes all over the city. The detective job included lots of overtime, and I was constantly getting called out for SWAT incidents. I was working more than 12 hours a day, and sometimes would be gone for days with just a few hours off in between. I started eating out twice a day. My bank account didn't seem to notice. I wasn't tracking my spending at the time, but I imagine the increase in spending was balanced by the extra income from all of the overtime.

I did notice a strange effect, though. Back when I was a street cop, I used to look forward to eating at my favorite burrito joint on days off. Once I could eat there three times a week as a detective, my enjoyment waned. This was the first time I consciously noticed my lifestyle inflating but not bringing about an increase in happiness.

My girlfriend and I began to get interested in personal finance stuff, and in the midst of paying down a 1,100 sq ft house in an inexpensive working-class neighborhood, we discovered FIRE.

We went hardcore, tracking every expense. Our food costs were steep. I began prepping a week's worth of meals on my days off, and started bringing my lunch to work everyday, along with a healthy stockpile of snacks for when I worked late. We made some tweaks, and my monthly expenses hovered around $1,000 a month. Per the 4% rule, my FI number was $300,000, and my projections showed I was just four years away from getting there. I went back to eating at my favorite burrito joint on the occasional day off. I started savoring it again. A little lifestyle deflation seemed to have actually increased my happiness.

We got married two years after finding FI. I cried tears of joy at the ceremony, having wed the love of my life. We had been dating for years, and married when we felt ready for kids. Both of us were committed professionals, my wife an engineer moving up at her company, while I continually took on more challenging assignments. We wanted to make sure we had a good footing professionally before kids. With both of us finally feeling secure at our jobs, we got hitched. Then our lifestyle inflated.

One day the SWAT team I served on was called to a house a few blocks south of mine to deal with an armed and barricaded shooting suspect. There were a lot of

I did notice a strange effect, though. Back when I was a street cop, I used to look forward to eating at my favorite burrito joint on days off. Once I could eat there three times a week as a detective, my enjoyment waned. This was the first time I consciously noticed my lifestyle inflating but not bringing about an increase in happiness.

good people in that neighborhood, but it was not a place we wanted to raise kids. A year after we married, we moved. We bought one of the smallest houses in a nicer neighborhood. The added costs brought my average monthly expenses to $1,250 a month. Just as I had got more than halfway to my FI number, I had a new one, and it was $75,000 higher.

We hadn't even started having kids yet.

We got used to the slightly larger house pretty quick, but I noticed that I felt much less stressed coming home to our new, safer, neighborhood at the end of a shift. This feeling has stuck with me over the years. Occasionally I'll drive by our previous house and thank my lucky stars our kids aren't growing up there. This was probably the first time I realized that spending more money in certain deliberate ways could actually improve our lives.

A couple years after moving, we finally had our first kid. Tied for first place on happiest moment ever. Looking at our financial tracking spreadsheet, the expense needle didn't move immediately. But it sure did when we started daycare a few months later. Like many parents, we were conflicted about handing our kid off to unknown people and didn't love the high cost of full-time childcare, so we started off with half days. With me working night shift and my wife working normal hours, we arranged it so our son was in daycare less than four hours a day. My wife would drop him off around eight, and I would pick him up before noon. I would get five to six hours of sleep if I hadn't had to work late, and then go straight into taking care of our son until my wife got home at 5 pm. We'd see each other for maybe 20 minutes, then I'd rush into work.

We did this for almost a year, and the dent part-time daycare put in our expenses was minimal. Mine climbed to near $1,500 a month, making my FI number $450,000. In addition to our young son getting up at all hours of the night, we were compounding our sleep deprivation by my night shifts and our refusal to keep our son at daycare longer. I worked half of the weekend, and my wife and I parented in shifts. We rarely saw each other.

Part of our rejection of more daycare was my motivation to keep expenses low. Though my wife and I tracked our finances together, we evenly split the household bills and costs associated with our son, but had separate tracking for our income, expenses, savings, and net worths/FI numbers. My wife, being the reasonable one, had lowered her savings rate after giving birth to accommodate eating out with her coworkers more frequently and indulging in purchases related to her knitting and crochet hobby. This kept her sane despite the increased stress of parenting. I went in the opposite direction.

I watched with fear as my FI number grew first when we moved, then when we became parents. I went hardcore, barreling past frugality into deprivation. My coworkers made fun of my rice-and-bean meal habit. I completely stopped eating out and volunteered for ever more overtime. I had no hobbies, and in my rare free time obsessed about how to lower my costs.

After all, if I could be happy in the Army eating cold chilli on the side of a mountain, I could surely maintain a sleep-deprived pace while I sprinted to FI with no ill effects.

I was wrong.

My wife's savings rate went to 60%, mine neared 80%. My numbers looked great on our spreadsheet, but my misery was bordering on burnout. I finally admitted we needed to deliberately inflate our lifestyles if we were going to maintain sanity.

It was ridiculous to not keep our son in daycare for a few more hours; he'd just be napping in the afternoons regardless if he was at home or daycare. Shelling out some more cash would buy me a few extra hours of much needed sleep. At the same time we were getting fed up with the way our parenting shifts were working. I was spending more time with our son, albeit sleep deprived, and my wife was feeling left out. Between parenting and my crazy job, I had no time to myself, let alone with my wife.

We decided to make some drastic changes that would push our FI date back but secure a better and more sustainable quality of life. We did the following:

1. Paid for full-time daycare, with our son going from 9 am to 3 pm.

2. My wife went down from 40 hours to 30 hours a week, which also reduced her pay by 25%. This gave her ten more hours a week with our son, money well spent. I also passed up a promotion, and instead volunteered for a slower-paced administrative position which kept me off the night shift.

3. I sought out a hobby that would get me out of the house once a week. I bought a new mountain bike for $1,300.

This purchase hurt, but I needed a relief valve. Before we became parents I'd tooled around the local trails on my 20-year-old mountain bike a few times. This crazy use of $1,300 increased my enjoyment of those nearby trails considerably, and became a great way to relieve some stress.

All of this upped my monthly average expenses to just over $1,700. New FI number: $518,000. I was bummed at seeing this on our spreadsheet. The same month my average expenses hit their new high, my net worth hit my old FI number of $300,000. It hurt. And then we decided to have kid number two.

Looking back to when we started thinking about having our first kid, we were more than a little naive about how we'd be able to keep expenses down despite adding a new member to our household. With a few years of parenting behind us, our eyes were wide open now. Thankfully both of us had been saving well over half of our income despite our constantly inflating lifestyle.

> If I could be happy in the Army eating cold chilli on the side of a mountain, I could surely maintain a sleep-deprived pace while I sprinted to FI with no ill effects.

We received progressive salary bumps and kept the big three expenses of housing, food, and transport low. Any spending outside of that was careful. But, with the birth of our daughter, my FI number moved again. It was worth it: Her birth was also tied for number one happiest moment ever. Man, I cried a lot on that one. Actually knowing what I was getting into probably made a big difference.

I suppose economies of scale helped with kid number two; even with two kids in daycare my average spending only increased to $2,250 a month, my FI number going to $675,000. I'd love to say we surpassed that new FI number a year after we met our daughter because of some great investing skills, but really we just benefited from the crazy bull market which everyone else who stuck with indexing through the pandemic experienced.

We realized that our inflated portfolios were nice, but a corresponding reduction in our assumed safe withdrawal rate was necessary. After running the numbers again, we realized I had amassed enough with a decent buffer to retire early from police work.

In March of 2022 I left behind a pension worth over a million dollars, but which would have required me staying on the force another six years to vest. Six more years of being half asleep while our kids grew up just wasn't worth it, not if I finally had enough money to make work optional.

A big reason I was OK with leaving was my experience of lifestyle inflation. I have felt the full spectrum of hedonic adaptation. In reviewing the happiest moments in my life, I was amazed I could be nearly as happy in the Army with a cold meal under a poncho on the side of the mountain as I could be in a climate-controlled hospital meeting the most important people in my life.

I had thought miserable experiences like freezing and starving in the mountains for months or serving in a combat zone would make every other minor inconvenience afterwards seem trite. I wish that were the case, but years later I still get annoyed by little things like getting stuck in traffic.

Happiness is relative to the amount of suffering at the time, not relative to life overall. That's why ten extra minutes under a poncho can be almost as amazing as meeting a new human. If life is a living nightmare, any minor improvement is cherished. But in the amazing first-world life I've been lucky enough to live, it takes something truly awesome to bring about the same amount of increase in happiness.

Realizing this made me understand that any extra spending on frivolous things was never going to move that happiness needle. Better to spend on the things that matter—time with family, freedom, and mental health.

## CULTIVATE INDIFFERENCE
## TO BIGGER, BETTER,
## NEWER

LAURA ROJO-EDDY

*Texas, USA*

**T**HE ONE FOUNDATIONAL attitude that put us (and has kept us) on the track to financial independence—before we ever heard of FI—was our indifference to the American cultural hunger for more, bigger, better, newer things.

We ignored traditional wisdom and advice from well-meaning family and friends like, "You should grow into your house payment." Such sayings seem to take for granted that you'll always be spending most of your earnings.

Instead, we bought what our families referred to as a "starter home." Now it's paid off. We're still there.

And instead of trading in our cars for new ones every few years, we buy used and drive them till they drop. We're not immune to the temptations of shiny new things, but it's easier if you get clear on the things that matter most to you. For us, that's travel. We prioritize spending on that over keeping up with the neighbors.

## SCRATCHING THE LIFESTYLE INFLATION ITCH WITHOUT INVITING DISASTER

### MRS. DINK OF DINKS ON A BUS

*Vermont, USA*

*dinksonabus.com*

BELIEVE THE TWO most important things to help prevent lifestyle inflation are:

1. goals
2. intentional spending.

For the longest time, I was on the hamster wheel of work and life, my identity completely wrapped up in my job. When I discovered FI, I thought it was great because I could stay on the hamster wheel—I'd grown comfortable with it in a way—and reach financial independence in the fastest time possible.

Then life abruptly threw me off the hamster wheel.

I found myself in a new career with a traditional 40-hour-per-week job, and I realized for the first time in my life that I had all of this *time*. I discovered passions outside of work. And I came across Slow FI, a new way of thinking about financial independence.

I drew up a financial freedom list—things I wanted to do or explore as I gained more time. I started to set goals for myself. One of these was to increase my income (by switching jobs or asking for raises), so that I could eventually go down to part-time work and still make decent money.

Without this, I would have just kept on working.

I also used intentional spending to avoid lifestyle creep. Because I was also paying close attention to my daily life and crafting it so that I enjoyed each and every day (thanks to Slow FI), I had a pretty good sense of what made me happy. So, I picked certain small things to spend on that wouldn't make too much of a dent in the budget, but would enhance my daily life greatly. For me, this meant monthly massages and hiring a house cleaner.

> When I discovered FI, I thought it was great because I could stay on the hamster wheel—I'd grown comfortable with it in a way—and reach financial independence in the fastest time possible.

I am scratching the lifestyle inflation itch, but I'm not breaking the bank or delaying FI to do so.

## GRADING OUR LIFESTYLE INFLATION EFFORTS

### MARK

*Madison, Wisconsin, USA*

WE STUMBLED ONTO The Simple Path to Wealth a few years ago when we were in our late 40s. One of my first goals was to figure out if we really had enough money to retire early. The answer was yes—largely because we had limited our lifestyle inflation to a reasonable level over the years.

Not that it was easy. We definitely went through a difficult phase in our 30s and early 40s. Many of my wife's coworkers were building new houses, some of them on a regular basis. We resisted that temptation (although we did pay for someone to install new siding). Instead we lived in an average-cost house (for our market), while earning a well-above-average income, and did most of the home improvement projects ourselves.

We also had relatively short commutes and didn't splurge on the types of cars or vacations enjoyed by some in our circles.

I do remember more than one conversation over the years that went along the lines of, "Why can't we have this, and why can't we do that?" We were mostly able to hold the line, but only mostly.

Some choices didn't help our financial situation. The major issue was kids' sports and other activities. Pro tip: Before you let your child fall in love with a sport, take the time to fully understand the costs. Some sports will run over $1,000 a month. Investigate. Discuss. Agree on limits. We didn't, and it led to a lot of bad financial choices for a number of years, and eventually some difficult conversations.

An overloaded schedule also led to a lot of eating out, bad for both our waistlines and pocketbooks.

So, when it comes to lifestyle inflation, I'd have to give us a C+. We avoided the bells and whistles that many in our income bracket went for, but we had a hard time bringing logic to decisions about what opportunities to provide for our children. We led with emotion on those. And, significantly, those decisions tied my wife to an employer where the average longevity was about three years. Her view was, "I'm working my ass off so my child can have this." Which was fine, but I'm not sure that any of us would say it was the correct choice today, not even the kids.

> I do remember more than one conversation over the years that went along the lines of, "Why can't we have this, and why can't we do that?" We were mostly able to hold the line, but only mostly.

In the end, the costs of children's activities will disappear (unlike a 30-year mortgage on a $750,000 house), but there is a price to be paid for lifestyle inflation, in more ways than one.

# LIFESTYLE BLOAT KILLS
# YOUR OPTIONS

CW

*Chattanooga, Tennessee, USA*

**W**E DON'T GET everything right, but one of the FI things my wife and I *have* gotten right over the years is keeping our lifestyle inflation low even as our incomes rose.

Thirteen years ago, some business partners and I started a software company and my wife and I immediately went to living on less than 20% of our previous income. We'd never have been able to take that risk if our lifestyles had gotten bloated.

In early 2021 (after more than 12 years of hammering away seven days a week), we sold the company. It was great for us founders to finally get made whole for all of the risk we'd taken over the years.

On paper, my wife and I have been FI since the deal closed, but it wasn't until we paid cash for the house we'd been renting that we actually *felt* that we were FI.

Interest rates were still in the basement at the time, and we could have easily gotten a mortgage. Any number of arguments could have been made that it was the wrong financial decision. But, for us, it was the right *money* decision.

I haven't sent a rent or mortgage payment to anyone in a year. Our living expenses consist of utilities, food, and not much else. And it feels amazing.

## LIFE-CHANGING ADVICE

LISA SCHADER

*California, USA*

*moneyfitmoms.com*

**M**Y HUSBAND AND I became young millionaires because a college professor gave us one life-changing piece of advice:

> "For the first ten years out of college, don't upgrade your lifestyle—continue living like broke college students and *invest* instead."

That professor had made a fortune as an investment professional and then became a college professor. We graduated from college, but never forgot his advice.

Avoiding lifestyle inflation wasn't easy—getting our first real paychecks out of college was exciting, and upgrading our lifestyle to match felt reasonable. But while some of our peers were buying cars or getting sweet apartments, we continued to live on the cheap.

We found the cheapest apartment in a safe(ish) area, packed our lunches, took public transportation to work, DIYed

> But because of compound interest, the opportunity cost of upgrading your lifestyle when you're young is astronomical.

home and car repairs (or traded services when possible), used thrifted or hand-me-down clothing and furniture. We basically just avoided shopping. When we *had* to buy something, we saved up for it, rather than using debt.

But living cheap was not the most important thing we did—the most critical step was investing that money instead.

That professor helped us avoid one of the most common financial pitfalls of youth: lifestyle inflation. One friend shared how he'd had a particularly lucrative college internship and consequently bought a BMW. Realizing the error of his ways, he sold it a year later. He calculated that driving that car for one year had cost him $10,000—but that was just the loss in value. Since he was 20 years old at the time, the opportunity cost of not investing that money was worth well over $500,000 of retirement money.

I think most sane people would agree that one year of car ownership is not worth half a million dollars. But because of compound interest, the opportunity cost of upgrading your lifestyle when you're young is astronomical.

## ONLY A MATTER OF TIME

RYQUIST

*Minnesota, USA*

**W**HEN I STARTED my career after graduation, my lifestyle expanded to match my new income. I at least made a good decision to reduce housing costs by living with friends, but I discovered a vulnerability that came with this choice.

Whenever one of us felt like dining out or grabbing a few beers, we would all do so together. We had adult jobs now, so each individual indulgence was within our means and could be justified on its own. It was the accumulation of these daily decisions that affected our accounts—and our waistlines. The latter finally instigated change. After an embarrassingly long time, I realized I was terribly out of shape and needed a new path.

Habits, both good and bad, tend to stack and working out made me want to eat a clean diet that would not squander the hard work. Good habits build on themselves like compound interest just as bad habits pile up like credit card debt. I also turned peer pressure on its head by involving my friends. We kept each other on track and made pacts, such as no alcohol for the first quarter of each year. It took a long time and there were plenty of setbacks, but I found a balance that works for me.

> Good habits build on themselves like compound interest just as bad habits pile up like credit card debt.

Food/drink is one of three major categories that define lifestyle expenses along with housing and transportation. These categories are so important because they make up the bulk of our spending and tend to repeat month after month. Controlling these costs provides a baseline budget that is likely to succeed. On the other hand, overspending in these categories will result in a high cost of living even if every possible luxury is minimized.

This was the best place for me to start because my efforts have paid off continuously. Buying a used car with cash, for example, provides years without monthly car payments. Learning to cook results in healthier and less expensive meals alongside the fun of developing a new skill.

A financial independence date is determined by savings rate which in turn is defined by income and expenses. I have found the greatest value in addressing lifestyle and its influence on spending. Frugality allows me to save more now, and means I will require less passive income each month in the future. Establishing a healthy savings rate and limiting lifestyle inflation make financial independence only a matter of time.

## LIFESTYLE INFLATION... SOMETIMES IT'S REAL MURDER

### CHRISTINA CONNALLY HONKONEN

*Knoxville, USA*

*pitchwirestudio.com*

I'VE ALWAYS HAD a penchant for the scruffy, do-it-yourself mentality so I was an easy catch for FI when I discovered the movement at 25 years old. Apart from occasional lapses into individual stock picking, I made good progress on The Simple Path to Wealth. My husband, Matt, shared my vision. Our basic approach was to keep our real estate costs low and pay off our home as quickly as possible, before aggressively funding our tax-advantaged retirement accounts.

In 2013 we welcomed our first child to our home, a craftsman-style adobe situated on the outskirts of an urban neighborhood. In retrospect, perhaps too much on the outskirts. We started witnessing blatant crime. Undercover cops would knock on our door and ask if they could park in our driveway.

We tried turning a blind eye to the drug drops and yelling matches around us until one morning we awoke to see yellow tape flanking our mailbox.

As I sipped my coffee, watching the scene unfold from my living room, I noticed a policewoman walk up and peek under a large tarp covering a big lump. I soon learned that under that tarp was the dead body of a man killed by our neighbor during a purported drug exchange. The victim, we were told, was murdered with a kitchen knife in a house roughly ten feet from our baby's nursery window.

That was how we learned that a cost-of-living increase is not necessarily a question of being tempted by a luxury car or private school tuition. Sometimes it can look like a dead body in your neighbor's front yard.

Matt and I went running, not walking, to the most expensive neighborhood in our city. We were worn out, tired of being scared, ready to position our child for a bright—and free!—public school education. And, most importantly, we wanted to enjoy walking in our neighborhood without fear.

We snagged one of the smallest homes on one of our favorite streets, at a price far higher than our first home but relatively affordable for the new neighborhood.

We have reaped many rewards from that decision over the years and I'm thankful we made it into the neighborhood before prices rose dramatically, as they soon would. Situated across from a river and numerous public parks, it is a truly magical place to live and raise kids. Our quality of life did not just improve, it skyrocketed.

And because we sunk money into our first home with those extra payments, we walked away with a sizeable sum and were able to put almost 25% down on our new home. A few years later, we would refinance into a 15-year mortgage, made possible by the equity we had accrued which created a manageable new monthly payment.

> We tried turning a blind eye to the drug drops and yelling matches around us until one morning we awoke to see yellow tape flanking our mailbox.

Another way to look at it, all that extra money we shoveled into our first house is the reason we will be mortgage-free at the age of 51. Not a bad time to cut out a giant chunk of your monthly living expenses.

Of course, our portfolio misses the mark of my original FI goals. Without a paid-off home, we never got the chance to aggressively fund our retirement accounts, at least not to the extent we could have done without a mortgage payment in those early years when compound interest provides such muscle. Today, a little under half of our net worth is tied up in our primary residence, not an ideal situation when you're aiming to meet the 4% rule.

But what comes with age is wisdom and a level of peace. We're not yet at FI, but we have financial flexibility and peace of mind. Messy situations have always been soothed by the fact that we never stopped investing in VTSAX. Our investment portfolio has achieved what they call Coast Financial Independence—where we no longer have to contribute to our investments to get to our goal in time—likely at an early retirement age.

## CONTROLLING LIFESTYLE
## INFLATION AFTER THE FACT

### BRIAN GRIESBACH

*Spanaway, Washington, USA*

**M**Y WIFE AND I never lived beyond our means—but I liked having things. We had a large house filled with furniture, a large garage filled with tools and toys. I had owned multiple boats, motorcycles, project vehicles—and tried hobbies from scuba diving to bicycling, RC helicopters, music, woodworking, and others I can't even remember.

All of this led to a huge accumulation of stuff. And that meant having a place to store it all. We lived in a much larger house than needed.

When I discovered FI, we started eliminating the accumulation. Moving house is a great forcing function for this. Each time we move I'm able to let go of another round of items.

Such simplification allows me to concentrate on a limited

number of hobbies and activities that I really enjoy. And, as it happens, many things can be borrowed or rented—instead of owned and stored.

It's controlling lifestyle inflation after the fact. But still pretty powerful for all that.

Before I knew about FI, I saved for retirement and things I wanted, but I had no bigger idea than that. Now, every financial decision I make brings me one step closer to true independence.

## I WAS A CHEAP ASS, AND I'M NOT PROUD

DAVID W BIAN

*San Jose, California, USA*

*www.linkedin.com/in/davidwbian*

I WAS NEAR THE end of graduate school, about to join the workforce, and I wanted to plan ahead. I'd be making "real money"—so I wanted to figure out what to do with it. I knew I needed to save, but how much would I need to retire?

If I worked for 40 years and retired for 40 years (if I even lived that long), I would have to save 50% of my income—and that was ignoring all other important factors like inflation, lifestyle creep, higher income, etc. While it would be possible to save that much, there had to be more to it.

That was when I came across JL's Simple Path and FI, and became obsessed with saving for retirement. I read everything I could find. I thought about how great it would be to not just retire early, but retire rich—and do what I want, when I want.

As soon as I started working, I set up my Vanguard and 401(k) accounts and started pumping as much as I could into VTSAX and S&P 500 index funds. I knew if I could keep this up, I could potentially retire in ten years somewhat comfortably or in 20 years very comfortably.

Life wasn't all good news, though. I struggled with spending money in certain situations. I hesitated to take my girlfriend at the time out to the movies even when I knew we would both enjoy it because, as the FIRE joke goes, "I could retire 52 seconds earlier" if I saved the money instead.

If you're thinking I was being a cheap ass—I was, and I'm not proud of it.

I knew it at the time, too. And I got to thinking about my psychology around money. I was so needlessly stressed about retiring early that I was stopping myself from enjoying life along the way. My obsession with financial security in the future had taken me far from doing what I wanted, when I wanted, in the here and now.

> I've come to realize that I should be optimizing for long-term happiness and not time to retirement.

Ramit Sethi has a concept called a Rich Life, which focuses on identifying the things you love and making decisions to spend money on those things, sometimes lavishly, while still saving for the future. I love this! If I can afford it, and it truly makes me happy or fulfills me, why shouldn't I do it?

This may be something as big as taking the opportunity to take the occasional amazing vacation with my sister, or as small as going to the movies just because I want to.

Some things cost money and others don't. I love learning new things like glassblowing and going to the gym. I also love listening to podcasts and hiking. There are plenty of people who are truly happy who live lifestyles that span the spectrum from minimalist to extravagant. I've come to realize that I should be optimizing for long-term happiness and not time to retirement.

Reaching financial independence earlier in my life would be

amazing, but so would loving my life along the way. Not only do I want the confidence to stay the course during this wild ride, but also the self-awareness to enjoy it too.

The Simple Path to Wealth doesn't require sacrificing your happiness for wealth—that's something I came up with all on my own. In fact, I believe happiness is one of the many reasons to walk The Path.

## YOU CAN BE FLEXIBLE, IF YOU'RE THOUGHTFUL

### LIZ, A PROFESSIONAL MARRIED MOTHER OF TWO

*Texas, outside a major metro area, USA*

**M**Y HUSBAND AND I are approximately eight years into our FI journey, having started in our mid-30s with $29,000 in retirement savings.

Flexibility is a big benefit of pursuing FI, and almost from the beginning we enjoyed the breathing room a little runway provides. Along the way we've had two children and each changed jobs three times. We have adapted to job loss, childcare challenges, and income volatility.

Once you know about FI, you cannot unsee it. However, after immersion in the framework, you realize there's flexibility there—you can deviate from some of its sacred teachings. In our case this is especially true regarding tax efficiency and spending less. I would love to pay zero taxes, but don't see that in my future.

We currently live off my husband's income and invest mine for sanity's sake (hello, steady paycheck!). With this we've had to give up dollar-cost averaging every two weeks and instead max out our Roth IRAs and my SEP IRA as money comes in. Once those are full we put a little into a taxable account. My attitude is that we don't know what the tax environment will look like 20 or 30 years from now, though I don't think taxes will be lower. Having different buckets of money will give us options.

> A lot of people would see this as lifestyle inflation but the reality is these choices in our minds were always non-negotiable.

FI flexibility has also allowed us to live out our values with relative ease, including not making decisions based on what costs the least. We believe the early years matter a lot, so we hired an in-home nanny for a year. We also send our kids to private school.

A lot of people would see this as lifestyle inflation but the reality is these choices in our minds were always non-negotiable. We started our FI journey before kids, and our expenses have grown quite a bit—though so has our income. We haven't been able to save the full amount of our income increases and may not be the most tax-efficient down to the dollar, but that's OK.

## I DIDN'T REALLY KNOW WHAT I NEEDED

JASON

*Austin, Texas, USA*

ONE IMPORTANT LESSON I learned is the difference between needs and strategies. Like many Americans, I was familiar with the needs-and-wants framework for spending decisions.

Anyone who grew up less than wildly affluent has asked themselves at some point: "Do I really need this?" when making a purchase decision. Although this old paradigm was useful for controlling spending, it left me wanting and with depleted willpower. Adept at material minimalism, I had little awareness of my underlying needs.

I first learned of the "needs and strategies" concept through the book *Loaded* by Sarah Newcomb. *Loaded* provided a new framework to think about needs. The book posits that all human desires arise from an underlying need, and all human behavior is in pursuit of satisfying a need. Rather than casting away a want as not necessary, determine what the underlying need is. It could be physical, emotional or spiritual.

Strategies are how we meet our needs. They can be financial or non-financial in nature. Financial strategies are only necessary to meet basic physical needs, such as the need for food, shelter or safety. Financial strategies aren't always necessary to meet non-physical needs. Often, *non*-financial strategies are more effective.

Developing an understanding of my needs and misguided attempts to satisfy them was a turning point on my path to FI. I was spending a lot on eating out and going out for drinks with friends. This habit left my body, mind and wallet in worse condition. I didn't realize that I was using a financial strategy to meet my need for friendship and connection. I changed strategies by joining a running club and organizing pot-luck get-togethers. These non-financial strategies enabled me to socialize, increasing both my savings and happiness.

The needs and strategies model prompted me to take a close look at what I value and enjoy in life. Now I can create new strategies that require less spending and are even more effective at meeting my needs. It is a valuable exercise in intentional life design. I am already benefiting from it on The Path to FI. In early retirement, I will use it to create strategies that drive happiness and minimize portfolio impact.

## THE POWER OF A
## NON-URGENT APPROACH

RYQUIST

*Minnesota, USA*

I HAVE LEARNED TO sleep on larger expenses two or three times. If I still want to make the purchase, I do so without regret. The value of this strategy is underlined by how hard stores work to encourage the opposite with impulse buys. Again and again we see flash sales and items with only a few supposedly left in stock, promoting urgency.

Take a non-urgent approach to acting on them. It'll steer you right.

# PART FIVE:
# *INVESTING*

# JL'S VIEW

## 1975: YEAR ONE FOR
## INDEX FUNDS AND FOR
## MY INVESTING CAREER

O N 1 MAY 1975 Jack Bogle founded The Vanguard Group and on 31 December of that year launched the First Index Investment Trust. This was the world's first retail index fund and was later called the Vanguard 500 Index Fund, which is still with us today. It was also called "Bogle's Folly" and Ed Johnson, then Chairman of Fidelity Investments, ran a series of derogatory ads calling indexing, among other things, "un-American." Mr. Bogle reportedly had those ads framed and hung in his office.

This creation of index fund investing is the single greatest gift to the individual investor in history. It is why I refer to Mr. Bogle as a fiscal saint. It is also why the investment establishment tried so hard to strangle the idea in its crib. They recognized the threat posed to their high-fee-and-commission hold on us small investors.

Purely by coincidence, the spring of 1975 was also when I bought my first shares of stock: Texaco and Southern Company. I would spend the next 25 years as a stock picker and, by extension, a picker of actively managed mutual funds run by stock pickers. I grew to be pretty good at it.

That is my dirty little secret. I actually achieved financial independence doing this before I embraced indexing. I mention this to make an important point. It's not like stock picking can't work. Done well, it can. It's just a whole lot more effort and expense for results that are almost always substandard compared to indexing.

I'm often asked what my single biggest investment mistake has been and it is this: I was far too slow in embracing index fund investing. For the first ten years of my investing life, I just didn't know such a thing existed. But even if I had, I'd not have been wise enough to embrace it. How do I know? In 1985 an analyst friend of mine introduced me to the concept. It still took me another 15 years to see the light. I made every argument imaginable to defend my old approach. Indeed, when I hear people arguing against indexing today, it is my own voice I hear in my head.

It is hard to think of those lost years. On some nights, typically when it is lonely and a cold, dark rain is rattling the windows— and I want to depress myself—I log on to an investment calculator and explore just how much further ahead I'd be had I been smart enough to embrace index fund investing sooner. And how much easier The Path would have been.

## THE ROLE OF INVESTING

As we discussed in the last essay, your savings rate is what powers your journey along The Simple Path. But it is a means to an end. It frees up some of your income for investments and, over time, it is these investments that will do the earning for you. You want this money to be working as hard as possible, and that means learning how to deploy it wisely and for the long term. Once your money is making enough money to support you, you have achieved financial independence.

# THE POWER OF
# INDEX INVESTING

Before Jack Bogle introduced index funds to the world, you either bought individual stocks and bonds you chose yourself, or you bought an actively managed mutual fund that bought them for you. You were charged high commissions and/or fees for this, which were themselves a drag on performance.

Mr. Bogle pointed out that picking individual stocks and mutual funds run by people picking stocks rarely outperformed the average return of the market overall—something that has since been repeatedly proven over decades of research. Knowing this, he reasoned investors would be best served by a fund that simply bought the entire index. The fact this also eliminated all those expensive managers and fees was icing on the cake. Icing that went into the investor's pocket instead of to the investment firms, and which is an analogy I have probably extended too far at this point.

To be clear, today there is an almost endless variety of index funds, each tracking just about anything you might imagine. But what we are talking about here are low-cost, broad-based index funds. Think the S&P 500 Index Fund, US Total Stock (or bond) Market Index Fund, a World Total Stock (or bond) Index Fund.

Let's take a closer look at what makes indexing so powerful.

1. When you buy a single stock, you are buying partial ownership of a specific company. For whatever reason, you think this company is going to do well. If you are right the share price should go up. But you may not be right. Turns out, choosing winners in the market is very difficult. Today's great companies might be tomorrow's Enron

or, less dramatically, Sears. And today's laggards might be tomorrow's exciting turnaround stories.

2. Companies have lifecycles. In the 1960s, General Motors was so dominant the thinking was no other car company could ever compete. The government seriously considered breaking it up. It didn't and, of course, other car companies figured out very well how to compete. They just happened to be Japanese. Sears, Polaroid, Xerox are some of the corporate giants of my youth now barely remembered. In the early 1970s there was a concept called The Nifty Fifty. These were the top blue-chip companies of the day and the idea was you could just buy them and hold them forever. Problem is, even the best companies don't last forever. There is an easier and better way.

3. With an index fund, you own a little bit of *all* of the companies that make up that index. If you invest in an S&P 500 index fund, you own a piece of the 500 largest publicly traded companies in the United States. If you own a US total stock market index fund—my slight preference— you own a piece of virtually every publicly traded company in the United States. That's about 4,000 companies these days.

4. Index funds are "cap-weighted," which simply means the larger the company the bigger a per cent of the overall portfolio it represents. Those companies that grow and prosper become a larger part of our holdings. Those that falter become a smaller part until they recover or drift away altogether, to be replaced by new emerging firms. Since the worst a company can do is to fail completely and lose 100%, and the best a company can do is to gain 100, 200, 1,000, 10,000% or more, this is a bit of a rigged game. In our favor.

5. I call the process above "self-cleansing," and it is what allows us to buy our index fund and hold it forever.

6. As long as there is a United States with a strong, viable capitalist economy, this process will continue. Of course,

nothing lasts forever and even the United States will one day go the way of Rome. Personally, I don't see that happening anytime soon. But if you believe that time is near—and some people do—The Simple Path isn't for you. You should be stocking canned goods and ammunition.

7. The United States is the only country in which I suggest an investor can own just their home country market. My international readers should look beyond their home country borders. For you, I suggest a Total World Index Fund.

8. The idea that you can't outperform the overall market might feel counterintuitive. It certainly did to me. That's what kept me a stock picker for far too long. It seems obvious, if you just pick a few really good companies, you'll outperform—or even if you just avoid the obviously bad companies. The word "just," though, is doing a lot of work here. Decades of research indicates that in any given year only ~25% of active managers will outperform the market. The further out you go, the lower the percentage. By 30 years it's less than 1%—statistically zero.

9. When you buy an individual stock, you have to be thinking about when to sell it. But your index fund is continually refreshed and renewed. Personally, I own the total stock market index fund from Vanguard—VTSAX. Other than selling a few shares while living on the portfolio, I'll hold it forever. This selling might amount to ~2% a year, with the dividends providing the rest of a 4% withdrawal rate. That's it. Easy-peasy.

10. Even though they rarely outperform the index, active funds charge a lot in the effort. Fund managers are very highly paid and they employ armies of analysts to try to beat the odds. But, as Jack Bogle once said, "Fund performance comes and goes. Costs go on forever." Index funds not only tend to outperform managed funds, they also don't have the drag of all those fees holding them back. That money stays in your pocket.

So, indexing is more powerful and it's certainly a whole lot easier. But is it too good to be true? Shouldn't something like investing be *difficult*?

No. Complexity really exists only to separate you from your money. Wall Street makes it complex because the more complex it is, the more likely we are to listen when they say, "Don't worry your pretty little head about it. We understand this stuff. Pay us our fees and we'll take care of it." But as we saw during the 2008–9 crisis, sometimes they create things they don't understand themselves. This would be bad enough if needing them were true. It's not.

The truth is, successful investing is the soul of simplicity.

## WHAT ABOUT VOLATILITY?

Indexing may be easy and powerful, but don't expect a smooth ride. Stocks are volatile. They go up ~75% of the time, which means the other ~25% of the time they're doing something you won't enjoy.

When the market plunges these days, it doesn't bother me. But that wasn't always so.

On Monday 19 October 1987 I went to work as usual. It was a busy day. Toward the end of it I decided to call my stockbroker, Wayne, for no other reason than I hadn't spoken to him in a while. He sounded harried when he answered the phone.

"How's it going?" I said cheerfully.

"You're joking, right?" came the dismal reply. "This has been the worst day of my life. Customers have been calling nonstop to yell at me."

In what was destined to be called "Black Monday," the market had fallen 22.6%. In a single day. The largest single day drop before or since. It was breathtaking, and terrifying.

I knew the right thing to do: Nothing. Stand firm, hold and

stay the course. Wait until the inevitable recovery. But knowing and doing are not always the same.

The market continued to drift down until finally, sometime in December, I lost my nerve and sold out. If it wasn't the exact bottom, it was close enough not to matter. Then, as if to rub salt in my wounds, it promptly turned around and began to rise again. I sat on the sidelines watching until it rose past its former high before I finally got back in. It was a harsh and expensive lesson.

But it took hold. Now I recognize, not just in my head but in my gut, that market drops and even extraordinary crashes are simply a normal part of the process. They are the price of admission if you want the outsized benefits of wealth-building that the market can provide.

Of course, this is easy to say. During the next market crash there will, as always, be panic in the air. The media will be filled with concerned gurus wringing their hands. But it's all just noise. You are best served tuning it out. Such declines are as normal as blizzards in New England and hurricanes in Florida. Scary, sometime dangerous, but always temporary.

## WHAT ABOUT MARKET TIMING?

Well, since the market is volatile, why don't we simply sell when it's high and buy back in when it drops—and repeat? That way we'd just sidestep those pesky plunges. That's got to be better than holding through them, right?

Why yes. That would be absolutely better. If it were possible. But it is not. No one can do this consistently. How can I possibly know that *no one* can do this? Simple. If anyone could, it would be far and away the most powerful fiscal advantage imaginable. Such a person would be a hundred times richer and far more lionized than Warren Buffett.

To be clear, some *have* done it on occasion. But to be useful, that consistency part makes all the difference. Let's go back to that crash of 19 October 1987.

On 12 October, just seven days before the crash, an analyst working for Shearson Lehman Brothers Inc. by the name of Elaine Garzarelli went on a cable news show and called it. This was a bold prediction, and spot on. She immediately skyrocketed in fame. Money poured into the fund she managed, which went on to *underperform* the S&P 500 by a dismal -43% over the next three years.

This is not to suggest Ms. Garzarelli got stupid. It simply points out making such calls consistently is impossible.

Think of it this way. At any given time there are so many people out there predicting what the market will do, someone is bound to get it right. It is like the lottery. If enough tickets are sold, someone will have the winning numbers. But we never think (I hope), "Wow, that person knows how to pick winning lottery numbers!" No, we correctly recognize that person got very, very lucky just because someone had to. So too when you hear some guru lauded for a correct market call.

In the midst of the Covid plunge of early 2020, people began commenting with disturbing certainty about how the market just had to go down further and how much longer it was doomed to stay down. How this time was truly different. I put a tweet up saying, "I've noticed there's a new symptom of Covid, clairvoyance." And, of course, the market promptly rallied back past previous highs, and did so in record time. Not because of my tweet, but simply because, as some wag once said, "The market will do whatever it takes to embarrass the largest number of people."

Timing the market consistently enough to be useful is impossible. What the market is doing at any given moment should have no influence on your investing. It has none on mine. The time to invest is when you have money to invest.

## DON'T OVERTHINK THINGS

The less you think about investing, the less you'll tinker with it. The less you tinker, the better your results. You need only get a couple of simple things right. Avoid debt, live on less than you earn, and invest the difference in broad-based, low-cost index funds. Stay the course and ignore the noise. As Jack Bogle once said during a market crash, "Don't just do something, stand there!"

Continue your regular investing schedule and celebrate periodic declines that let you buy shares "on sale." Keep investing and these drops become your friend.

People routinely object. "Only one fund? What about diversification?" Back when I first started investing, this was the advice for building a diversified portfolio: "Pick seven or eight sectors and one or two stocks in each. This will give you a total of ~10–16 companies which is the most you can reasonably be expected to follow as closely as you'll need to and you'll be well diversified."

With VTSAX I own ~4,000 companies. Job done on the stock diversification front.

For many advisors this 100% stock allocation feels far too aggressive. They are not wrong. It *is* aggressive. With this allocation you're not diversified across asset classes, but I'm OK with that. This is about building your wealth, and stocks perform best over time.

But this will be a volatile ride and if you want to smooth it out a bit you can add bonds with a Total Bond Market Fund. But understand the price you pay will be lower long-term performance. The more bonds you add the smoother the ride, and the lower your returns over time.

Of course, for every objection that I'm too aggressive, I get another complaining, "You're way too conservative! If you tweak it this way or that you could get a better result. Crypto! Gold! Commodities! Puts! Calls! Penny stocks! Meme stocks! Beanie

Babies! If you leveraged your investments, think how much more you'd have!"

You can choose to be more aggressive or more conservative than what I suggest. Your call. But in my experience, this is the sweet spot—powerful in terms of results but not crazy with risk. That's why it is what I tell my daughter to do, and why it is the investment approach recommended for The Simple Path.

## HOW MY ADVICE CAN LEAVE YOU BLEEDING AT THE SIDE OF THE ROAD

Before you embrace this investing approach, you must be absolutely sure that when there is a market correction (-10%), a bear market (-20%+), or a market crash (-35%+) you will stay the course. You can expect it to be terrifying, but when all the pundits are screaming "This time is different! Sell!" you must ignore the noise. You must know in your head—and in your gut—that these events are a perfectly normal part of the process, the price you must pay. Your reaction must be to embrace the wonderful buying opportunity they represent and keep on acquiring more shares.

Be absolutely sure about this. Make no mistake. This approach *does not work* if you panic and sell. Do that and it will leave you bleeding by the side of the road.

## RULES FOR THE ROAD

- When you own a broad-based US total stock market index fund, you own a piece of virtually every publicly traded company in the United States of America and everyone from the CEO to the factory floor is working to make you richer.

- A US Total Stock Market Index Fund holds ~4,000 stocks, which means you have broad diversification.

- If you live outside the United States you'll want to look at a total world stock index fund.

- Picking individual stocks *can* work—but it's harder, more expensive and will almost always produce worse results.

- Index fund investing is easier, cheaper and more powerful.

- Effective investing is the soul of simplicity.

- Complex investments exist to enrich those selling them.

- Bear markets, corrections and crashes are all to be expected. They are a normal part of the process and enduring them is the price you must pay for the long-term results stocks can provide.

- When these happen it is critical to stay the course and ignore the panic all around you.

- Market drops are a gift. They allow you to buy shares "on sale."

- No one can time the market.

- The less you tinker with your investments, the better your results.

- Do not invest until you are absolutely sure you will stay the course when times get tough. If you panic and sell, my advice will leave you bleeding by the side of the road.

## "DON'T LOOK FOR THE NEEDLE IN THE HAYSTACK. JUST BUY THE HAYSTACK."

## —JACK BOGLE

# THE STORIES

## WHY WEREN'T WE RICH AFTER TWO DECADES OF INVESTING?

JUSTIN HALL

*Arlington, Virginia, USA*

*LivingTheFIghLife.com*

I THOUGHT MY WIFE and I were doing everything right to achieve a rich, free life. Avoid debt—check! Spend less than we earn—check! Invest the surplus—check! So, after almost two decades of investing, why weren't we rich or at least well on our way?

When I calculated our net worth 19 years after we started investing, we had invested $103,000 into IRAs, but their value was only $92,000. We had actually lost money!

I'd also lost $15,000 out of $50,000 invested in a taxable mutual fund account and all of the $5,000 invested in individual stocks. I thought I had done my homework. I had read an investment book and several articles on investing, and sought advice from friends, but it wasn't until I found JL's Simple Path that I finally understood that my investing problem was... *me*.

I have been frugal and a great saver my whole life, but—as you can tell—a terrible investor. I was working hard to invest for the future but never getting there, always panicking and selling whenever the market tumbled, waiting and reinvesting cautiously long after the market recovered.

Here are the most egregious examples of my rocky investing.

In 1997, I purchased 1,000 shares of Boston Chicken (later known as Boston Market). We lived in Boston at the time, and I loved our nearby Boston Chicken restaurant. I was convinced that home meal replacement was a growing trend and great investment. Unfortunately, the company was cooking more than delicious chicken. Just weeks before I purchased the stock (and unbeknownst to me), the firm revealed it was recycling money by loaning to its franchisees to build new restaurants, masking its true, troubling financial picture—huge debt.

> I didn't yet understand how to hold and wait for a recovery. In fact, many of the remaining companies, such as Amazon and eBay, would eventually fully recover and make a lot of money.

Boston Chicken soon filed for bankruptcy.

I watched that stock drop from around $5 per share to pennies as the company financially collapsed. Believing that I simply needed to learn more about stock investing, I read *The Motley Fool Investment Guide*. It was no fun to read their take that delicious chicken does not necessarily make a great investment. I learned that picking individual stocks can be very risky.

Not to be deterred, I continued to closely watch the markets for three years, saw their year-over-year gains, and thought, well, we can't miss out on the tech stock boom. So in January 2000, after the Y2K scare passed but right before the dotcom bubble burst, I invested a quarter of our net worth ($50,000) into mutual funds (half in a tech fund and half in an S&P 500 index fund).

Yep, I bought high.

The value of my shares burst along with the bubble. I held them for a measly four years, and when there was little to no recovery, I sold our shares, locking in a $15,000 loss. I didn't yet understand how to hold and wait for a recovery. In fact, many of the remaining companies, such as Amazon and eBay, would eventually fully recover and make a lot of money.

Luckily, we left alone our only remaining investments—our IRAs—and they continued to grow... until the Great Recession hit.

In September 2008, when the Great Recession was in full swing and the stock market was way down, I convinced myself and my wife that we needed to pull our IRA investments to safety and avoid further "losses." So with much angst, I transferred our IRAs into money market funds and locked in losses of approximately 25% each. The recession made me wary of the market, so I kept our investments in money market accounts until February 2014, when I felt I couldn't let the market rise without us any longer. By then, the market had long recovered, but my jitters remained. I was certain (as were many pundits) that the market would once again drop.

Finally, in early 2018, I found the FI movement and gained a new perspective of how to build our financial future. I now understood the importance of investing in broad-based index funds and paying low investment fees. But most importantly, I learned how to hold (and even buy) when the market is falling, and sell (rebalance) when it is up.

My first big test was in March 2020 when the pandemic hit and the market plummeted. In the past, I would have pulled out my money after it dropped precipitously, but now I didn't sell. In fact, I confidently optimized our available investment dollars and shifted into more stock. I now trusted that, eventually, the market would rise again. In early January 2022, I rebalanced our portfolio, selling stocks at their peak and buying government securities (I needed to wait on bonds as interest rates were rising). In early June 2022, when the market dropped 15%, I shifted funds from government securities to buy stocks "on sale." When it further dropped into bear market territory, I purchased more stocks at a deeper discount. If it drops past 25% or even 30%, I'll do it again.

Since finding JL's Simple Path, our stock portfolio has increased by 60% and we have achieved financial independence. I am no longer investing with angst, leaving behind a trail of lost opportunities. My wife and I are investing thoughtfully, our eyes on the horizon, confident the market will eventually recover. Our two children, both in their early 20s, are getting a great start to a lifetime of smart investing.

## HIGH FEES ARE NOT A REQUIREMENT

### BRIAN

*Pennsylvania, USA*

I HAVE ALWAYS BEEN a bit of a spreadsheet nerd. Every decision my family made, whether large or small, was accompanied by a rating system based on the numbers. However, the most important money decision—where to house our investments—was a blind spot, and the exception.

For almost 20 years of investing I actually assumed that paying advisor fees was a *requirement*. Then I discovered JL's Simple Path in summer 2019.

Later that summer I moved most of our investments to low-cost trackers. Learning the 4% rule, and running our family's numbers, I realized that my wife and I could retire in our early 40s if we wanted. And we could do this with three school-aged children!

The rest, as they say, is history. In 2020, we paid off our mortgage. In 2022, we took a three-month family sabbatical in Europe.

We continue to use our FI planning and knowledge to live a debt-free, financially healthy lifestyle.

## HOW TO THINK ABOUT FINANCIAL ADVICE SO IT REALLY WORKS FOR YOU

### NATHAN MCBRIDE

*Utah, USA*

FOR AS LONG as I can remember, I've been fascinated with money. When I was a kid, I would regularly retrieve all of the money I had stashed away in various places around my room and carefully lay it out on my bed into neat piles as I counted it. I felt some sort of accomplishment tallying up how much I'd saved from my allowance, birthdays and Christmases.

I saved throughout my childhood, and kept a basic budget when I left home for college. I thought I had it all figured out. It wasn't until I gained some professional experience in the finance industry that I realized just how much I didn't know.

My second year of college I took an internship with a large financial planning company. Throughout my nine months there I learned all about life insurance, how to sell it, and how to get repeatedly hung up on while trying to sell it.

I also learned a bit about investing.

As it turns out, many of the funds I was learning about were expensive front-end loaded mutual funds. Of course, when I was told how much commission I would make if I sold them, I thought they were great!

It wasn't until a few years later that I started to call into question the role of a financial advisor and challenge my understanding of money and finances as a whole.

If asked, I would be willing to bet that the majority of people seek financial advisors either because "that's what you're supposed to do" or because "I barely know a thing about investing, where would I even start!"

However, it can easily go wrong when an advisor is making decisions for *your* future with *their* best interests in mind.

Because of this I decided to take a different approach. I look at financial advice as similar to tutoring in, say, calculus.

In the beginning everything seems difficult, almost like a foreign language. So you find a tutor, a professor, or even just a friend to help you study and test your knowledge. Eventually you reach a point where you understand the basics and can navigate some problems. Then things get more complex. You need more help as concepts build on concepts.

> It can easily go wrong when an advisor is making decisions for *your* future with *their* best interests in mind.

In the same fashion, a financial advisor can be a kind of financial tutor.

They can guide you in building a solid foundation—then, once you get a good grasp of the basics, you can take the reins, checking back in when new problems present themselves.

I was lucky enough to make friends with one of my mentors during my internship. Now he is someone I can check in with every once in awhile, bounce ideas off of, and discuss upcoming events in my life that may require a reevaluation of my current financial plan. Exactly what I need.

## I THOUGHT I NEEDED ADVICE—
## I JUST NEEDED CONTROL

### GREG WINDSOR

*Christchurch, New Zealand*

I N MID-2020 MY father told me and my two brothers that he was going to sell the family holiday home, and that he would like to split the proceeds between us three as an early inheritance. I ended up with $150,000. And I didn't have a clue what to do with it.

The term deposit rates for savings in the banks weren't very high at the time. After looking around on the internet, I figured the best thing to do was to talk to a financial advisor. I was nervous about investing. I had always thought of putting money in the stock market as a bit like gambling.

I was told by an advisor that as I was only investing around $150,000, I would be limited to the New Zealand market at first. Once my finances hit the $250,000 mark, the advisor could then spread the money into the international market as well, including the US.

I ended up staying with this investment firm for about 12 months. During those 12 months I didn't invest any additional money, because I didn't understand anything about dollar-cost averaging. I thought that, when the market dropped, not only did your money decrease, but also the number of shares you have. I wasn't aware that when the market went down, it was only the value of the shares that decreased.

I had no idea what a dividend was either.

Even though I was investing $150,000 with a popular New Zealand investment company, I wasn't given any advice on anything to do with investing. I can't even count how many stressful days and nights I had watching the daily stock market and listening to the news about "a great day for the stock market," followed by "a bad day for the stock market."

Approximately ten months into this stressful investment journey I came across JL's Simple Path at last. I started to hear about things called dividends, dollar-cost averaging, index funds. It all sounded... simple, not stressful!

After a little more investigation I found out you can easily invest in the US stock market in New Zealand. In particular, I became interested in a fund that follows Vanguard's S&P 500 ETF. The fees for that fund in New Zealand were about a quarter of the fees I was paying to my financial advisors.

I now had the 4% rule firmly in mind.

Before learning of this, I thought that paying around 1.5% annually to the financial advisors was a bargain considering the amount of money they could potentially make for me in the future. Now I realized that 1.5% in fees was actually over a quarter of my future income.

> Approximately ten months into this stressful investment journey I came across JL's Simple Path at last. I started to hear about things called dividends, dollar-cost averaging, index funds. It all sounded... simple, not stressful!

Perhaps the biggest thing I learned when I found The Simple Path to Wealth was how to mentally handle investing in the stock market. After ten months of investment stress, it changed my life to know that, in your wealth-building phase, a correction, bear market, or—God forbid—a market crash has its positives.

You can now purchase shares "on sale."

I had the confidence to take my money back from my financial advisor and go on my own. In the end I chose to invest solely in the S&P 500. I have an automatic payment going into that fund every fortnight, and all my dividends are reinvested back into my portfolio. I'm currently "enjoying" a bear market and its discounted prices.

## I USED TO THINK ADVISORS
## WORKED TO MAKE ME RICH

### JASON MARTIN

*Maricopa, USA*

I AM ONE OF those fortunate Americans who will have a municipal government pension waiting for me in a few years. Unfortunately, my pension caused me to be somewhat apathetic towards other aspects of my investment life.

Early on in my career, I asked newly retired coworkers what they would do differently if they could go back in time. They all said the same thing: Put more into their deferred compensation account. These public sector 457 accounts are like private sector 401(k)s, but designed to supplement pension payments in retirement. I was wise enough to listen to those retirees and consistently put at least a small portion of my check away into it, even though I had no idea where that money was going.

The account slowly grew over time, and I put a portion of every raise into it too. Before long I had a sizeable nest egg.

In 2015 a financial advisor specializing in "public safety" retirement solutions came knocking. He promised better returns than what the city's limited plans were offering. It helped that the advisor was also a coworker who was doing this as a side hustle. Why wouldn't I trust him?

> The FI way has given me the discipline and mental fortitude to lash myself to the mast during downturns in the market and view them as opportunities to build more wealth.

We sat down and I signed forms detailing my risk tolerance. They showed me how I would someday be very wealthy. They moved my money from the city's 457 to a self-directed Schwab account, and got started buying all kinds of mutual funds, stocks, and who knows what else. It seemed so complicated; I was just glad they were there to help make me rich.

Then 2020 came along and there was a sudden interest in the stock market due to apps such as Robinhood. A few of my friends were buying and selling stocks on their phones like it was a new type of video game. Of course, I was intrigued and downloaded one of those apps and started playing around with small amounts of money. I lost some and earned some, but I was hooked on learning more about the world of stocks and investing.

One day I opened my 457 and looked at the history of my account. I had been consistently charged fees for years, even when I was losing value!

I called up my friend/financial advisor and told him I wanted to start taking a more active role in what I was investing in. The whole process of me finding things to invest in and them complying with my wishes had become such a hassle, and I was getting frustrated. It was like I had no control over my own money.

By late 2020 I was listening to every kind of investing book or podcast or video I could get my hands on. Eventually this quest led me to JL's Simple Path.

The more I learned, the more I realized how easy investing really is. The people managing my money made it seem more complicated than it had to be. I learned about index funds and expense ratios and fees, and how those fees were dragging my portfolio down.

It took about three months to get the guts to fire my advisor and start controlling my own money. It was a little scary at first, being responsible for such a large sum of money, but my new knowledge settled me as I sold off highly priced mutual funds and stocks and shifted to Vanguard's Total Stock Market ETF.

I went with VTI because it has a slightly lower expense ratio compared to VTSAX and, because I'm forced to use a Schwab account through my employer, there are additional costs to buying VTSAX through them.

Now with only a few years left before I can retire, I feel confident and in control. The FI way has given me the discipline and mental fortitude to lash myself to the mast during downturns in the market and view them as opportunities to build more wealth. I am eternally grateful. Even though I have a pension, my retirement accounts represent generational wealth for my family.

## THE PROBLEM OF SELLING

### BEN SHEARON

*Sendai, Japan*

*retirejapan.com*

**A**FTER 15 YEARS of investing and eight years of running a website about personal finance for residents of Japan, I realized that some of my investments were not fit for purpose.

Drat.

Until very recently I was pretty happy with my portfolio. We own a core of index funds, with a dividend-paying stock portfolio on the side.

My investing philosophy so far has been to buy things and never sell, reinvesting any dividends that come along.

This approach has worked pretty well. So far.

However.

I have been thinking about what retirement might look like, how we might start selling our investments in the future to generate funds to live off, and what rules I could make to help me make effective decisions.

And I realized that while I have effective rules to help me buy investments, I don't have any idea of how we are going to go about selling them.

Pretty much everyone who is anyone in personal finance or investing says the same thing: Invest in low-cost index funds, automate it as much as possible, and then ignore your investments.

And if we had done that I believe we'd be in a better position.

So if you are just getting started or you are looking to increase the amount you invest every month, please consider sticking to the basics: low-cost diversified index funds, one stock and one bond fund. Make clear rules for yourself on how you will invest *and* how you will spend.

And you won't end up like me.

## MY $2,000 NIGHTMARE

### RACHEL HERNANDEZ

*Texas, USA*

*www.mobilehomegurl.com*

**B**ACK WHEN I was just starting out, I bought a mobile home for $2,000. As a real estate investor, this sounded like a great deal—so cheap. But that's exactly the problem. Just because something is priced low does not mean it's a good deal. I learned this lesson the hard way.

The lead came through a park manager. He told me all about the home and the seller, who wanted to sell asap. She was a single mother who had been living there for less than a year and had fallen behind on the lot rent for the park.

I made an appointment with the seller to inspect it. It was a two-bedroom, one-bath mobile home located in a manufactured home community—small, old, built in the 1980s. There wasn't any central heating or air conditioning, unlike some mobile homes I had bought in the past.

The seller was asking $4,000. We negotiated back and forth, eventually settling on $2,000. I was ecstatic. Sounds like a bargain, right?

Little did I know how hard it would be to sell this home. It was located in a low-end park where I would not do business today. Back then, I was still green and new. All I saw were dollar signs. I figured I could easily sell it and move on.

I was wrong.

Because of where it was located, it only attracted unreliable prospective buyers. The park manager insisted I just sell the home using owner financing, but if I did that I'd still be on the hook if they did not pay me and the park for the lot rent. Which would lead back to square one.

The park manager didn't see the problem. "You can just take back the home and find someone else." But I didn't plan on doing business that way. I wanted to sell the home and be done with it.

I wanted a qualified buyer. Unfortunately, it turned out that was never likely in that park. I tried to find buyers in nicer neighborhoods. One was a lovely family looking for a home for their mother. I had sold them their place in another park. When they came to see this one, they politely asked me if I had anything else for sale in a different community.

That was how I learned the importance of location in real estate. You can always change a house, but you can't change a neighborhood. Or can you?

I held out as long as I could. The home was vacant; I was throwing away money every month on lot rent. At one point, someone stole a window air-conditioning unit out of the home. I had to do something.

So, I decided to sell the home cheap. I found an investor. He bought the home for cash—and moved it out of the park and onto his own land. I guess that solved the location issue!

## THE RELIEF OF INDEXING

### JEN HSIN CHAN

*Taiwan*

I HOLD A FINANCE bachelor degree from the National Taiwan University, but I never heard of index funds and passive investment during my student years. Like my fellow classmates at this elite school, I believed stock picking to be easy—and beating the market a piece of cake.

After college I invested in individual stocks and bought high-fee mutual funds. My investment performance was poor. Sometimes money came easy, but I lost quickly by attempting to time the market. It was all so unpredictable. I got drawn into technical analysis, studying graphs and patterns. My investing performance didn't improve. I was exhausted.

> Approaching my 40s, I don't worry for my retirement years—because the collective drive of human beings to improve and create value is on my side, and in my portfolio.

In 2014, when I finally learned about passive investment and index funds, it was a relief—and a release from pain and confusion. Since then I have invested in the Taiwan market's symbolic index fund, Yuanta Taiwan 50 (ticker :0050), to track

TWSE Taiwan 50 index companies, and held worldwide index funds from Vanguard.

I think the biggest advantage to embracing passive investment is I can finally concentrate on my full-time job—with no need to worry over markets or what the media makes of them everyday. I'm free. While still seeking superior returns, I can live a life.

I am very happy to admit the collective wisdom of the market is enough for me. I have no inside information or extraordinary technical analysis skills. I earn income, save 70–80% of my salary, and invest in index funds. Approaching my 40s, I don't worry for my retirement years—because the collective drive of human beings to improve and create value is on my side, and in my portfolio.

## THIS ISN'T MEANT TO BE TOO EXCITING

### KINGSLEY EZENWA

*Calabar, Nigeria*

UNTIL RECENTLY, INVESTING in stocks wasn't easy in my part of the world (Nigeria). It was seen as something only meant for the elite. Thankfully, that narrative is rapidly changing— and I am more than excited to be part of that movement.

My journey towards financial independence hasn't been easy. I have made lots of unwise decisions, and have many regrets. But I hope my story can inspire others to take action.

Money always interested me growing up, perhaps in large part because my dad was so bad with it. I learned first-hand what I shouldn't be doing with it from him. A lack of basic money-management skills makes for dire outcomes, and it soon extends to other areas of your life.

So I always saved hard, ever since I was a kid, to try and avoid that. But with time I realized that, if I wanted to reach my goals faster, I needed to multiply my savings. That was how I discovered the stock market.

In Nigeria, there is a strong preference for individual stocks (particularly growth stocks) over investing in an index. And for many years, I pursued—and recommended—active management. Then I lost all my savings (meant for university) in 2020.

It was one of the toughest periods in my life. But at this time something beautiful also happened: I discovered JL's Simple Path.

My portfolio now probably looks incredibly boring to most people in Nigeria or further afield: just VOO and BND. But I know now that true investing is not meant to give you a rush of excitement. If it does, something's wrong.

I can happily say that I am in a much better position. I get to sleep well at night knowing that an index is doing all the heavy lifting for me. It makes staying the course a lot easier.

## JUST DO IT SCARED

LISA SCHADER

*California, USA*

*moneyfitmoms.com*

**I** STILL REMEMBER WHERE I was sitting in our tiny apartment when I called Vanguard and opened my Roth IRA. I was so nervous—which is insane. I had just graduated with a master's degree in tax accounting and passed all my CPA exams!

I think it was because of impostor syndrome. I felt like, who was *I* to open an investment account? I was almost completely broke.

I remember the woman on the other end of the phone being really kind and helping me figure out a fund I could buy based on the lowest minimum investment. It was nerve-wracking. But I love the Glennon Doyle quote, "If you can't beat fear, just do it scared." So, even though I was an anxious mess, I did it. We started investing through both our IRAs and 401(k)s.

> I love the Glennon Doyle quote, "If you can't beat fear, just do it scared."

The long-term result of investing early was life-changing. Almost exactly ten years after we graduated from college, our net worth hit $1m.

## ENJOYING MARKET FALLS

### ANDY LYON

*England/UAE*

*Twitter @mrlyonresources*

I HAVE ANOTHER 20 years of work in me, and before I found JL's Simple Path I'd have been dreading the current market drop. Instead, I'm excited. I hope it stays like this for a couple of years so I can buy more index funds via Vanguard and help build more wealth when markets rise in the future.

Unfortunately, I see friends and family panic-selling and missing out on this opportunity.

## MY GUT SAID SOMETHING WAS WRONG—SO I DID THE MATH

MB—MYFICAPSULE

*Minnesota, USA*

**M**Y WIFE AND I had come to the conclusion we were likely done with our financial advisor. It was probably time to manage our own money, now that we'd found the FI community. We'd had enough of the heavy fees inside of mutual funds and watching our investments lag behind a roaring market.

I called our advisor but only got his voicemail. I left a message. I think he could tell from the sound of my voice that I wasn't calling with anything great to say. But I wasn't actually going to fire him there and then. I wanted to tell him I was 70% of the way to a decision. My plan was to give him a shot to defend his role. I didn't want to be hasty.

> The math said something was wrong. And my gut said something was wrong. That feeling is gone now, and I love it.

But I just couldn't get hold of him after that. Normally I could text or call and get a rapid response; now it took two whole days. Even then he said he was really busy, but we could set a time to speak soon. I gave up, and recorded a voice memo on my phone telling him our plan, then texted the file to him.

We finally connected again four days later, but he claimed he hadn't listened to the memo. I recapped where we were. I still said we were only 70% of the way to a decision. I wanted his take.

His response was long and drawn out. But I will always remember the first part: "If you want to go chase returns in index funds, be my guest."

It was the first time I had heard index investing described like that. I tried to tell him respectfully that my understanding was that index funds simply tracked the market. There was no chasing. Mutual fund investing, on the other hand—with its high fees for active management, not to mention my advisor moving us in and out of funds all the time—seemed a much closer fit for that description.

We agreed to disagree, but afterwards the more I considered the sheer absurdity of what he had said, the more certain I was it was time to part. I wasn't chasing returns—all I wanted was the market average.

I had a few insurance policies with the advisor that I wanted to keep, but I wrote an email to him after that to cancel everything else. I never heard back. Not even a brief acknowledgment.

I moved over to Vanguard, upped my savings rate, and built our net worth. Eventually the silence from the advisor got too much, and I pulled my bigger policies that were still with him, even though it meant losing $6,000 of premiums.

This break-up was a tremendous weight off my shoulders. The math said something was wrong. And my gut said something was wrong. That feeling is gone now, and I love it.

## SIDE HUSTLES AREN'T AS EASY AS EQUITIES

SWARNADIP CHATTERJEE

*Kolkata, India*

EQUITY IS THE only place where you have "passive" income in the truest sense—your money works to make you more money. Other sources of so-called passive income—side hustles like YouTube—often actually require enormous investments of willpower, energy, and time. And the last of these is your scarcest resource.

Personally, I have found that reducing expenditures and increasing my investments led to a better life than working round the clock, at weekends, on multiple jobs, all in the hope of one day working less. It can make sense for a time—but it's easy to get trapped. Life is about relationships.

## YOU SHOULD BURN YOUR BOATS

MATT

*USA*

IT'S 2016. I'M working in a busy ops center for the government. It's not going well.

Our fourth child is on the way, and while we love each of them and want their happiness and health, it occurs to me that I don't want to do my job forever. I see coworkers older than me, doing the work for over 30 years, presumably because they must.

No thanks.

My way of life demands devotion to country, reticence to discuss details, and the ability to avoid trouble. While a pension should keep me off the breadline, it won't be enough for me to live on without some extra juice. It behooves me to avoid debt and risky financial mistakes, and while that disposes me to a high credit score it doesn't mean I know anything about saving money.

Case in point: When I started government service in 2011 I had a choice of C, S, F, I and G funds in the Thrift Savings Program (TSP). At that time, the share price of the C fund was almost exactly that of the G fund. It was explained to me that the C fund was more volatile than G, so I thought: "If this is my money, why on earth would I pay $17 a share for this C fund if the G fund is safer and only costs $15?"

Yeah, you know where I kept my money. Just enough to get the 5% matching contribution. For years.

I had an investment advisor. I was dimly aware that I needed financial guidance, so why not have someone tell me where to invest? I'd pay a small commission for that peace of mind. I only knew that I didn't know enough to have a better plan. I had stopped making contributions, so my advisor would occasionally call and saw away at me in ten-minute chats about the ways in which I was missing out, and that I needed to get serious about investing. It felt spammy, and it stuck in my craw.

As the wise say, chance favors the prepared mind. On that busy ops floor, I met a new colleague. He used spreadsheets and cFIREsim (cfiresim.com) and terms I didn't understand to determine when he could leave. Not retire, *leave*: Get up and walk away when he had enough.

I didn't think it possible, let alone on a government salary, and wasn't a pension the reason I worked for the government in the first place? At first blush it seemed a foolish pipe dream, but this colleague was no fool. My foolishness, on the other hand, was obvious enough to him that he introduced me to JL's Simple Path.

> It behooves me to avoid debt and risky financial mistakes, and while that disposes me to a high credit score it doesn't mean I know anything about saving money.

As an adult, there are not many times when your mind cracks open, pours its contents out before you, and allows you to rearrange it entirely.

JL's Path was doable for our circumstances. I had monstrous childcare expenses, a reasonable house in an affluent area, and a car loan. I had whole life insurance policies, some money tied up in a previous employer's state-run pension system, plus the investment advisor-controlled Roth IRAs and some related errata. Crucially, I also had the will to make many changes, drastically and without delay. I got to work.

The car loan was paid; the insurance policies were cashed; expenses were kept at bay. Yet, make no mistake: that was the easy part. I had to overcome a lot of fear to get fully on board. What if this was all nonsense? Was I a sucker? Many have gone astray following whims and trends. But I asked myself: isn't that what you were doing beforehand anyway?

I did more research. A Frontline documentary on the retirement gamble was instructive. A hilarious John Oliver episode on retirement was well timed. Yeah, index funds were efficient, and compounding interest was a miracle. There was no other feasible way to get where I wanted to be. I was already behind the curve. I cut every last rope that bound me, one at a time.

I started with the index funds I already had: the TSP. I was 100% G Safe, I was told. Safe from what? The compounding effects of inflation and maximal growth? I told myself: You have a pension and social security. That's your G fund now. I switched to the 100% C fund and started buying more than the 5% match. I watched the color wheel of my shares switch from the Kelly green of G to the ochre brown of C. The TSP palette did not match the go-go changes I was making, which made this feel all the more subversive.

Next, those state-run pension dollars. I learned that I had about $60,000 in them. For this sum I could expect a future pension of $800/month. That sounded nice. The pension program worker made it sound like I was giving up a sure thing, pulling out my contributions like this. But $800 also sounded like a lot less than I'd need. I found the forms I needed to add it into the TSP. One big pot, compounding and growing for years in a way I understood. In the TSP, I watched my ochre pot grow as the new funds hit my C holdings.

Lastly, those advisor-controlled funds. I knew this siren call would be strongest. The advisor had an interest to keep me and his funds, and would use the prior years of service and mutual history as anchors and leverage. But I win 100% of the gunfights I avoid. The money had to go to Vanguard VTSAX.

I started there and worked backwards, tasking Vanguard to do the lifting. I waited for the funds to transfer, knowing the advisor would reach out the moment they moved. Sure enough: An email at the crack of dawn, tinged with opprobrium at my lack of decorum.

> My advice: Go all-in on the change. The absolutist, burn-the-boats approach sounds radical, but the shores on which you will find yourself are not.

I could have replied with an angry screed. Instead, I thanked him for his years of service. He had, in fact, taught me a lot: not what he wanted me to know, but that I didn't know enough to find a better plan. In the space between my desire for something simple and his looming expertise, that small gap for chance and the prepared mind.

I'm still working in the same place as I write. It's much better now, in crucial ways.

I wish I could tell you I'm FIRE. The purists would mark me down as "Dumpster FIRE," if they'd call me anything. We have allowed ourselves a few indulgences along the way, like a slightly bigger house that we love. We won't get to FI in time to hang out with our teenage kids on a lazy Tuesday, or give a savage middle finger to the workaday life anytime soon.

No, it's more like this: I max out my C fund contributions every year, and we max my wife's Roth IRA as well. Our expenses are in check. We have enough and the mortgage will be paid off ahead of schedule. I do my job without desperate need for promotion, and I can take off on a lazy Tuesday to hang out with kids if I choose. If I don't quit or get fired, I can walk away at the minimum age with a reasonable pension, healthcare coverage I can take with me into retirement, and enough money to draw 3.5–4% from every year, without worrying if it will last.

I watch the markets and the related financial fuss with the

bemused disinterest of a Zen master. I watch the magic of compound interest and share that knowledge with my kids. There are no guarantees, but what I now know to be the end-state freed my mind from future worries about having enough. I can focus on my family, here and now with the time I have, with one less existential worry. If I'm lucky enough to grow old, I can live out my days without being a burden to those I love.

My advice: Go all-in on the change. The absolutist, burn-the-boats approach sounds radical, but the shores on which you will find yourself are not. These are low-cost index funds, after all. And you won't be alone when you get there.

## A MILLION IN SEVEN YEARS

ALEX

*Sydney, Australia*

**$** 1 MILLION IN seven years. Sounds impossible? I'd agree. But I still did it.

Did I plan it? Nope. Could it be planned? Maybe.

I certainly didn't expect it to happen, even after I set out to achieve it.

I managed to become a millionaire in my 30s and theoretically could retire 40 years earlier than what's considered normal. I don't come from a wealthy family. I have inherited nothing but good health and the luck of moving to a great country as a kid.

I have not started and sold a business. I have not been to university. I have no high-paying career in banking, tech, law, or medicine. In fact, I wasn't a brilliant student. I didn't enjoy school very much, and left as soon as I could.

I didn't make a lucky investment. Actually, I made some bad ones. After the Global Financial Crisis, I borrowed money to trade speculative shares from 2008 to 2012.

I lost everything I had, and more. But I am grateful. I was still young. And it forced me to turn my life around.

> Compared to the dangers of debt, the dangers of taking chances in your career when young are minimal, and the upsides are significant.

I decided it *really* wasn't fun being broke. I set myself the following three simple goals: get out of debt, save money, learn to invest properly. It was tough, and took time. But it gave me a vital foundation.

I became established in my early career, debt-free and with some savings to hand, and I knew now that "investing properly" looked like JL's Simple Path—not leveraged trading.

I decided to aim for a million. And it kind of still blows my mind to think I managed to do it. The best bit is I had a lot of fun on the way and didn't feel like I was sacrificing my 20s and 30s just to save money.

Here is what I learned:

**1. Focus on what really matters: Make more money.** You probably underestimate how much more money you can make by taking more risks. Compared to the dangers of debt, the dangers of taking chances in your career when young are minimal, and the upsides are significant.

Make it your top priority, way above skipping takeout coffee or living in a campervan to reach FI.

Cutting expenses is good, but becoming more valuable is far more effective. It's also the easiest way to avoid lifestyle inflation. Instead of trimming your outgoings, keep them stable and boost your income.

**2. Learn, but take action.** You need to learn and have goals and values that will bring you happiness and meaning, but you also have to take action. Everyone has dreams; most don't do anything about them. Knowledge never leads to results. Only action does.

**3. Track your cash flow.** You can only manage what you can measure, as they say. If you don't know where your money's going, you don't know how to optimize things.

And when it comes to optimizing, people mix up goals and values a lot. Reaching FI is a goal. It's not a value. However, if you track your spending you can see what's aligned to your values, especially by asking the following questions.

- What do I want to do?
- Why do I want those things?
- How am I going to get there?
- What is out there that I have not yet discovered?

If your spending isn't in line with your answers, cut it.

**4. Please don't waste time trying to pick stocks or time the market.** I say this not only because I lost everything I had trying it. But also because, if you reach FI in a short period of time, guess what? *Your investment return will be almost irrelevant.* Compounding is powerful—but it really starts taking full effect after several decades. Making a good salary and having a high savings rate will be what gets you there.

> Knowledge never leads to results. Only action does.

In the short term, doubling your income is much easier and safer than trying to double your investment returns.

**5. A certain ratio, not income, will make you feel rich.** I have a million in my bank account but it doesn't make me feel rich. What did make me feel rich was when I made $10,000 but spent only $5,000. The ratio between your income and your expenses is what will make you feel wealthy. It's pure math, really.

If you can live on half of your income, after just one year you could take a full year off with no work. But if you save only 10%, you would need to save for years before such a sabbatical. (Not nine, because you'd expect some returns on your investments.)

**6.** Often even 60-year-olds don't have 20 times their expenses covered, so anyone pursuing FI who achieves this ahead of time can be rightly proud. But, in the end, **most people don't run out of money but time.** Enjoy the journey.

**7. F-You Money feels better than FI in many ways.** When I had my first $100,000 saved I knew I'd be fine no matter what. Every $100,000 since has been diminishing returns.

Ultimately, I would leave you with this thought. We all have one life. Don't ruin yours to reach FI. Imagine you only need ten years to get there, but those ten years have to be a hell of self-sacrifice.

It's not worth the bad memories of a decade, or the loss of your youth. Instead, avoid debt and make good decisions and improve your value in the marketplace—then go for FI.

## IT'S NEVER TOO LATE
## FOR EARLY STEPS

### RECENT RETIREE

#### *USA*

I AM A 67-YEAR-OLD, recently retired, married woman. For most of my life I have been in the dark regarding my financial well-being. Yes, my husband and I contributed the full amount that our employer would match to our 403(b)s, and would periodically look at those funds. But that was about it.

We always have lived frugally, with little or no debt—and none at all right now. Over the years we might occasionally meet with financial advisors, including the one provided by whatever company was overseeing the 403(b)s. Most of the time we found it overwhelming, complicated, and stressful to think about. We were always inclined to put off doing anything. It was easier to *not* think about it!

It wasn't until my husband (who worked for the same employer as me) became disabled that I began paying a bit more attention. Still, even then, it was the same story—this is just too complicated and stressful. We have time.

We never fully trusted *any* financial advisor we met with. Admittedly, we were clueless about anything of this nature, but we could never quite shake the feeling that they were not really doing much for us *and* it was costing a good amount of what little we did have.

> Most of the time we found it overwhelming, complicated, and stressful to think about. We were always inclined to put off doing anything. It was easier to not think about it!

Finally, I ran out of time. As I neared retirement I was forced to face what I had been ignoring my whole working career. I began reading as much as I could and tried to educate myself. I found an article written by Warren Buffett about index funds that made a whole lot of sense to me. Then I happened upon JL's Simple Path. Managing our own money became a lot less scary when I finally saw the FI community already doing it. It was so simple I knew I could stay the course.

Which was immediately tested. The pandemic broke out just as I began retirement. However, we got through.

I write this because I want to urge younger people (my own kids included) to educate themselves early on and not be afraid of investing like we were. Our biggest mistake was being way too conservative back then (due to our own ignorance and some bad advice our portfolio had been 50/50 in equities and bonds since we were in our 20s!).

I don't pretend to fully understand the world of finance by a long shot, but JL's Simple Path to Wealth is simple—so there isn't a whole lot you have to understand. I now feel confident that what we do have is invested about as smart as it could be.

*Lastly, the wisest kind of investment… an early one:*

## HOW TO IDENTIFY THE FUTURE MILLIONAIRES OF AMERICA

GREGORY EDWARD BRENNER

*Houston, Texas, USA*

IT WAS THE spring session in 1996, at my first four-year college after attending a junior college for two years. I remember being seated in the large auditorium and being somewhat intimidated by how many students were in the basic management principles course. The professor started the first class by talking about our financial future and assigned a task for us to complete by the end of the semester. Each student would be required to open an IRA (individual retirement account).

Over the next few weeks I researched the task and took $200 from my savings account and opened up a basic IRA with Fidelity. Easy-peasy! Although $200 was a lot of money for a 21-year-old.

On the second-to-last day of the course, the professor followed up on the IRA assignment. He asked all students who had completed the task to stand up. I quickly got to my feet, assuming all 200+ other students would do the same.

In total, maybe ten stood.

Red in the face, I wanted to sit back down as quickly as I could. But the professor went on to talk about the power of compound interest—and had all the students clap "for the future millionaires of America."

Just over 25 years later, that same Fidelity account—transferred to my 401(k) plan through T. Rowe Price—hit the precious seven-figure mark. It was amazing that it had all come to pass.

I tried valiantly to reach my old professor at my alma mater but had no luck. The gratitude I have for him is enormous. Hopefully he knows his basic assignment helped pave the way for my financial future.

# PART SIX:

# F-YOU MONEY

# JL'S VIEW

## GIVE ME THE FI, YOU
## CAN KEEP THE RE

I HAVE LONG HAD an uneasy relationship with the acronym FIRE—Financial Independence Retire Early.

On the one hand, it is very clever and certainly memorable. On the other, there is the implication that if you FI the RE part must naturally follow. For me, that has never been the case. I enjoyed my career and I liked working. I just didn't want to have to do it all the time. Way back in 2012, Mr. Money Mustache asked me to write a guest post. I called it, "It has never been about retirement."

Then there is this silly bit of nonsense:

Leave your regular job and do something different like blogging, podcasting, carpentry, writing, boat building or whatever and those Mr. Money Mustache has christened "The Internet Retirement Police" will be all over your ass. You will be labeled a fraud. For them, the only acceptable form of retirement is playing golf and sitting on the beach drinking pina coladas. That's fine if that's what you want. But over the past decade I have met countless folks who have "retired." Every single one has gone on to do interesting and productive things, and some of those things even (gasp!) earn them money.

This is why I am all about the FI part and indifferent to the RE.

Achieving FI is all about having options. It means being able to choose how you spend your time. That might mean a RE of pina coladas, beaches and golf. Or of new exciting productive and possibly profitable things.

But here's the cool thing. You can enjoy many of those options even before you are fully FI. There is an interim step on The Path. I call it having F-You Money.

## DISCOVERING
## F-YOU MONEY

As I described earlier, when I started my journey there were no guideposts. No internet. No way to find and connect with like-minded people. I was alone and wandering in the wilderness. I had watched my father's health collapse and with it our family's financial fortunes. I learned it was a fiscally precarious world and I resolved to insulate myself from those risks as best I could.

I had no awareness of concepts like financial independence or retiring early. I just knew it was a mistake to assume I would always be able to work, let alone have (or want) a job. My solution was to save 50% of my income and invest. It never occurred to me there might be a name for this, let alone what that name might be. Until I read *Noble House*.

*Noble House* is a novel that came out in 1981 as the sequel to *Tai-Pan* (1966). In it, author James Clavell introduces a character whose stated objective is to have "F-You Money." For her, this is ten million dollars and it means having enough to, well, say "f-you" whenever, wherever and to whomever she feels the need.

I'd never heard this concept before—let alone expressed in such a salty and memorable way. It crystallized what I was working toward, even if I still had no notion of a finish line at the time. There was no FI community, no awareness of a formula for how much was needed to never have to work again, no Simple Path— just the route I was slowly discovering by myself. But now, at least, the destination had a name.

When I am working I tend to do it intensely. This has its pluses. It is very productive and effective. Your employers and partners love you for it. It is also unsustainable. There is no balance and it leads to burnout. Looking back, I realize I was good for about four to six years. If I wasn't smart enough to step away after that, my performance would erode and my employer would slowly wonder what had happened.

The least amount of time I ever took off with F-You Money was three months—we made our way as far north as Hudson Bay that summer. The longest was five years—a little longer than I would have preferred, but it took a while for a new job offer to come my way. I pursued, unsuccessfully as it turned out, other business interests. We got pregnant and our daughter was born (stuff happens when you have time on your hands). My wife quit her job and went back to school and graduated. We decided she'd be a stay-at-home mom. We had no income at all. And it worked.

While for Clavell's character F-You Money was her endgame, I always thought of it as an interim step. For me:

- F-You Money = Enough to make bolder decisions, but not enough to live on forever.
- FI = Enough money that the money it earns is enough to support you, plus a little bit more. (The now-classic formula is 25× your annual spending; that is, enough so that such spending equals no more than 4% of your invested assets.)

# F-YOU MONEY
## IN ACTION

While I hadn't yet heard the term, the first time I had and used F-You Money was with that $5,000 (~$30,000 in 2022) mentioned in my essay on freedom. It was not only enough to travel to Europe with a leftover cushion to find a new job upon my return, it was enough to embolden me to make the decision to quit to do it. That decision, in turn, put me in a strong enough negotiating position to not only get to travel but to keep the job.

With each passing year my financial resources grew stronger and this increased my life options. Over the years I have stepped away from jobs numerous times. Sometimes to travel, sometimes to pursue other interests, and sometimes just because it was time.

One of the most enjoyable parts of working on *Pathfinders* has been seeing the many varied and surprising ways other people have used it too. As the stories in this part will show, the deployment of F-You Money often leads to more rewarding jobs or situations—both financially and psychologically. Sometimes it lets you walk away from six-figure paychecks and be more than OK. Sometimes it provides just enough to keep you going while you find something different or explore something new.

Often, you don't even need to spend it. Just knowing you have it allows you to be stronger in the world. Someone in debt is simply far less free. One of the worst ways—but perhaps little considered—is how much the need to service those debts restricts them from taking even modest risks in pursuing more joy in their life, let alone addressing things like toxic work environments.

# RULES FOR THE ROAD

- Achieving FI is all about having options. RE is just one.

- Freedom doesn't only come at the end of The Simple Path when you've achieved FI.

- Along the way you'll steadily be acquiring F-You Money, and the freedom and options that come with it.

- F-You Money is not enough to never work again.

- But it does allow you to step away whenever the situation calls for it and it makes you stronger in the world.

- It allows you to be freer and bolder, able to speak up, take risks and be more independent.

- Surprisingly little F-You Money is surprisingly powerful.

- Every step you take along The Path builds on those you've taken before.

- As your F-You Money builds, your freedom and options expand, and it leads inevitably to being fully FI.

## "LACK OF MONEY IS THE ROOT OF ALL EVIL."

### —GEORGE BERNARD SHAW

# THE STORIES

## SH*T HIT THE FAN MONEY

RYAN J

*New Jersey, USA*

**M**Y STORY IS about F-You Money with a twist—I like to call it **Sh*t Hit the Fan (SHTF) Money**. It's not merely an emergency fund, though that helps. It's about having enough not *just* for saying what needs to be said, but for doing what needs to be done when sh*t has hit the fan.

With SHTF Money you have time to take stock without needing to completely stop your progress down The Simple Path to Wealth. And sh*t *will* hit the fan in your life. Like a recession, it's just a matter of when.

Overall, I had a lot of luck that led me on to JL's Simple Path before I even knew it by name. I wasn't poor, wasn't rich, had good parents, a decent education, and several incidents of lucky stumbles in college that provided good financial influence. Like knowing how much more important it is to be in the market as soon and as long as possible, rather than trying to time the market and pick just the right stock. I also had a natural tendency to maximize my dollars via investing or paying down debt with anything extra.

Given the above, plus an engineering job right after graduation, most FI community members would probably think I'd be retired in no time.

But something soon happened that forced me to change course.

I was busy trying to run a financially efficient household, paying down both my fiancée's and my student debt (a total of ~$170,000 in ~5 years). My attitude was that, "No money should just sit in cash unless it is part of our emergency fund needs." Shortly after paying off all our loans, we began to max out everything—IRAs, 401(k)s, and HSA. And about six months before the wedding we saved up for... I had what would later be determined as a manic episode with psychosis.

A few weeks later, on Mother's Day, I had another. I was given the diagnosis of Bipolar Type 1.

Essentially, I went through my "quarter-life crisis." It's not important why—I honestly don't know. They came on quick, with seemingly no provocation. I would go on to have another two, much more severe, episodes a year and a half later, requiring much longer hospital stays and an eight-week outpatient recovery.

My suspicion is that a lot of these were due (at least in part) to poor work/life balance. I have not had an episode for the past six years. Coincidentally I moved to a different employer six years ago.

After getting a diagnosis following the second episode, I was compliant with my medication (although it took a few to find what worked best), and I am still compliant today. Surprisingly, I needed a mental breakdown before experimenting with drugs. I also now volunteer in the mental health community.

Our wedding was pushed back a couple of times because of these episodes. Some advice my wife and I appreciated was that, "Big life changes take about a year to fully adjust to—getting married and adjusting to this diagnosis are pretty big life changes, so maybe just focus on the mental health management first."

We did eventually get married. Then a year into our marriage my 30-year-old, seemingly healthy, wife got diagnosed with stage-three colon cancer. She had colon surgery, six months of chemo, and a kidney surgery (a scan showed there might be something there too). She also froze her eggs due to concerns that chemo might prevent us from having kids in the future without the help of health insurance.

> Being on a path toward FI—not quite at FI—has given us the freedom and time to focus on ourselves and our own recoveries without the additional stress that the need for money can cause.

We are all doing fine now. In fact, we had our first child about a year ago! We went through these challenges, with the support of friends and family, all before Covid, and I think it left us better prepared than others for the pandemic in terms of our mental and physical health, as well as self-care routines.

I bring up these challenges not to seek attention (most friends and colleagues don't even know of my mental health challenges), but because I was once asked an important question by my younger brother: "How were you able to pay for stuff during that time? Aren't hospital bills expensive?"

Yes, yes they are. We hit our $10,000 max-out-of-pocket amount on our HDHP a few times, but when you are saving one person's entire salary, in a two-person household, you have options. I honestly didn't sweat a single medical bill. I might call and question a few things, but then just sent the payment. I don't think we even touched our emergency saving account, we just cut back on our taxable investment savings, and maybe our 401(k) savings, while still keeping any matching contributions.

If we ever do truly "retire" we even have about $30,000 in receipts so we could technically draw from our HSA tax-free before the 59.5-year mark.

Being on a path toward FI—not quite at FI—has given us the

freedom and time to focus on ourselves and our own recoveries without the additional stress that the need for money can cause. The crises that we faced actually helped by testing us and giving us confidence that we were doing well with our savings.

Once we weathered the storms, we were able to really chart our course more intentionally toward FI. The SHTF Money helped with our sense of security; F-You Money helps with our confidence.

The goal for me has never been achieving FI—but to achieve balance. You need to save and prepare for the uncertainty of tomorrow, while enjoying the time you have today.

## NOW I ONLY WORK FOR EMPLOYERS I RESPECT

DANNY

*New York, USA*

SHORTLY AFTER GETTING married in late 2013, we made the decision to tackle our car loan (~$15,000) and mortgage debt (~$150,000). Besides my full-time job, I made the decision to go back to my childhood job (caddying).

Surprisingly, that's where I received the most criticism from friends and (select) family members. Questions included: "Why are you taking on a second job?" And: "Danny, why are you being so *responsible*? The debts will be paid off over time."

Well, we eventually paid off all of our debts in late 2016 simply by living on less than we earned. We saved about 50–60% in those three years, applying a majority of it to the debts. Additionally, I was promoted at my job, and given two raises.

Our debt payoff was extremely beneficial in the coming years. In late 2018, my wife and I had our first child. Also, around June 2019 I was promoted for a third time at work. A normal person would be excited by this. I was not. I knew it would mean more responsibility and hours with a less-than-friendly boss at work.

I had to do something.

Luckily for us, we had been growing a substantial pile of F-You Money after paying off those debts. My personal savings rate shot up to slightly over 70%. We were in a wonderful position for exactly this challenge.

> When I told my boss the news I would be leaving in February 2020, he was shocked. As he so eloquently put it, "You're walking away from a six-figure paycheck with no immediate plan of finding another job. Are you sure that's what you want?"

When I told my boss the news I would be leaving in February 2020, he was shocked. As he so eloquently put it, "You're walking away from a six-figure paycheck with no immediate plan of finding another job. Are you sure that's what you want?"

I did try to negotiate alternative working arrangements, but we were just too far apart.

When my wife was laid off from the same company, my boss offered me a second chance. I declined before he finished his sentence. He needed me more than I needed him.

After February 2020, we became millionaires. My wife made the decision to be a stay-at/work-from-home mom. I have changed jobs four times, thanks to having the freedom to only work for who I respect.

Eight months after I left, my boss was fired.

## MY F-YOU FUND CAME IN HANDY
## WHEN I LEAST EXPECTED

LAURA C

*London, UK*

I'D DILIGENTLY SAVED a F-You Fund over the years. Being worried at the start of the pandemic, I kept saving until I had a year's worth. I knew it probably didn't make the most financial sense. Three to six months was the usual suggestion.

I had no idea that I was on the verge of a breakdown.

I was mentally unwell for the first time in my life. I got signed off from work for two weeks. But it was six months before I went back on a staged return.

Of all the irrational worries I was unable to corral with rationality, money didn't stop me sleeping at night, it didn't make me despair. Friends and family were concerned about how I'd survive financially. "There's a mortgage to be paid! You have a sole income! What'll you do?"

But the one thing that *didn't* play on my mind was if I'd be OK financially while I wasn't working. It was the only aspect of life that felt under control.

> I'm gradually getting back to work. And if it gets too much? I've still got six months' worth of the F-You Fund and I'm not afraid to use it.

I'm gradually getting back to work. And if it gets too much? I've still got six months' worth of the F-You Fund and I'm not afraid to use it.

I am privileged that I was able to save that amount. But I worked hard (too hard in hindsight) for that money. I earned it—and getting well again was the best thing I could have spent it on.

## I HAVE FOUND THE ULTIMATE
## STRESS-REDUCTION DEVICE

### BRIAN GRIESBACH

*Spanaway, Washington, USA*

IN 2015 MY wife and I moved 2,500 miles across the country for a job opportunity in the greater Seattle area. We had always been good savers, were on our second financial advisor, and were hoping to retire early at 60 instead of the more typical 65+.

After about a year and a half we noticed that our 401(k)s were out-performing the small amount we had in a taxable account managed by our financial advisor. He had helped us by encouraging us to max out our Roth IRA and 401(k) contributions, but the checks we were sending in every month sat in a money market fund.

I started researching options to make the leap to managing our own financial assets. The idea of F-You Money really resonated with me. I wasn't passionate about my work and couldn't get the extended time off I wanted to pursue my interests.

In 2017, I fired our financial advisor and moved everything over to Vanguard. I was amazed by the amount we were able to save now that we had a tangible goal of FI. There have been some bumps along the way, but through lifestyle reduction and diligent savings and investment our net worth has grown significantly.

> It's impossible to know how the future will play out, but the comfort of knowing we'll be OK financially has been a significant stress reduction.

We're going to stop working soon and take a whole year off to slow travel. I never dreamed I would have this kind of flexibility 20 years before I planned to traditionally retire. I just wish I had discovered this path sooner.

It's impossible to know how the future will play out, but the comfort of knowing we'll be OK financially has been a significant stress reduction. I hope more people take control of their financial futures and pursue the things that make them happy.

## HOW F-YOU MONEY MAKES
## YOU REALLY FEEL

### CHAD, FLOREM AND TRIPLETS

*California, USA*

IN 2008, THE housing crisis had a domino effect. People were laid off. Voluntary furloughs took effect. Streets were lined with foreclosed signs. My husband was often away training for his eventual deployment. I was responsible for bills, the mortgage, two auto loans, a student loan and credit card debts.

Not knowing when the economy would improve made me feel like we were underwater in a storm.

> F-You Money. It's more than a phrase; it's a ticket out of the rat race.

For my sanity, I started reading financial blogs about being debt-free. Cutting back on unnecessary spending was a good start but not enough. I started reading blogs about FI one afternoon and came across the concept of F-You Money.

It hit home how, despite being a loyal employee, I was merely a cog in the wheel. With a net worth in the red, my employer owned me.

All of a sudden, I had this urgent need to be financially independent.

After discussing it with my husband, we moved our Roth IRA, savings and money market accounts to VTSAX. When we pivoted from spenders to investors, our money slowly but steadily began to build real wealth thanks to compound interest.

F-You Money made us feel proactive, resilient and unbound. In 2022, the economy is tanking again—but this time we are not as vulnerable. Our young triplets are seeing and enjoying the benefits of F-You Money. It's more than a phrase; it's a ticket out of the rat race.

## I ACQUIRED F-YOU MONEY BY MISTAKE—THEN I USED IT

### MR. NEWFARMER

*Austria*

F-YOU MONEY HAS given me the freedom to completely change my career path, to pursue what I love, to make the world greener, and to be my own boss.

I spent my 20s absorbed by career advancement and 60-hour weeks for a global consulting firm. Fortunately, I accidentally kept my living costs as low as a student's all that time. I was happy, why spend more? So when I discovered FI, I was ahead of the game. I was still nervous about walking away from the position I had gained from all that work. But I had accumulated F-You Money by mistake, and could use it.

I now run my very own small-scale organic food store. Instead of being away from each other the better part of every week, my wife and I are co-owners of our own business. Partners in crime—both in private life and in business.

Even though we have not yet met our FI number, we already reap so many benefits from living the FI way. My suggestion to you: Do not continue to work overtime until the day you reach your FI number and then suddenly stop working altogether.

Instead, see FI as a continuum.

What would you like to do once you reach FI? What would change in your day-to-day life? Think carefully whether there are activities you could already start to include in your life before then, even though you are "only" part way through your FI journey. Then continue to build in even more flexibility into your schedule as you progress further. That way, you do not "push your happiness into the future," as a saying here in Austria goes, but you live your life to its fullest today.

## MY F-YOU MONEY LET ME TRY
## EARLY RETIREMENT

### WILLIAM R

*Minnesota, USA*

**F**-YOU MONEY GAVE me confidence to take chances I never would have dreamed of. For instance, I was able to slowly test out early retirement. I began to feel that a two-day weekend was not enough time to recharge for another week of work. I decided to ask for Fridays off. After all, it was mostly a wasted day at work. People went through the motions, but everyone was focused on the weekend.

I had been working at my job for almost ten years and built a reputation for being reliable. We agreed upon a three-month trial, but everything went smoothly and we never went back to five days a week. The one extra day every week that I had to myself was incredible. I was able to focus on my gardening, run errands, clean the house, or just take a day off to rest and recover. It was truly liberating—a feeling I will never forget.

When I was able to retire in my early 30s, I wanted to do it differently. I knew from experience that, with the standard two-week notice, a lot of a person's unfinished work is left to people already overwhelmed with their own tasks. I saw myself that this always added a lot of stress in the office, and could lead to panicked decision-making.

> F-You Money gave me confidence to take chances I never would have dreamed of.

Although I was unhappy in a corporate environment, I loved working with my colleagues. They were the ones who would feel the brunt of my departure.

So, instead, I gave my employer a two years' notice.

I had one final safety check. When I gave my notice, I requested one month of unpaid time off to get a glimpse into early retirement. This would allow me to make sure I was cut out for this, and it also gave my employer the chance to evaluate the gaps they would need to fill in my absence.

The month away from work confirmed it was exactly what I needed. I never second-guessed my decision as the next two years passed.

Perhaps very few companies would allow such flexibility. However, before I had F-You Money and dared to ask, I would have counted my company as one of those inflexible firms. F-You Money gives you the power to find out.

## WE'VE HARNESSED F-YOU MONEY
## REPEATEDLY—HERE'S HOW

### DIANDRA & BRAD

*Wisconsin, USA*

*www.thatsciencecouple.com*

ABOUT FOUR YEARS down the road towards financial freedom, we realized we were not going to get there overnight since we never made crazy high incomes.

We both worked in the biotech field, which had decent benefits but raises that barely kept up with inflation. We had paid off our debts, saved more than just 10% in our 401(k)s, and started to build that six-month cash cushion.

While sitting on a pile of cash feels good, we started to see opportunities pass us by. If money is supposed to be a tool, then why don't we use it? I felt stagnated in my career, working in a high-stress environment, undervalued.

So instead of staying, I thought, why not take the leap and see if I can find something more fulfilling?

**Activate F-You Money episode 1:** May 2018. There was an opportunity at a small start-up my former coworker had moved to. She said, "You can have that 'scientist' title you want, and you'll make more money." Staying at my current job would have been the safe route. Higher ups were telling me "If you take that job, you'll never be able to make that kind of money again with your credentials." Sure, it was high risk, but I had a safety net (my F-You Money) in case it didn't go well.

I interviewed and got an offer I couldn't refuse. In one fell swoop I made over a 50% raise and got the title of scientist I always wanted. I took the next few months to stash away as much cash as possible, as if the company could go under at any time. I invested hard and fast, and maxed out my 401(k) for the first time ever. I even saved to buy a used vehicle outright (my indestructible economy sh*tbox, the Prius). But one of the most important things about this job transition was that it got us comfortable with the power of F-You Money.

**Enter F-You Money episode 2:** July 2018. A few months later, Brad had been working towards a master's degree for some time, but he needed to take time off work to focus on his final research project or he wouldn't be able to graduate. Equipped with the power of F-You Money, Brad asked his managers for the option of part-time work. The answer, no. "We need you full time."

Of course, this would be a disappointment for some, but we turned it into an opportunity—to activate the F-You Money. If it's full time or no time, then how about no time?

Brad turned in his resignation letter and took the semester to work on research. A few months later, with diploma in hand, we knew he had made the right decision. After graduating he even got a chance to work for the National Park Service (one of his dream jobs) because of the cash cushion he had created.

**F-You Money episode 3:** February 2019. F-You Money had one more major role to play: going back to school. While I enjoyed my new high salary, there was an emptiness inside of me. I wanted to change the world and really make a difference in individuals' lives, but I felt like I needed a PhD to do that.

I applied to programs and continued to stash up money. When I got accepted into a program, I transitioned to part-time and partial remote work in the pre-pandemic world. I was starting to buy back my time.

With F-You Money, Brad was able to take a mini sabbatical and take eight months off as we relocated for my program in August without worrying about getting a job right away. Now he is at his highest salary ever and building up his F-You Money again.

At the time of writing, I'm in the final year of my PhD program, doing research on diet and lifestyle, and I've started my own evidence-based nutrition coaching business. None of which would have been possible without F-You Money.

We saved, we invested, and we changed the course of our lives. Good luck to those on The Path, and don't forget if you're stuck in a rut, you can always harness the power of F-You Money.

# PART SEVEN:
# STAYING THE COURSE

# JL'S VIEW

## PERSISTENCE ON AN
## UNUSUAL PATH

I N A BOOK filled with great stories, in this part we come to a few of the most inspirational.

To reach any destination, you must keep moving forward. You must stay on the route, returning to it when you've taken a wrong turn or ill winds have pushed you into the weeds.

In the next few pages you'll read about staying the course while nearly losing your job as a front-line doctor during a pandemic, when disability strikes, when your country is invaded by a hostile army, when your country is the invader and becomes an international pariah, and when everything simply just goes wrong over the decades.

Thankfully for most of us The Simple Path is a whole lot smoother. It certainly has been for me. But that doesn't mean there aren't temptations and frustrations along the way. The whole world out there is, after all, telling us we're doing life all wrong.

*You deserve a break today, this too could be yours with our E-Z financing, you will be irresistible with this scent, this car, these clothes, this liquor...*

On The Path, you're a unicorn. The people around you are more likely than not to be confused at best, and possibly even hostile to the choices you're making.

Frequently I am asked if the FIRE movement is destined to take over the world. To those of us on this Path, it just feels so much better. But my voice, and those of others writing in this space, is but a teaspoon in the marketing ocean of the larger culture. We are more at risk of being lured off The Path by that culture than it is of being overly influenced by these ideas.

## IT AIN'T ALWAYS EASY

If you are just beginning on The Simple Path full of optimism, excitement and dreams of what financial independence is going to feel like, the idea of straying from it might seem laughable. The Path is simple, after all. You've read all about the concepts, ideas, benefits and approaches it entails. You've hoisted your pack— suitably light and holding only what you really need—onto your shoulders and you are ready to get moving. You are clear on the plan and now all you need do is execute it. One foot after the other. Simple.

True enough. But a map is a map and life is life, and sometimes life gets in the way. Unexpected obstacles appear, detours beckon, streams need fording. You can get lost if you're not careful. You might just get a little tired, pause for a rest, and find it has gotten cold and dark when you wake.

That's OK—happens to the best of us—as long as you get up, shoulder your pack once again and keep moving.

Persistence is what gets you there. Staying the course.

# THE APOGEE OF HUMAN TOLERANCE

One of my favorite books is *Sapiens* by Yuval Noah Harari. If you are interested in understanding why we humans are the wacky creatures we are and why we believe the wacky things we do, this is the book for you.

One of the key reasons we've been such a successful species is our remarkable ability to create stories. We've used them over time right up until today to cooperate with each other and to shape our world. Mr. Harari makes the case that perhaps the most powerful of all these stories, myths if you will, is that of money. From *Sapiens*:

"Money is the apogee of human tolerance. Money is more open-minded than language, state laws, cultural codes, religious beliefs and social habits. Money is the only trust system created by humans that can bridge almost any cultural gap, and that does not discriminate on the basis of religion, gender, race, age or sexual orientation."

By way of illustration, he also tells this story:

"When ISIS conquered large parts of Syria and Iraq, it murdered tens of thousands of people, demolished archaeological sites, toppled statues and systematically destroyed the symbols of previous regimes and of western cultural influence. Yet when ISIS fighters entered the banks and found…"

Well, what they found were piles and piles of pieces of paper and on these pieces of paper was the awful propaganda of The Great Satan itself. Images of past leaders, and religious and political writings. So, of course, they promptly burned them! Right?

Oops. Sorry. I get excited. Here, let's let Mr. Harari tell it…

"… stashes of US dollars covered with the faces of American presidents and English slogans praising American political and religious ideals, they did not burn these dollars. For the dollar bill is universally venerated across all political and religious divides. Though it has no intrinsic value—you cannot eat or drink a dollar bill—trust in the dollar and in the wisdom of the Federal Reserve is so firm it is shared even by Islamic fundamentalists, Mexican drug lords and North Korean tyrants."

## THIS TIME ISN'T DIFFERENT

Perhaps the most common force that knocks folks off The Simple Path is fear. Fear mostly around the volatility inherent in stock investing. We've covered this already, so I won't belabor it here. But it is critical enough and dangerous enough to warrant a few more words.

When the market takes a major plunge the common wisdom too often becomes "This time is different." Sure, they say, all those *other* times the market recovered—but this is *a depression.* Or *a housing collapse.* Or *stagflation.* Or *a war.* Or *a bank run.* Or *a pandemic.* Or, or, or, or…

If anything, such alarmist assertions tend to mark the beginning of a new surge up. Witness the great bull market that followed the now infamous 1979 *BusinessWeek* cover headline: "The Death of Equities."

Markets crash from time to time. It's what they do. Enduring this is the price we pay for the long-term wealth-building gains it provides. The triggers may be different—but the fact that a collective representation of commercial endeavor is occasionally reevaluted in light of unexpected information is a feature, not a bug. Our capitalist system is dynamic—continually adjusting and adapting to new ideas and situations. Individuals are able and encouraged to create solutions to problems and they are rewarded when they succeed. It has built a world from which we all benefit.

No, the world is not perfect. But before you fall prey to the drumbeat of pessimism that seems all too pervasive, here's a thought experiment. Imagine you could be born at any time in history. If you chose any time but now, well, I suggest you brush up on your history—and what our world is really like today. *Factfulness* by Hans Rosling is a good place to start.

## KEEPING IT SIMPLE

There is another guy writing in this FI space. Good guy, and smart. He makes the case that, by adding a couple more specific funds he's identified to my recommendation of just a single total stock market index fund like VTSAX, performance can be slightly enhanced. You'd then rebalance these funds as needed to keep the allocation percentages in line with his recommendations. Played out over a couple of decades, this slight extra performance can have a meaningful impact on the end result. Backtested, his research shows this to be true. I have enough respect for him to take him at his word on that. So why don't I embrace this seemingly better approach?

The most obvious reason is that backtesting might not accurately predict the future. While true, that also feels like a bit of a copout. Here's the more important reason: Very few people are likely to hold four or five funds, rebalance them as required, and make no other changes over the decades this will take. Why?

Because this more complex approach encourages—indeed requires—people to tinker with their investments and, as we discussed earlier, the more you tinker the less well you are likely to do. Moreover, this particular tinkering is asking them not only to continue to hold asset classes while they are doing poorly, but to shift money to them from those that are doing well when that happens. Human nature being what it is, folks are more likely to do the very opposite.

With every slight drop in the market I get panicked comments that indicate just how hard it is to get people to hold just one fund and stay the course. This is why I refer to my daughter's lack of interest in investing as a superpower. It makes her, and folks like her, less likely to tinker.

Theoretically, this fellow's approach might well yield a better result. But the more complex a thing is, the more likely it is to fail. This is The Simple Path to Wealth because in the real world simple is more powerful, easier and more robust. This is not always an easy path. No sense in making it more difficult with complexity.

# RULES FOR THE ROAD

- We are unicorns in a broader culture that encourages a very different approach.

- Staying on The Path isn't always easy.

- Unexpected obstacles appear, detours beckon, streams need fording. It can get cold and dark.

- Persistence is essential.

- When you get pushed or lured away, you must find your way back and continue the journey.

- Money is the single most powerful tool we have for dealing with this complex world we have created.

- "Money is the apogee of human tolerance."

- Market drops are normal. It wasn't different last time and it won't be next time. Only the trigger will change.

- There is no better time to be alive than right now.

- Adding complexity for a theoretically better result is unlikely to work over time in the real world.

- Because The Path is simple, you are less likely to tinker and more likely to stay the course.

- The Simple Path is indeed simple, but even so it can take effort to stay the course and continue the journey. You must tune out the noise, return when you have strayed, and remain persistent.

"CONSIDER THE MOSQUITO. HE SINGS AT HIS WORK AND HE KEEPS EVERLASTINGLY AT IT. THE ONLY WAY TO STOP HIM IS TO KILL HIM."

—JT FISHER

# THE STORIES

## FOUR THINGS THAT HELPED US STAY THE COURSE

HEMANI & TANUJ

*London, UK*

THERE WERE FOUR key steps that helped us stay the course. **The first was avoiding lifestyle inflation from the beginning:** We made sure to only buy as much house as we needed, with a focus on low day-to-day living costs. For example, borrowing less than two times our income and choosing a location where we could walk for all our needs. This choice then compounded to mean our car expenses were super low too, and we got healthier with all the active local travel.

**The second was getting our savings rate right:** With a starting rate of 50%, we increased to a peak of 90% during the pandemic lockdowns, as many of our costs dropped to zero. This was also partially possible due to a focus on increasing our income by finding better-paying jobs and seeking freelance work as side hustles.

**Third, carefully keeping our heads in the ground:** We avoid the news and have our stock market index investing on autopilot. When others tell us about falls in the stock market, we secretly feel excited—it's on sale, and we're already automatically buying.

**Finally, occasional deployment of F-You Money:** Knowing with confidence that our financials were solid, we have been able to leave bad jobs or environments to clear our heads. We then always found something else afterwards that was much more enjoyable and higher paying.

We have been able to help others in profound ways they often do not even realize, all due to our financial means, experience in finding value, and flexibility in how we spend our time.

## STAYING THE COURSE IN WARTIME

ROMAN KOSHOVSKYI

*Lviv region, Ukraine*

*www.youtube.com/c/RomanKoshovskyy, mykrp.com.ua*

I AM A 30-YEAR-OLD pursuing FI in Ukraine. It's an interesting time to do so, with my country at war. But it's always been a little different here.

Until a 2017 change in regulations it was hard to find equivalent investment vehicles to the ones most popular with the international FI community. There are still far fewer than the US, but it's possible to open accounts in US or European-based brokerages.

A lot of people have done so. But many still hadn't before the war. They blamed circumstances, the economy, corruption—what was the point? They didn't understand that some things are only improved from the bottom up, with small mindset and habit shifts. At least that's been my experience.

The war, of course, has thrown everything into the air. But I am keeping to JL's Simple Path as best as I can.

I am always researching and analyzing data on my FI journey. But I also try to keep things simple and fun. I stick to all the classic FI principles—diversifying investments, taking a long time horizon, thinking like an owner of the world's businesses, avoiding debt, spending less than I earn and investing the rest.

> Some risks are much more significant than the economy. Your life, and time with your loved ones, are much more precious than all the money you will ever earn.

I also like to remain a little flexible and keep learning. I know I won't necessarily get it 100% right, but I will be much better off in 15–20 years than many. I enjoy sharing everything I can with my Ukrainian peers to help them find financial freedom too.

Here are some key things I have learned from my pursuit of FI in Ukraine, which I hope will help others stay the course no matter where they are:

- **Diversification isn't just a fancy word.** At the time of writing, Ukrainian bond and stock markets are not functioning properly (only war bonds are allowed for trading), so parts of my capital are frozen and could be gone forever, or the future payments could get restructured. That's the risk I took with some home-country bias. Fortunately, I don't have all my eggs in one basket. Thanks to my assets abroad and brokerage accounts in the US that I opened before the war, I can continue to contribute to my retirement portfolio and buy good assets with lower prices in the current drawdown.

- **Disasters can happen, and insurance and backup plans can only protect you so much when they do.** You have to have cash on hand and some liquid assets for the ultimate curve balls of life. Only invest money you won't need even in the direst of circumstances—cash you definitely won't need to touch for maybe even 20 years.

- **Move fast, but think slowly.** In hard times the urge is to follow the crowd. That's how you fall into common traps—piling up perishable food, converting currency when exchange rates have been driven ridiculous by fear, ignoring air-raid sirens because everyone else is. It's better to evaluate your options before acting.

- **Some risks are much more significant than the economy.** Your life, and time with your loved ones, are much more precious than all the money you will ever earn. Wartime refreshes your perspectives and shifts your priorities.

If I had known war would really break out, would I have moved more of my assets abroad? I don't know. I love my Motherland, and I am working—as are my friends—to prosper it now and in the future. We don't know how life will unfold, but I will do everything in my control to keep to JL's Simple Path to financial freedom.

## WHEN YOUR COUNTRY BECOMES
## A GLOBAL OUTCAST

ARTEM VORONOV

*Naberezhnye Chelny, Tatarstan, Russia*

*www.voronov.net*

I LIVE IN THE center of Russia with my wife and nine-year-old daughter. When I was in elementary school in 1991 the Soviet Union, where I was born, broke up into several countries. In the decade that followed, my new country, Russia, went through a painful transition to a market economy and integration into the world community.

Democratic momentum and political reforms, as well as the first economic collapse in my memory in 1998, eventually led to an unprecedented economic recovery in all sectors. International companies opened local industries, wages rose, ordinary people could afford to buy previously inaccessible commodities, a new car and more comfortable housing. During this golden era, I graduated from university and began my professional career in the automotive industry.

Although my income never grew as quickly as when I started out, my spendings were always less than my income. I remembered the example of my parents, whose bank accounts were devalued by hyperinflation after the collapse of the USSR; all subsequent financial opportunities passed them by. Today they live on a social pension and are completely dependent on the state. Compared to them, in my old age, I always wanted to have wider choices: the opportunity to move to a warmer climate with F-You Money, for instance. $250,000–$350,000 would be enough for me. I began to think about ways to invest my savings.

At the beginning, I had no clear plans and continued to spend a little more than I should have, and save a little less than I could. I have long been acquainted with the stock market, and tried active trading and investing in individual stocks. Without a strategy, I was afraid to invest a large amount, so I did not achieve any results—except to waste my time.

Meanwhile, the government of my country has taken a number of adventurous geopolitical steps, accompanied by a continuous depreciation of my income from increased inflation and a falling national currency. The more my lifestyle deteriorated, the more active the propaganda. I saw how dissenting mouths are shut up, and democratic institutions are methodically dismantled. In such an environment, it became obvious that investing requires global diversification into assets supported by economic freedom and property rights. My current life in Russia was still comfortable, I loved my homeland, but my view of the future became rather gloomy. Sooner or later I expected a failure of economic policy. I could not imagine the reality of the military catastrophe before that.

Around 2014, I came across JL's Simple Path. That's how I became an index investor. Whenever I tried to be smarter, I got worse results. Possibly my biggest mistake was taking lightly the recommendation to invest in Vanguard funds—instead, I opted for the UCITS ETF on the broad US stock market, domiciled in Ireland and available for purchase through a Russian broker.

My choice to invest through the Russian stock market was justified, among other things, by tax benefits for Russian residents, as well as by the fact that a significant amount is needed to open an account with a foreign broker. We also have investment accounts like IRAs with a tax deduction on deposits and the ability to sell stocks tax-free after three years. As long as the tax benefits exceeded my fund's fees (TER = 0.9%), I planned to accumulate about $150,000 in it over several years, and then transfer these funds to a foreign broker and buy a low-cost Vanguard index fund.

But this was not destined to happen.

The outbreak of armed conflict between Russia and Ukraine was unexpected by most people, myself included. The severe international backlash that followed led to a halt in communications between stock markets and the continued disruption of economic interconnections. This caused processes that neither I nor the FI community could have imagined. Hopefully humanity will pass these times with as few casualties as possible, lessons will be learned, and the perpetrators will be punished.

At the moment, the trading of my ETF from Russia is completely frozen, as is the access of foreign investors to Russian stocks. True cross-border risk has materialized for me. Can I get my capital back one day? I hope so. Meanwhile I have to leave my $47,000 portfolio alone—almost all of my personal savings. Currently my asset allocation is nearly in line with Warren Buffett's famous recommendation of 90% S&P 500 and 10% US government bonds. Who knows, maybe after retirement, my daughter or I will regain access to assets worth millions.

Certainly this will not happen until the authoritarian government of my country changes.

It was probably a mistake to strictly follow the rule of not panicking or selling. It works well to overcome psychological handicaps during financial panics—it helped me stay on course during the Covid sell-off in March 2020. But it kept me from being able to maintain control of my capital before the bridges were raised.

> I saw how dissenting mouths are shut up, and democratic institutions are methodically dismantled. In such an environment, it became obvious that investing requires global diversification

After such a blow, it took time to pull myself together. But now I have started collecting emergency funds again and gradually investing in the remaining available index tools.

Today, foreign brands are closing production and leaving my country at an accelerated pace. Output in the automotive industry has collapsed by 80%. I still have a job, and my wife has her own small business, we live in our own house and we have no debts.

I have no doubt about humanity's ability to cope and thrive, and that markets will recover. During the last 15 years I feel I have already experienced every threat possible: financial crises, climate disasters, pandemics, even war. I probably won't raise an eyebrow when aliens arrive. The world is still out there, and the S&P 500 is higher than it was when I started out.

I am anxious about the future of my country and do not want my daughter to grow up with a sick ideology, isolated from the rest of the world without prospects of a decent standard of living. Recently, I have been thinking more and more about emigration, although I am still indecisive—today a Russian passport is unwelcome almost everywhere.

I keep walking, and I understand better that JL's Simple Path to Wealth needs both the strong legs of the pathfinder and strong tarmac underfoot if you are to succeed.

I still hope the best lies ahead, and I believe I have time to see it one day.

## STAYING THE COURSE AS A FRONT-LINE DOCTOR IN A PANDEMIC

EDWARD KIM

*Connecticut, USA*

**A**FTER A SIX-YEAR long-distance relationship, I had proposed and just started a new job. My fiancée and I were both doing separate medical residencies and fellowships for six years apart in Michigan and New York. We finally moved to Connecticut, and were getting settled into our new lives together. I was looking into the best funds for my 403(b), when I discovered JL's Simple Path.

I increased my contribution rate and invested my 403(b) in S&P 500 index funds. I also started a brokerage account at Vanguard, and started contributing to it in VTSAX. Then the Covid-19 pandemic hit, and I was thrust into the eye of the storm.

As an infectious disease physician, I saw every patient with a Covid diagnosis at the hospital. The hospital, in the meantime, was furloughing people and cutting salaries because of the sudden dearth of elective surgeries and non-Covid patients. The hospital even threatened to furlough me in the middle of the pandemic.

The stock market had entered a bear market, and was also down 34%. I absorbed myself in FI materials, stayed the course, and did not withdraw or alter my investments.

During that time, some of my co-physicians refused to see patients and continued to work from home. Another colleague and I were the only ones seeing every Covid patient in the hospital and clinic. I felt that it was our duty to help as many patients as possible during a time of great need, but it meant that a workload that was meant to be divided among seven physicians was being done by the two most junior physicians.

After two years on the front line and feeling burned out and unsupported, I applied for a new position. By then, vaccines were available and hospitalizations were finally declining. My retirement accounts had recovered. Staying the course provided me with the reassurance to look for a job with better work/life balance.

## WHEN EVERYTHING GOES WRONG

TOM

*USA*

**F**ROM 1947 TO 1969 I lived at home with my brother. We were children of two strict Catholics, who were themselves children of the Depression—to say we were repressed is probably an understatement.

We were both taught to save. I started to work at 13, in a retreat house refectory. I saved every dime in a local savings and loan. It was cool to watch the deposits build up little by little.

I went to a Catholic grade school and an all-boys Catholic high school. Both cost money.

In 1965 I started at Wayne State University. I had some help from my folks, but paid for books, transportation, lunches, etc. myself. I lived at home and commuted.

I worked every summer as well as stashing money away for the next school year. I dated, hung with friends, and had an active, fun college experience even though it wasn't at the ivy-covered walls of a major university away from home. I thought it, at the time, to be, well, normal.

In 1968 I bought my dad's used 1965 VW for $500. I finally had "wheels." When I graduated, I had $2,000 in that savings and loan.

In June, I graduated. In August I got married to my little Irish lass, "MA." In September I reported to active duty at the Basic School, USMC Training Center in Quantico, VA. Life was good and I was finally on my own.

After living that restrictive, home all the time, life with my parents, I was free at last and MA was pregnant. I was going to be a father. From 1969 to 1992 were the MA years.

I started to want things my parents would never let me have. A brand new Pioneer sound center complete with amp, turntable, reel-to-reel, cassette player, top-of-the-line speakers, etc. I found an old oak roll-top desk I liked for $300. And so on.

The two grand melted away; but I was an officer in the Marine Corps. I had a regular paycheck of $5,000 a year. Saving somehow didn't seem so critical, retirement was 20, 30, 40 years away. I might not live that long.

Pretty soon we were living paycheck to paycheck. Credit was easy to get and easier to use. We started to build up a little debt, not much, but a grand or two. Didn't seem like any big deal.

I got out of the Corps in 1973, and got a great job with M-corp for $12,000/yr. Two grand more than I made as a 1st Lt in 1972. In 1972, "B" was born too—I now had two wonderful daughters. I bought a house in Detroit for $20,000.

I did a fine job at work and in 1976 got promoted to field development manager. I wasn't sure about leaving our friends and family. I went to Chicago, went to Mass at the Cathedral one Sunday, and prayed to the Lord to ask if this was right for my young family. The usher interrupted my prayer and tapped me on the shoulder and asked if my wife and I would take the offering up at the Offertory. I took that as a sign—a "Yes."

So I took the promotion and moved to Chicago. We still had a little debt. Couldn't seem to pay those damn cards off completely every month. The house in Detroit we sold for $18,000, buying high and selling low.

I did sign up for payroll savings at this time. Our new house in Naperville, IL cost twice as much as our house in Detroit—$40,000. The mortgage payment was twice as much, and obviously I wasn't earning twice as much. I had to commute into the Loop (downtown Chicago) every day too. Still, it was a great community, right in the old part of town.

Costs were increasing while I wasn't keeping pace. We had

kids to raise, had to "keep up" after work, in the neighborhood, etc. My payroll savings were about 5% of my income, maybe 6%. My wife decided to go back to school. I had my first college education to pay for.

In 1979 or 80, I left M-corp to work for V-corp (as office manager) for like $35,000, over $10,000 more than I was making at M-corp. It sounded like a good deal. I took it. And it lasted for a year—my first real setback.

I had conflict with the two owners. They didn't like the direction I was taking the office. I scrambled and M-corp took me back. They were more faithful to me than I was to them. Still, they knew I was talented and hard-working. I was now the advertising/sales promotion manager at $27,500. They even bridged my time so I didn't lose my ability for vesting.

In 1983, a couple of months short of my tenth anniversary at M-corp (and vesting), I was pursued by R-corp in Bridgeport, CT. They treated me like a king. MA and I loved the area, the job was a new challenge. It seemed like the right thing to do.

I even had another sign from God that it was the right move. A rainbow this time.

We sold the house in Naperville for $60,000. Off to New England in 1982. Bought a house for $85,000 in Newtown, CT, using the 20 grand as the down payment. Loved it.

The job lasted two and a half years: R-corp went bankrupt due to asbestos litigation. Bummer.

Still, that year (1984), I got a call from a friend who worked at RR-corp. He wanted to know if I'd like to talk to a recruiter in New York about an opening as a VP at RR, working on the C-corp business. I said sure. In 1984 we headed back to Detroit.

Bought a home in upscale Birmingham, MI for $120,000. My wife now had a job at DT-corp as an auditor. RR helped get her transferred to Detroit as well. We were on our way.

Two jobs, nearly $90,000 a year. Wow! Things went well, the girls graduated high school and went on to MSU, I now had two college educations to pay for, work was hard, my wife and I hardly saw each other. In 1987, my dad died; in 1989, my mom died.

In 1990, MA asked for a divorce. She said I was mad all the time (maybe I was just sad). Didn't know what I wanted I guess, except I didn't want the divorce. Anyway, after the dust cleared I still had a job, had to sell the house, didn't get much more than we paid for it (those were recession years), and I walked away with about $24,000 left in my personal nest egg after she took her half and we paid the lawyers.

I put the money left in four diverse money market funds and let 'em alone. In 1990 I met "A" at work, 23 years my junior. She loved me, I rented a house in Birmingham and she moved in. We had a ball. Life was good again.

In 1990, RR took me off C-corp (where I was happy) and put me on new business because I was "so good at it." I hated it. In 1991 I asked for some time off, I was burned out and I wanted back on C-corp. They said "no," I said I quit. A and I loaded up an '89 Jeep Cherokee and set off to see the back roads of America. We traveled all of 1992, camping and backpacking. I'd do it all again.

A new young lady, a mate for the rest of my life. That's what I thought. The year off taught us a lot about each other, we loved each other, we knew we'd make it. No job, but who cared, we'd find something—and finally, in 1993, we did.

By then, A was pregnant with our first son. I found a job with an old buddy repping auto parts and pickup-truck-bed liners in Baltimore. We bought an end-row townhouse in Towson, MD, and settled in. "G" was born and all seemed well, until my boss said he couldn't afford me and my $30,000-a-year salary anymore.

No problem: I found a new job at a little ad agency in Winchester, VA. Sold the house in MD and rented one in VA. Good move, because that $40,000/yr job only lasted a year.

Did I mention, I had to cash in my money market funds one at a time between 1992 and 1996 to survive, for down payments and the like?

It's now 1995. I find a great new job in Ohio at U-corp calling on an old RR client, FM-corp. I knew this was going to last, so I bought a nice house in Cuyahoga Falls. "Z," my second son, was born there. We were happy. I turned 50 and started to worry about retirement. Then 1997 came round.

I couldn't stand my boss and the owner of U-corp anymore. I started looking again. Thank the Lord, I had earned a $20,000 bonus in 1996. Money in the bank, and to pay off credit cards.

Guess who wanted me back in Detroit? Good old RR. Off we go, one more time. Motown here we come. Back on C-corp, back with our friends (A's and mine), we are happy. And we buy a house in 1998 in Milford! Wow, my home from 1998 until 2013. Longest place I ever lived continuously. Used what was left of the U-corp bonus as the down payment.

Everybody was making money and life was good. I got back to the ad agency grind and A stayed at home and raised the boys… until 2002 or so when she started back to college at Eastern. Another college education! No problem, we'll just refinance, the house is appreciating.

A buddy of mine from BB-corp becomes president at YR-corp and he wants me to join his team as a VP—an honor and more money. Off I go to YR. Well, that lasts two years until he gets canned and of course all "his people" get the ax too. Out of work in 2001. Takes me almost a year to find a new job.

When I left BB and went over to YR, following my buddy M who became CEO of the Detroit office, I took around $40,000 in 401(k) money. In two years or so I managed to add another $50 or $60K. On M's advice, I invested those dollars with a money manager for one of the big investment companies. In a couple of years he lost about $80,000 of my money. That hurt. He kept telling me it was just a blip in the market, it would come back (e-boom and bust time period). Anyway, easy come, easy go.

I spent money I had set away for retirement. So now I was 55 with a young wife, two sons and no nest egg. Guess where my new position is? Back at BB, but this time as a lowly account supervisor. I am being punished.

They put me on the C-corp business. I work hard and help

build the business. They finally promote me to VP again in 2003. Making $80,000/year, $1,400/year mortgage, helping A through school. She graduates in 2006 and guess what... she files for divorce. Takes half of what I have in my 401(k). I think the house is appreciating—I keep that, buying her out of her half. Pay lawyers. And child support... life gets kinda sucky.

To make things worse, in 2008, the bubble bursts, I'm screwed, C-corp goes bankrupt, fires all their vendors, sticks everybody with debt and now I'm 61 and no one wants or needs a 61-year-old account man. I'm saddled with debt, get deeper in debt, house depreciates, can't sell it.

I hang in with part-time jobs and Michigan State Unemployment Insurance until 2012 when the answer hits the proud old Marine officer... I have to file for Chapter 7.

I take my SS at 62, since I can't wait until 65. I collect a small VA benefit of $132/month for hearing loss during my USMC years. I also have a $400/month pension from RR.

I find the Swede, fall in love again, find a part-time job at a museum and historical farm as a historical presenter working on the farm, and life is good again. Since I don't have dollars, I have learned not to worry about it.

I have my health (and VA Health Benefits), great friends and relatives, wonderful kids and grandkids, a job I love that gets me outside and provides plenty of exercise, a roof over my head and a woman who loves me. What else do I need?

I make about $2,500/month with my PT job, my VA benefit, my RR pension and my Social Security. I'm a lucky guy.

*A version of this essay was originally published on jlcollinsh.com*

## THE 1% RULE FOR PAINLESS PROGRESS

TOM BENSON

*Houston, Texas, USA*

EARLY IN MY career I started saving in my company 401(k) to get the company match. Over time, I would increase the amount saved by 1% whenever I got a raise. I ended up saving the max amount allowed for many years—and through all types of market conditions (1985–2001).

The majority of my contributions were invested in a low-cost S&P 500 stock fund and small-cap fund (to match the total market).

I never "missed" the 1% of my raise that I put into my 401(k), and this simple strategy allowed me to comfortably retire at age 58 with more money than I ever expected to have after a career of 35 and a ½ years.

## MAKE A GAME OF IT

### TODD HAVENS

*Los Angeles, California, USA*

*thinkwealthybook.com*

TEN YEARS AGO, instead of gathering all my friends together to ring in my 40th birthday, I escaped with my partner on a getaway cruise. It felt like there was nothing to celebrate—I was embarrassed that I still owed $25,000 in student loan debt and had nothing—zero—saved for retirement. (The three-day cruise was dirt cheap and we won $200 in bingo the first night, though, so happy birthday to me!)

As fate would have it, the next year I fell into a six-figure job where I started hammering away at the debt each month while simultaneously maxing out my company's Roth 401(k).

I had been interested in changing my financial fate—wanting more than the paycheck-to-paycheck lifestyle that my parents had struggled with—so I was primed to follow the great advice and examples of my favorite personal finance books. I even set my final student loan payment to hit on 31 December that year so I could start the new year completely debt-free. (And I've never looked back.)

We kept our expenses low and, for a few years before our daughter was born, we made it a game to see how much money we could stuff inside various tax-advantaged retirement accounts. It didn't seem like we were socking away that much money (and I'd swear on my living mother's grave that it wasn't), so it's quite unbelievable what a long-term investment horizon coupled with tax-advantaged investments can do for a family because, by retirement, if not sooner, we will be millionaires, if not multi-millionaires.

The persistent investing in low-cost index funds works. It works wonders. And it works the same for everyone.

## WHEN DISABILITY STRIKES

### TUCKER

*Ottawa, Ontario, Canada*

*postmorbus.com*

*"Motor Neuron Disease. Type: Primary Lateral Sclerosis."*

**I**T WAS A handwritten note. The neurologist, I guess, thought that reading it would somehow soften the blow. But those seven words would change my life forever. I was 42, a wife, and a mother of a seven- and nine-year-old. So I did what anyone would do in that situation: burst into tears.

Imagine, for a moment, if all of your expenses suddenly shot up by 30%. Could you manage that? Does your FI budget include not being able to do a lot of things for yourself? Imagine if you couldn't clean your own house let alone do routine maintenance. Imagine if going to a grocery store required all the energy you had for the day. Imagine having to choose either doing the laundry or playing games with your kids after dinner.

What if you had to completely renovate your home so you could live there: ramps, a walk-in tub, higher toilets, lower counters, grab bars everywhere? The thought alone should send your head spinning. I know the reality spun mine. Tyrion Lannister said it best: "If you're going to be a cripple, be a rich cripple."

Before that day in 2018, I had been no stranger to the concept of financial independence. I managed to be frugal in my 20s and 30s, and frugality and budgeting allowed me to have a small business in my late 20s which I packed in to become a stay-at-home parent. My husband worked incredibly long hours for a start-up in California. So I took over all of the house and childcare and tried to make his paychecks go as far as they could. We scrimped and didn't even have a car until my eldest was six months old, and even then it was a second-hand one.

We mostly biked or walked everywhere, cooked from scratch, and took advantage of free programs with the library or pre-school drop-ins for entertainment. We didn't save a lot during those years but we lived lean and managed to pay our bills, kept a roof over our heads and food on the table.

When our youngest was two years old, I decided that four years out of the workforce was long enough, not least if we wanted to hit our retirement goals. Social media was just taking off, and I soon found myself helping organizations build their presence online. I managed to finagle contracts from September to May, taking summers off with the kids. Because I didn't need to work—we could get by on one salary—I had options. I turned down less lucrative contracts in favor of waiting for more interesting and higher-paying ones. With this strategy, I effectively doubled my salary in less than five years.

With more income, I decided to dip my toes into learning about investing. That was when I discovered the FI community and the magic of index funds. We were walking JL's Simple Path in earnest now. In 2015 I was hired to head the social media team of the largest Canadian government department. It was a ton of work but within six months I had full benefits and a pension plan. This allowed me to buy back my pension for the years I had worked on a casual contract basis.

Two incomes, two kids in school, our retirement goals getting steadily closer—it was an exciting time, and we looked forward to the future. But I had noticed some worrisome health changes. I booked appointments and tried to figure out what was happening.

Since 2013 I had noticed that my gait was changing and often I'd feel tingling in my legs. I was running fairly regularly and walking during my lunch hours but it seemed like I was stumbling more often, and soon those stumbles turned into outright falls. In the fall of 2015 I had an MRI. They discovered that I had slipped disks in my neck and, as Occam's razor would dictate, the cause was probably some pinched nerves. The neurologist then referred me to a neurosurgeon and I was booked in for surgery. Luckily, my benefits had just kicked in. Unluckily, four days before neurosurgery I fell and broke my ankle. So within four days I had two major surgeries.

If that wasn't enough, from 2016 to 2017 I ended up having three ankle surgeries, including a full reconstruction, as my ankle refused to heal. My husband ended up having to take care of me and our children, all while working an intense full-time tech job. In retrospect it was the darkest year of our lives. We struggled to keep our heads above water.

Just after we came out the other side and were hopeful that things would settle down, our home rental arrangements fell through. We had been saving for a down payment, but were priced out of our current neighborhood. Two weeks before Christmas 2017, we moved in a whirlwind of stress. Meanwhile, I was going through a restructuring at work which came with its own stresses.

And then that familiar tingling came back, this time in my arms. Back I went for MRIs and myriad tests. And eventually the results came in, and I was handed that piece of paper with my diagnosis.

If ALS is rare, PLS is even rarer: It's estimated that only 500–

2,000 people have PLS in the US, and around 50–200 of us in Canada. There is no known cause, no known cure and no known treatment. It typically has a normal life expectancy, and only affects upper motor neurons (which control voluntary movement, like walking) while ALS affects both upper and lower motor neurons (which control involuntary movement, like breathing).

The next six months I went to appointment after appointment and filled out what felt like a million forms. It left me completely drained. Luckily, because I had excellent benefits I also had disability insurance which paid out 70% of my salary after 13 weeks. Meanwhile, I could get employment insurance for a quarter of what I had been making at my job. Having run out of sick leave and vacation leave, that was my only option.

Fortunately, we had made a point to live off of one salary, so despite some adjustment to our renovation goals for the house, we were OK. I was approved for short-term disability, but after a period they forced me to medically retire. Remember those pensionable years I bought back? I am glad I bought them because I will get that indexed pension until I die, and then my husband will get a portion of it. It's not a huge amount but it also allows me to keep my inexpensive medical and dental benefits and a small life insurance policy.

> Around 6% of Americans will experience a temporary disability each year, and in both the USA and Canada almost half of people 80 or older have some kind of disability. Yet, almost no one plans for the fact that disability might affect them.

According to the CDC, 26% of Americans have a disability and in Canada StatCan tells me 20% of people here do. Around 6% of Americans will experience a temporary disability each year, and in both countries almost half of people 80 or older have some kind of disability. Yet, almost no one plans for the fact that disability might affect them. When people do worst-case-scenario budgets they often include DIYing a lot of things they currently farm out.

In my worst-case experience, we had to hire *more* people to help us manage everyday tasks.

Hilariously, though, I am retired. Not exactly as planned—but retired nonetheless. The caveat is that my disability income ends at 65, so I have to plan for that as well as plan for my husband's early retirement. He loves his job and plans to work for a while longer but we also realize that this could change at any minute. Luckily, when you live your life with a built-in savings rate, it's easier to switch gears when things go awry. On that note, here are some lessons I've learned:

- **Focus on financial independence and not early retirement:** No one knows what the future holds, so obsessing about it means you may miss other opportunities to add value to your life, such as starting your own business or traveling. Giving yourself options should be your biggest goal.
- **Investigate disability insurance:** If your employer doesn't cover disability insurance it might be worth investigating it until your savings rate covers your salary. An individual plan can be organized to only cover a certain amount of years or a certain salary amount.
- **Buy the most useful mobility devices you can afford:** I walk with a carbon-fiber sidearm crutch. Sure, it was about a hundred times more expensive than the cheap ones you get at the drug store, but it makes getting around so much easier. The scooter I bought folds up so I can still travel, and it is light enough that I can drag it in an emergency. Sure, I could get a cheaper version but only if I wanted to limit myself to very basic activities. These tools are my legs, and it's a place I refuse to cheap out on; they allow me to live my life.
- **Always save something:** Even if your salary is low, or if you are living off of one salary, save whatever you can— even if it is a small amount. Don't give up just because it

isn't a huge sum. Small, regular amounts can lead to big gains long term.

- **Marry well:** I have watched people lose their partners as soon as they become disabled. Often, the writing had been on the wall for those marriages for a long time. Our crisis made our marriage even stronger. We had to dig deep to come through the other side of a heinous couple of years.

- **Social capital is as important, if not more important, than financial capital:** If you are working long hours with retirement in mind and not supplying energy to the people in your life then you could find yourself at the finish line alone. Don't miss years with your kids by taking up a time-heavy side hustle. Don't avoid going out with friends because you're obsessively frugal. Almost all of our friends are childfree and work high-salaried, professional jobs. When our kids were young we always made time for house parties and brunches but skipped the expensive dinners. Almost every night after dinner we played board games and read books with our children, even if it meant our house was a disaster. When everything went sideways for us, our friends built ramps for our front door and showed up and unpacked our house for us when we moved and were exhausted. Our tween/teen children still hang out with us after dinner (so far!). I encounter so many people with PLS who didn't put work into their relationships who find themselves sick and alone. The time to work on your relationships is always *now* and *constantly*.

- **Don't wait to live:** The perfect example of this is people who wait until they're retired to travel and then have a major event prevent them from traveling. I have always traveled, but now it is much more difficult and not being able-bodied means I have to forgo certain sites.

- **People are generally helpful and kind:** In the West we put a premium on individualism and being self-reliant. One of the largest psychological changes I had to go through was learning to ask for—and to accept—help. The reason I can still do dragon boat paddling is because my team helps me in and out of the boat. On a recent trip to Denver the airline staff helped me to get my stuff on the plane. When I have asked strangers to assist me, they always have. The hardest part is getting over yourself and your erroneous adherence to doing everything yourself. Regardless of whether or not you are disabled, this rule applies.

- If you are diagnosed with something, **look for the outliers.** Medicine is great at managing trauma and emergencies but for long-term, chronic illnesses there is a gap in knowledge. To be fair, they are doing the best they can with the info they have but the more rare your disease, the less info there tends to be about it. In my case, I got a lot of advice that was given to ALS patients because the two diseases are similar—but, unfortunately, a lot of that advice is bad for PLS patients. Thankfully, a search in a PLS group led me to people who were managing to stay mobile with a combination of off-label drugs and physiotherapy. I mimicked them and have managed to hit a maintenance plateau with my mobility.

- **Take advantage of government programs:** In Canada, I applied for the Disability Tax Credit, which is worth $8,870 as a non-refundable credit that I can also transfer to my husband. I also have a Registered Disability Savings Program account which matches my contributions dollar for dollar (and if your income is lower you can get $3 for every dollar you put in!) and is allowed to grow tax-free. In the US, there are similar programs worth investigating.

- Finally, if you do find yourself facing down life with a chronic condition, **allow yourself to grieve.** You will eventually learn to live with it, switch gears and move on. I promise. But it's important to take the time to learn how to face a future that looks different than the one you imagined.

# PART EIGHT:

# FAMILY

# JL'S VIEW

## PARTNERS, KIDS
## AND PARENTS

**I**N THIS SECTION we have stories from The Path revolving around family. Partners who are on board, or not. Lessons we learn from our parents, intentional or not. There is even one about how FI can support a relationship with a big age difference.

And, of course, kids. Sharing The Simple Path with them, traveling with them, walking The Path as a single parent. Yes, despite what the naysayers claim, you *can* FIRE with kids.

Family. Sometimes our biggest support and greatest joy. Sometimes the source of pain and restriction. Sometimes both.

We've already discussed how walking this Path makes you a bit of a unicorn: confusing and sometimes even off-putting to those around you. This certainly applies no less when those people are family. With the best of intentions they can try to pull you off The Simple Path even as you try to introduce them to it.

## MY FAMILY

If you have read this far, you already know my failed efforts to show my young daughter The Simple Path to Wealth are the origin of the blog, the books, the Chautauquas, the interviews. Now an adult, she likes to remind me of the wonderful benefits that have come from her not listening to me. Had she done so, none of those would exist. There would be no *Pathfinders*. Then too, had she done so, I'd have fewer grey hairs.

But, as you'll hear her say in the chapter with our interview together, these ideas were sinking in over the years. Indeed, she was shocked to learn in college that not everyone had been taught this stuff.

Like her, I too was a product of my upbringing. Watching my father's health fail, and our financial life with it, was a scarring event. But those hard times taught me valuable lessons I have since used to my benefit. Lessons my parents never intended perhaps, but ones they taught me anyway.

## STOCKS

It is interesting what we absorb and why. I remember my dad talking about the one and only time he bought stock shares. I might have been ten. The market was hot, he had some extra cash and a business associate gave him a lead or two on a couple of sure winners. They tanked, and I remember him saying "The stock market is rigged. It is nothing more than gambling." Since then, I have watched many others buy on hot tips, lose and come to the same conclusion. They, and he, are wrong of course. The stock market is an incredible wealth-building tool.

What they were right about, but didn't say, is that buying stocks on hot tips is a very bad idea and very much like gambling.

How I managed to learn the hot-tip lesson without being poisoned on the market I can't say. But it has served me well.

## DEBT AND CARS

One thing my parents got right was debt. Other than mortgages on the first two (of three) houses they owned, they never had any. The last house they paid for with cash from the sale of the paid-off house before. For everything else it was simple: If you couldn't pay cash you couldn't afford it. I guess going through the Depression and World War II offers some important lessons.

Other than occasional mortgages on houses, I've also never had debt. Not even a car payment. My dad didn't teach me how to buy debt-free cars, I just watched how he did it.

My dad used his car for business and he bought a new one every five years. He drove Plymouths and he'd decide what model he wanted and go around to the local dealers and say, "This is the car I want and I'm buying it today. Give me your best price and, if it is the lowest, I'll be back with cash." Unlike today when dealers make money on the financing, cash in those days was a negotiating advantage.

The moment he bought a new car, he started saving for the next one. Instead of making monthly loan and interest payments to the bank, he made those monthly payments to his savings account. The bank paid *him* interest.

This begs the question, how do you get that first car? You do it by buying really junky, old, cheap vehicles for cash and ~~enduring~~ enjoying those while you save the money to buy better ones. That's what he did, so I did it too. It works. I commend it to others. Unless, even better, you develop a taste for cheap cars and just stay with them.

# THE JOY OF EARNING

My father was a manufacturer's rep, mostly representing various lines of housewares. Each year these companies would send samples of their new products. My dad would then give the old samples to my mother who'd run an ad in the local paper and sell them.

One year he had a line of fly swatters. The old samples of these weren't worth enough to pay for an ad so they gave them to me to sell door-to-door. I was thrilled. I was also five or six years old. As I type this a few things occur to me.

- These days, you can't imagine sending a five- or six-year-old out to knock on strangers' doors. You'd likely be arrested for child endangerment. But this was the 1950s and those were different times.
- Thinking about the five- and six-year-olds I've come across over the years, I can't imagine any of them being excited about doing this to earn money. Or even caring about money. But I was. Not sure where this came from. But I'm glad it was there. I loved selling those fly swatters and I loved the feeling of earning my own money.
- I remember I sold them for five cents each, a small price to kill the flies in your life I'd say. But I also remember that most people said no. Looking back that seems odd. I like to think I was a moderately cute five-year-old. It was just a nickel (56 cents in 2022). How do you say no to that? Evidently, easily. Ah, well, it was a great life lesson. You gotta knock on a lot of doors and hearing "No" doesn't hurt. You just move on and keep looking for "Yes."
- This also has gotten me thinking about the town where I grew up. Today it is a ritzy suburb of Chicago. Back then I remember it as a place with boarding houses, abandoned houses (haunted houses to us kids who broke into them on dares) and vacant, overgrown lots to get lost in. Maybe that nickel/56 cents was more precious than it seems today.

## UNIVERSITY

While in good health my father was hard-working and prosperous. His business was successful and he renovated the old house where I grew up himself. He bought those new cars, plus a second-hand one for my mother. We even went out to restaurants a few times a year, which was pretty rare back then as I recall.

He put both my older sisters through college, but when my time came the money was gone. This was a mixed blessing. On the one hand, I have always taken pride in having put myself through college. It is a wonderful feeling.

On the other, I was envious of my coworker David in the Jewel food store. We both stocked shelves there during high school, but his parents were going to pay for his college. Where my money bought room, board, books and tuition, his bought a bright red 1967 Plymouth GTX 440. If you are ever wondering what to get me, I'll take a mint one of those.

## "WE ALL HAVE OUR
## CROSS TO BEAR"

The quote in the heading above was a favorite saying of my mother's. She meant everyone, even those who seem most favored, has their challenges. Envy is pointless. And those who seem less favored, and whose challenges are more obvious, can turn them to their advantage. We all must play the cards we are dealt.

To be sure, there are people whose cards are so bad that The Simple Path described here is not possible. But if you are able to read this book, that's not you. You are perfectly capable of following this Path.

Our challenges are what make us. Those described above, along with a few others, certainly made me. One of the key things successful people worry about is how to raise successful kids when you're wealthy and the challenges are too few. It is a real issue. "Rags to riches to rags in three generations," as the saying goes. According to a recent survey, only 2% of today's millionaires come from the upper class. Another 19% come from the upper middle class. 79% come from the middle class and below. This, of course, runs counter to the popular narrative that most wealth is inherited.

Truth is, most wealth is earned by people like us.

Makes me wonder, if my dad hadn't smoked and if we'd remained financially secure, would I have appreciated how important money really is? Maybe if you want your kids to be rich, you are better off not being so yourself.

## RULES FOR THE ROAD

- Your family can be your biggest support or your biggest hindrance. Sometimes both.

- Either way, your family will influence your journey on The Simple Path.

- We are all products of our upbringing.

- Difficult experiences can forge our strength.

- Our life challenges help form what we become.

- The outcome depends on how we choose to play the cards we are dealt.

- Life made too easy can be a curse. This is why so many self-made wealthy people worry about their kids.

- Families often provide deep inspiration, and patterns of thought and behavior that are enormously helpful on The Path. They often also propagate poor attitudes, ideas and behaviors we must recognize and reject.

"WHATEVER COURSE YOU DECIDE UPON,
THERE IS ALWAYS SOMEONE TO TELL YOU
THAT YOU ARE WRONG."

—EMERSON


"HAPPINESS IS HAVING A LARGE,
LOVING, CARING, CLOSE-KNIT FAMILY
IN ANOTHER CITY."

—GEORGE BURNS

# THE STORIES

## THE POWERFUL INFLUENCE OF
## A SIMILARLY MINDED SPOUSE

TEANNA KEITH

*Bakersfield, California, USA*

**M**Y STORY SPEAKS to the powerful influence of a similarly minded spouse. At least when it comes to finances—debt, especially.

I made a list the other day. It compared my financial life in 2012 with 2022. There's a big difference, mainly because I was in a different relationship at each point in time. The attitudes and decisions of 2012 were absolutely a result of my marriage then (2001–12). And those of 2022 are absolutely both our doing today (2014–forever!).

In both snapshots, our combined income is good and there's a mortgage. But in the old relationship we were spending $1,500 a month on car payments, had put down 0% on the house, were running 0% credit cards to pay for remodeling in addition to six credit cards for monthly spending, had no Roth accounts, no SEP, a minimal emergency fund, $60k of student loans, no savings…

We dreamed of a vacation home, but it was just a dream.

Now we pay cash for all vehicles. We've paid off all our student loans. We've put down 20% on our home on a shorter-term loan. All remodeling is done with cash (which gives us great discounts). We've had no credit cards since 2014. We fully fund our Roths and SEP each year, have a six-months-plus emergency fund, and decent savings.

And we've been able to put down 20% on a lake house.

Making good money is one thing. It doesn't guarantee you independence. Choosing what to do with it is everything. And having a spouse with the same attitude to financial freedom is priceless.

## PLANNING RETIREMENT TOGETHER

### FLORENCE POIREL

*Thalwil, Switzerland*

*www.linkedin.com/in/florencepoirel*

**W**ITHIN THREE MONTHS of having moved to Switzerland, I met my partner, Jan, who happens to be 17 years older than me. And as we started talking about our future together, I realized that, if I wanted to enjoy the best of our lives together, I would have to retire much earlier. If I retired at the regular 60-something, Jan would be close to 80 years old. What kind of activities would we do then?

That's really when I joined JL's Simple Path.

Most FI resources are US-centric, so it took me a while to find European and/or Swiss-based resources, and begin my own personal FI planning. I then began building out my spreadsheet with multiple formulas to calculate my FI number, before expanding to visualise net worth growth and forecasting net worth at different ages for potential retirement.

Which was when it really hit me: Savings accounts alone would never get me where I wanted to be.

> Pursuing FI pushes you to think about what you want to do with your life, and to define your values.

I started small, investing €20,000 at first. From the start, I only invested in ETFs, because I had learned from all the FI blogs that they were the go-to. I am also quite risk-averse, so their diversification really attracted me, while the notion of passive investing into a set portfolio appealed to my lazy side.

After six months or so, I felt more comfortable with the market's ups and downs, and decided to invest a bit more. Now, probably 70% of my net worth is invested (counting my company's shares too).

It took me a while to build my portfolio, and I changed its composition as I got a better grasp of my needs and values, and a deeper understanding of fees and taxes. It took me a while to identify the best ETFs to invest in for Europe/Swiss-based investors too.

When the market dropped, I kept investing serenely into stocks while they were "on sale."

Meanwhile, we rent our property, preferring being able to pick up and go as we please. This also makes geoarbitrage possible. There are many different tax areas even within the Zurich canton in Switzerland. We moved to the lower-tax town of Thalwil, one of the best things we have ever done—more space, better views, the same monthly rent, yet much lower taxes. An upgrade while saving money!

In the space of a year, I went from never logging into some of my accounts, to educating myself on multiple aspects of financial planning and forecasting my investments for retirement. This has been life-changing. I focus so much more on my own well-being, how I decide to live day to day, without trying to do it for someone else—just truly for myself and what I want life to be.

I've managed to increase my net worth by over 400% in five years. But FI is much more than numbers. The real gold on JL's Simple Path is the life conversations. Pursuing FI pushes you to think about what you want to do with your life, and to define your values.

As a woman, it hasn't always been the easiest thing to talk about. Some people find planning your life to be disturbing in a way. But it brings depth and clarity like never before.

My partner and I see eye to eye on spending, on what we will do with our money when we die, and on the future—we're planning our retirement activities together already. But my numbers are my own numbers, and I will be able to remain a strong independent woman no matter what.

## MARRIED, BUT ALONE
## ON THE SIMPLE PATH

### PADDY TSIGANE

*Montreal, Quebec, Canada*

**M**Y FI JOURNEY started about six years ago when I quit the job I've had for 13 years. My wife and I wanted to get closer to our relatives, so we moved our family from the city of Montreal, Quebec to a more rural region an hour's drive southeast.

Quitting my job left me with a decision to make: Keep the

company pension as it was, or take the money out and put it into a Lock-In Retirement Account (LIRA).

I realized I really had no idea what to do.

I just didn't know much about managing my money, besides putting some aside for a distant retirement. I was 47, with about $200,000 in savings and mutual funds. So I put the LIRA in another mutual fund for the time being—but promised to educate myself.

And that's when I found JL's Simple Path.

> Although I'm married, I'm alone on The Path to FI for the moment: My wife, though pretty good at saving, doesn't share my cost-cutting approach to increasing our savings rate and accelerating FI.

The concept of FI made perfect sense to me! I calculated my savings rate, my net worth, and opened an investing account. I moved my savings and investments to this new account and started experimenting with ETFs. I realized how poorly I'd been advised by various mutual fund sellers over the years, most of them advising me to put my money in high-cost mutual funds—including some speculative precious metal funds.

Although I'm married, I'm alone on The Path to FI for the moment: My wife, though pretty good at saving, doesn't share my cost-cutting approach to increasing our savings rate and accelerating FI.

We're at the stage in life where our children probably cost us the most: braces for both our girls, special glasses for the oldest, many after-school activities. So I'm able to reach a savings rate of about 40%, no more.

Being 53 years old, and aiming to not have to work for a living at 60, I still have a few years ahead of me to save the most I can. Fortunately, the house will be paid for in two years, which should free up some more money for saving.

Before the recent debacle on the markets, I had doubled the money I had six years ago. Taking advantage of this ongoing "sale," I keep buying mainly one asset allocation ETF (VEQT.TO) and one global ETF (VXC.TO). Hopefully, my net worth will recover and rise to reach my goal of $1m before I'm 60.

## TWO BRIEF VIGNETTES FROM "THE GODFATHER"

JL COLLINS

*South Dakota, USA*

A S I WAS reviewing this collection of stories as the book came together, it occurred to me I might have one of my own to add.

More accurately, two brief vignettes from when I was in my 20s.

The first concerns a woman I was dating at the time named Diana.

As far as I recall, she and I never discussed money but she must have noticed something. One day she mentioned that she was getting deeper in debt and asked if I would review her spending with her.

Diana had come from a very poor background in rural Ohio and never had the chance to go to college. But she was smart, hard-working and enterprising.

This was in the days when secretaries were common and in demand. She picked up those skills in small-town Ohio, moved to the big city of Chicago and landed a job as a legal secretary. Within a few years, and by the time we met, she was in charge of the secretarial staff of a major law firm. She was making excellent money.

She shared her income when we sat down together, and

I wasn't surprised she was having difficulties. I could see the lifestyle she had put together: the large apartment, the new car, the clothes, the travel.

Going through item by item, I'd ask what she spent on each. The conversation went something like this:

"Well, my rent is $xxx, but I make $xxxxx so I can afford it."

"OK."

"My car payment is $xxx, but I make $xxxxx so I can afford it."

"OK."

"My last trip cost $xxx and the one before it $xxx, but I make $xxxxx so I can afford it."

"OK."

"I need professional clothes for my job and I spend about $xxx a month for those, but I make $xxxxx so I can afford it."

"OK, and I think I see the problem here. Yes, you make $xxxxx and that means you can afford any of those $xxx things. More than one in fact. You just can't afford them all."

Now this might seem obvious to those of you reading. It felt obvious to me. But let's not be too quick to judge. For a poor girl from rural Ohio getting a taste of the big city and its temptations, it is not hard to see how that connection would be easily missed.

In the ten years I've been writing my blog, I've seen it missed by many people. And most of those refused to accept it even when it was pointed out. Not so Diana.

Even as the words left my mouth I could see the light go on in her eyes. She changed on a dime and never looked back.

———

My second story is considerably briefer.

A few years back my wife Jane and I were at Chautauqua.

One of the attendees asked, "Before you were married, did you guys discuss money frequently?"

"We are very compatible on the subject of money," I said. "In fact our views are almost identical. Since this is so important, and since it never actually occurred to us to discuss it before marriage, I have always considered this to be great good luck."

I had fielded this question many times over the years and this was my stock response. But this was the first time I had delivered it in front of Jane.

She leaned back a bit and stared for a moment.

"What are you talking about?" she said. "On our first date you told me I should be saving 50% of my income."

Which, as it turned out, she already was.

## MEMORIES OF MY FATHER HELPED ME PURSUE FI

### CHRISTOPHER JOHNSON

*North Salt Lake, USA*

YOU DON'T NEED a flashy reason to be on JL's Simple Path to Wealth and I am grateful for that.

My introduction to the personal finance world came when I was about to leave my first job. An older coworker of mine pulled me aside and offered me some advice: "Don't cash out that 401(k). Invest it in index funds and never touch it. You can pull it into your own IRA, but don't you dare blow that cash."

I had no idea what an index fund was. When I asked, another coworker pointed me to a famous FI blog. I will never be able to thank them enough. It was like a drug. After that, I read every FI blog and book I could get my hands on.

Here I was, young, newly married, no kids, and ready to do whatever it took to retire early. I wanted to avoid the 37-year grind I saw my father go through with the same company. By the end of it, they were treating him like garbage—he held on, got his pension, watch, and a swift kick to the curb.

I never forgot how tired he seemed during those later years. FI seemed to offer a way to avoid all of that. So I was hooked.

There was just one problem: My wife and I had bought a house, and my wife liked it. To be honest, I did too. We were already cautious by nature so we didn't overextend or anything like that, but that mortgage was always there and any FI calculations would have to take that into account.

I can't remember how many times I fantasized about selling the house, buying a trailer, and running off to...

Actually, I had nothing. No secret plans. No Peruvian mountains to climb. No second career as a professional bagpiper. Nothing. FI was just a way to avoid work. It wasn't enough to motivate us to sacrifice the house or do anything else extraordinary. The numbers we needed to hit FI with the house were just so far away. Certainly too far to sprint.

We settled into our suburban lives and I gradually began to think of FI more as a way of living than a way to avoid earning one.

Thankfully, we both had pretty strong desires for stability and safety. To this day, every time we go out to eat, my wife asks if it's OK to buy a drink or dessert. I credit most of our good decisions to her need for security, and my own need to provide that for her.

That desire for safety led us to paying off our house early after making our usual retirement contributions. We knew it was mathematically wrong, but the idea of being nearly bulletproof was something we both were willing to sacrifice for. (I say mathematically wrong because investing those same funds would have yielded much higher returns over the long run. Our mortgage rate was a paltry 4.25%.)

Armed with a wall chart of bad guys from old-school Nintendo games, we started that seven-year journey. Every month, we'd cross off a bad guy for each $1,000 we paid down on the house. It sounds silly, but seeing progress gave us energy to keep going.

Seven years is a long time to stick to anything and we needed all the motivation we could get.

During those seven years, life threw us a few financial curve balls. I switched jobs, joined a start-up that failed, and was a founding member of another. Start-up land may sound surprising to you, but we felt like two jobs and decent savings gave us the freedom to swing for the fences... and possibly strike out.

I remember the day my coworkers and I found out that we had no money left. No warning from the higher ups, just a meeting to let us know that paychecks would not be coming. There was palpable panic in the room.

If the statistics regarding how many households in America live paycheck to paycheck are true, that panic was completely justified. I had never been so grateful to be on The Path.

> I gradually began to think of FI more as a way of living than a way to avoid earning one.

We also were thinking about expanding the family. We had decided to just let things happen whenever they did. Turns out, they wouldn't just happen. Infertility comes in all shapes and sizes, but all of them are expensive. Doctor visits, surgeries, IVF, transfers, miscarriages, deliveries... everything had a price. Our son cost about $50,000 to get out of that petri dish, and he is worth every penny.

Our journey to parenthood had more obstacles than we could fathom, but money wasn't one of them. Miscarriages are expensive, financially and emotionally. Can you imagine adding a $3,000 hospital bill that you can't pay on top of the emotional trauma of finding out that your unborn child is gone? Being on The Path meant that my wife and I could focus on caring for each other, instead of bills.

The point to all of this is that life throws surprises at you. Money can solve a pretty hefty chunk of those problems, but not all of them. For the things that money can't handle, you need money to not be a problem. Infertility and job loss is bad, infertility, job loss *and* money problems is so much worse.

Now that we have our son, our lives are much more expensive, but they are much more meaningful. Living well below our means allowed my wife to reduce her hours to spend more time with him at home. Luxury at its messiest. He also lives in a home that belongs to his parents, not a bank. With no mortgage, our savings give us a much longer runway should things go sour again. All the while, we invest as much as we can in all three of the tax buckets, looking forward to the day we wake up financially independent.

We still aren't planning to retire early and we still have no plans for what to do when we get there. I've often wondered if we are doing it wrong because we don't have a big **why**. I asked JL about this during a recent virtual Chautauqua and was lucky enough to get a response. I think I'll end my story with his words:

*"Remember that from the very beginning of stepping on The Path, you are a little bit stronger than the day before."*

That's enough for me.

## AIMING FOR FI BEFORE
## MY YOUNGEST HITS 18

### LISA FROM BALTIMORE

*Baltimore, Maryland, USA*

*Nponfire.wordpress.com*

I AM A SINGLE mom to three kids who are 10, 13, and 16.

I started my journey on JL's Simple Path with a goal to reach financial independence by the time my last child reached age 18. I am now already almost there.

In the past five years I have cut my spending, increased my

savings, and moved all of my retirement accounts into low-cost, index-based funds centered mostly on the US and international stock market.

I did have one lapse in judgment in March 2020 when I moved some funds out, thinking I could time the market—never again! Even with recent downturns I rarely check the balance of my retirement account/brokerage as I know I am almost ten years out from stopping work.

I have started teaching my children about saving, investing, and intergenerational wealth—they each have a Roth IRA and I match any funds they earn and choose to put into it. With college coming up quickly, we've also discussed how saving wisely can lead to fewer student loans.

## I LEARNED A CUSTODIAN MINDSET
## FROM MY PARENTS

TIM DE PRIJCKER

*Antwerp, Belgium*

EVER SINCE I was a child I have been following the financial markets, together with my father. He started to invest in the early 1990s, and I showed interest as well. Teletext and the newspaper were our main pieces of information. Individual stock picking was the way to go, then mutual funds—always without any benchmarking against a decent index, thus not knowing how much we underperformed.

My parents bought a car dealership in 2000 (aged 46), and spent much of their time managing this business for its first decade.

Business went well. Private bankers approached my parents and persuaded them to invest their surpluses in equity funds.

These funds were global and 100% in equities, and my father was investing for the long term—so some of our approach was right. But, years later, when we found JL's Simple Path, we discovered the virtues of low-cost index fund investing for the first time. My father likes to walk the talk. So he switched 95% of his portfolio to a small number of global ETFs following MSCI indexes.

When my father started suffering health issues, I took over the family business. My mission was clear: Improve the business, make it attractive, then sell it. Successfully concluding this was a real milestone for us all.

Thanks to walking The Simple Path already, I was armed to invest the funds that came from the sale of the company. Without FI principles, this would have been a painful exercise, with private bankers keen to convince me to invest with them. I would probably have been flattered to have "made it" in life—finally a client of interest to private banking! Luckily we have been able to avoid that.

My parents have had a great life, in which they were able to avoid debt (except housing), save, invest, and allow enough lifestyle inflation to enjoy themselves. Meanwhile, over the years, a nice investment portfolio piled up. My father never touched it, since there was other income still coming from the business.

In talking with my dad the past few years, it became clear to me that he considered himself (and my mother) as *custodians* of their portfolio—not owners. True to that, the portfolio was officially gifted to my sister and me earlier this year.

Now I am a custodian of this capital too. My wife and I will stay the course, while managing lifestyle inflation and bringing our FI number down. When the time is right, I intend to financially educate our children. I will consider my personal finance mission accomplished when they see themselves as custodians too.

Not having to worry how our money is invested frees up a lot of time—invested in active parenting, permaculture and food forest gardening, volunteering, marathon running, and developing a holiday home rental business in southern Spain.

# IN OUR HOUSE, MONEY
# IS AN OPEN SUBJECT

### ATA ATANASOV

*North Bethesda, Maryland, USA*

*www.acompactlife.com*

**D**O YOU WANT to be truly wealthy?

I think we all do. It's not about fancy cars, luxury homes, private jets—it brings you freedom to do what matters the most to you.

I want to convey this message to my kids as early as possible because I believe it is a great way to live.

In our household, money is an open subject. Our little ones are starting to understand the meaning of savings, investing, and spending sparingly. They know what it takes to earn, how to go about saving, and most importantly what happens when money is invested.

Even though they do not have a bank account, they have a Roth IRA account with Vanguard. Whenever they receive money, I make sure 30% of it gets to the investment account.

> Hard work produces income. Saving produces options. Spending doesn't produce anything.

Once they've spent their money, it's gone forever. On the other hand, they can watch their invested money grow. They can immediately grasp the benefits of automatic investment, understand what happens to their money if left alone, and know exactly how much money they have available.

My wife and I discuss all small or big purchases openly with our kids. I know that if they see us make smart money decisions, they will be more likely to do the same. Over the years, as our earnings have increased, our spending habits have been pretty constant. This shows our kids that we don't acquire new things just because we have more money.

Once our basic life needs are met, I think it is important to give away our surplus to a meaningful charity. It is money well spent, and brings me the most satisfaction. Right now we are making monetary donations to Doctors Without Borders, but we have our kids pick out a cause that is important to them and donate part of their money to it too.

Ultimately, money is something you can master. The sooner you understand this, the more control you have over your life.

Hard work produces income. Saving produces options. Spending doesn't produce anything. But you have total control over your spending habits; never let anyone else tell you otherwise.

## PURSUING FI ALLOWED US TO TRAVEL THE WORLD WITH OUR KIDS—BEFORE WE FINISHED

ANTHONY ST. CLAIR

*USA*

*learnersandmakers.com*

ORDINARY PEOPLE CAN work toward extraordinary goals. In the dark, exhausted, we locked up our house for the last time. After loading up our remaining car, the four of us stared at our home. My wife and I had lived in this single-story, mid-century ranch for 16 years. I'd proposed to Jodie here. We'd shared meals and time with friends and family. This house was where our son and our daughter had grown from babies to full-on kiddos.

Now, our home was something we stared at as we drove away. The back of the car held four backpacks, two carry-on rolling suitcases, and a few thises and thats of things we hadn't had time to go through before leaving.

Even Connor, now ten, choked up. His seven-year-old sister missed our elderly cat, who had gone to live with neighbors. Jodie and I squeezed hands for a moment, as I turned onto the highway and headed to our new lives.

Then we smiled.

It was time for our worldwide family traveling adventures to begin.

Our family is not rich (well, not yet, but we're working on it). Over the past ten years, we have worked toward a family goal that my wife and I set long before we started our family. Even while dating, Jodie and I talked about how, someday, we would travel the world with our children for at least a year. Now, we were starting that journey.

This decade of prep had not exactly been smooth. After a few years of planning (and setting aside some F-You Money), in 2011 I had left an unsatisfactory job to set up shop as a full-time independent writer and content creator. Later that year, my wife and I also welcomed Connor into the world, and Jodie took unpaid maternity leave from the music-teaching business she ran.

Over the next few years, we struggled a lot financially, even before Aster completed our family in 2014. Debts built up. We worked to grow our businesses, but we had always prioritized spending as much time as possible with our kids. Jodie and I understood all too well that childhood was when we would have the majority of our in-person experiences with our children, and we were determined to make the most of it.

For a while, our travel dreams felt out of sight. Yet we knew we weren't just working toward a big family goal. We were also providing a sort of living experiment for our kids. Our hypothesis? Ordinary people could work toward extraordinary goals.

We wanted Connor and Aster to observe, and hopefully one day to understand, that a fulfilled life means knowing what you want, setting goals, and doing the work to turn your priorities into reality. As each child matured, we worked money, spending, and saving into those conversations. When each child turned five, they got their own weekly allowance.

> We wanted to travel the world with our kids so they could further develop their own sense of what matters to them in the world and in their lives. As they grow up, they can better understand how to focus and work toward what they want and need as adults.

Our family table discussions regularly included topics such as intellectual property, compound interest, total stock market index funds, what a Roth IRA is, and above all, how we were making our big family global travels happen.

Over the past few years, we transformed our finances—while working from home and homeschooling both kids from preschool onward. Our debts were sorted. Jodie had also decided to make a career change, and we began working together on content creation based around family travel and accessible travel. We invested in total stock market index funds (and when interest rates suggested it was favorable, parked some shorter-term assets in US Treasury Series I Bonds). We learned to travel hack with credit cards, and we developed a list of countries we wanted to visit.

Our last step of trip prep? Emptying out our home so we could rent it out while we were abroad.

Then, as we came into the latter half of August 2022, we closed one chapter in our family's lives, and started a new one full of world-schooling, remote working, and location independence.

Mexico. Thailand. New Zealand. Costa Rica. France. Uruguay. Ghana. Japan. Just a few places on a long list of countries we wanted to experience together.

Why travel the world with our kids? Because travel has always been a priority for us. We love how travel expands our perspectives and teaches us about other people, the broader world, and our own wee selves. And we wanted to travel the world with our kids so they could further develop their own sense of what matters to them in the world and in their lives. As they grow up, they can better understand how to focus and work toward what they want and need as adults.

Our decade of work had begun with a big dream, endured through lots of toil and work, and now had come to fruition.

As we left our home behind, on that dark night after weeks of work getting it ready to rent out, we smiled. Our passports were ready for stamps. Our hearts and minds were ready for new experiences. And we were ready to share this amazing world with our children, all the better to prepare them for the capable, caring adults we could see them growing up to be. We were still just ordinary people, but as I looked in the rear-view mirror and caught my children's eyes, I could tell they knew we were beginning something extraordinary.

# PART NINE:

# ENDGAME

# JL'S VIEW

## ARE YOU SEEING WHAT I'M SEEING?

So you are walking along The Simple Path to Wealth, dealing with obstacles as they come and otherwise enjoying the sunshine and the exercise of your ever stronger financial muscles.

Then one fine morning you'll rise from bed, stretch and greet the new day happy to be alive. You'll shrug on your pack, take a few steps down The Path and suddenly realize you have come to the end. You have arrived at that mythical land of financial independence.

Not quite believing it, you pull out your calculator and run the numbers. Then you run them again. Maybe you pull aside a trusted friend, show them the numbers and ask, "Are you seeing the same thing I'm seeing?"

# I'M A LITTLE SLOW

My own story is like that, but a little more embarrassing. In my defense, as I've said before, I was wandering in the wilderness. I didn't even know there was a path, let alone a destination. Nevertheless, one day, there I was. Even though I didn't know where I was. Confused? So was I.

You'll recall, back in 1989 I quit my job and began what became the longest "sabbatical" of my career. It lasted five years.

As the years dragged on, I wasn't worried, even as my wife quit her job to go back to school and our daughter was born. No income. More expenses. But I knew we had F-You Money.

One time during my annual year-end review of our finances, I noticed something interesting. While we had no income and were spending even more than before with new school and child costs, we ended the year with more money than we'd started with. "That's odd," I thought. I ran the numbers again. Same result. This was three years into this income-free zone, so I pulled out my numbers from the first two years. While I hadn't even noticed it at the time, they both showed the same thing. More money after a year's worth of spending.

I sat back in my chair staring at these numbers a while. "Well, that's remarkable," I remember thinking. Mind you, not remarkable enough to call my wife in and say, "Hey, look at this. Pretty remarkable, eh?"

Not remarkable enough to take the next small mental leap to realize this meant my money now made enough money by itself to meet our needs. And, oh by the way, this means you never have to work again.

Nope. I folded my expense and investment papers up, put them away, and went about my day. Yep, I'm a little slow.

I simply had no frame of reference for what had happened let alone what it meant. It didn't occur to me that I had become financially independent—that wasn't a term I'd even hear until decades later.

## ALMOST MEXICO

A couple of years later, still no job in sight, we started talking about moving to Mexico. We'd traveled there, liked it, and met some interesting people along the way. We figured we and our young daughter would learn Spanish, experience a new culture— and who knew what adventures would present themselves. Then the next new job came along and, of course, I took it. It seemed the obvious choice. Mexico slid off the table and disappeared under the waves, to mix a couple of metaphors.

Looking back, I have no regrets. I liked working, enjoyed my career, and a new job is what I wanted. But I do wonder: What if I had a fuller understanding of what those figures were telling me? An awareness of the 4% rule and how to quantify how much is enough? What if I had been introduced to the concept of financial independence? Would Mexico have gotten a closer look, and where might that have led?

I'll never know but I have learned not to assume, had we taken the fork in the road not chosen, things would have been better.

## I DIDN'T KNOW, BUT YOU DO

I arrived at FI unaware of both its meaning and the incredible range of options it offers. I just didn't know, but you do.

You will have walked this Path with intention and you will have arrived at FI deliberately. Now, stretched out before you, a multitude of new paths and new journeys beckon. You are free to choose whichever speaks to you. You are free to pursue one, set it down and try another.

Continue a career you enjoy, as I did. Pick up and move to your Mexico, wherever that might be. Become a nomad and wander the world. Buy that little cabin in the woods and grow your own food. Write that novel. Build a house with your own hands. Launch that new business. Join that NGO. Or just sit for awhile, bask in your accomplishment, and think it over. You've got time, and you own it now.

I've come to this point twice in my life. The first time was when I graduated college with my degree in English Literature with not a clue as to what I was going to do and dead broke, paying for school having drained every dime. It was exhilarating.

The second time was in 2011 when I quit my last corporate job. I'd quit many before, and been kicked to the curb once as well. But this was the first time I'd left with no intention of working again. Now, having the time, I started writing those letters to my daughter and then...

...well, you know now what happened then. It has also been exhilarating.

Based on what I read in the FI community these days, this sudden freedom can be a source of considerable angst. It doesn't have to be. Take a deep breath. Relax. You got this.


## THESE STORIES

In these stories here at the end of *Pathfinders* you'll find tales of what it is like to retire early, and what it is like to reach FI and not retire at all. Or to retire to a new career. Stories about the uncertainty of ever making it, and of using what has come to be called "lean FIRE" to escape.

These—as well as all the travelers' tales that have come before—hopefully show the only limits are your imagination. Reaching FI is a big deal—an awesome accomplishment—especially if you've walked The Simple Path over a long period of time. Think of it like turning the page. Your next adventure starts now, and you can see how some of your fellow travelers have done it by turning *this* particular page.

# RULES FOR THE ROAD

- If you choose to walk this Path, one fine day you'll be financially independent.

- Being FI opens up whole new worlds and options.

- Quitting your job is only one of those.

- Keeping a job you love is another.

- There is no rule on The Simple Path that says you have to stop working once you are FI.

- Being FI rarely means being inactive.

- It means owning and controlling your time to use as you see fit.

- Where The Simple Path ends, you'll find the juncture of the many other paths being FI opens.

- This can be a source of angst.

- It can also be a source of exhilaration.

- The only limit is your imagination.

"THE REASONABLE MAN ADAPTS HIMSELF TO THE WORLD: THE UNREASONABLE ONE PERSISTS IN TRYING TO ADAPT THE WORLD TO HIMSELF. THEREFORE ALL PROGRESS DEPENDS ON THE UNREASONABLE MAN."

—GEORGE BERNARD SHAW

"LIFE SHRINKS OR EXPANDS IN PROPORTION TO ONE'S COURAGE."

—ANAIS NIN

"TRESPASSERS KINDLY REMEMBER TO CLOSE THE GATE."

—SIGN ON AN IRISH GATE

# THE STORIES

## RETIRING EARLY TAKES COURAGE—
## HERE'S HOW WE'RE DOING IT

### SCOTT AND CINDY

*Los Angeles, California, USA*

**M**Y HUSBAND AND I are in the midst of retiring early right now. Scott quit his job a month before I wrote this. Next month, I'm doing the same!

Arriving at this moment was the easier part of FI. To actually pull the trigger and retire was the difficult bit.

It's hard to be mentally and emotionally ready. I am very much a creature of habit. I have very little tolerance for risk—I don't even enjoy roller coasters. I like the security and comfort of a stable job and reliable income. The idea of not having a paycheck every two weeks was absolutely terrifying. It made me want to puke.

I drove my husband crazy hemming and hawing about whether to quit our jobs or to keep working for another year or two.

Then one day I was expressing my fears to my mom. Her

response: "Oh, c'mon! You are way too young to have this kind of mentality! Now is the *best* time to take a chance and see what happens. You are only in your 40s. You are still so young. You're acting like you're older than me and I'm 70 years old! Don't be such an old fuddy-duddy."

*"Don't be such an old fuddy-duddy..."* You know what? She was right. I was being a lame stick in the mud. Did I really want to spend the rest of my life working? Did I want to pass up the chance for freedom just to cling on to safety? Was I really going to let my fear of the unknown keep us away from the greatest adventure we could embark on?

Now was indeed the best time to give FIRE scenario a shot. What did we have to lose?

If something goes haywire, what is our worst-case scenario? Having to go back to work? Isn't that everybody else's everyday scenario?

And yes, we are still young enough that, if it doesn't work out, we will have time to change course. Am I really going to let my mother think that I'm an old fuddy-duddy? Absolutely not!

Retiring early takes courage. You have to be brave enough to do something very different from what is "normal." But isn't that what life is all about? To take chances and to learn from it—to truly live our lives and to be fully engaged and awakened to experience it all. Stepping away from the daily grind and retiring early will give us that opportunity.

> What is our worst-case scenario? Having to go back to work? Isn't that everybody else's everyday scenario?

Seeing what we will potentially gain from retiring early instead of looking at what we are technically losing really changed my perspective. Instead of worrying and stressing, I am now looking forward to what's to come. Instead of boredom or the dread of another day at work, I have a sense of anticipation and wonder. I can't wait to go on this early retirement adventure and see where life will take us.

# IT'S AS SWEET AS I THOUGHT
# IT WOULD BE

## MICHAEL QUAN

*San Diego, California, USA*

*www.financiallyalert.com*

G ROWING UP, I had the privilege of seeing my uncle retire in his late 30s. His life was full of joy. He would take his kids to and from school, go on many vacations, and had the freedom to do anything he wanted at any time. I saw this freedom and I wanted the same.

It wasn't until middle school that I realized how he was able to live differently to everyone else. He had figured out how to make his money work for him. He was no longer trading his time for money, rather his money was earning for him 24/7.

Observing my uncle gave me a big advantage. I knew that living an unconventional life of freedom was a real possibility. So, I got busy learning everything I could about money. I read countless personal finance books, attended wealth-related seminars, and asked my uncle lots of questions. He told me his secret to early retirement was investing early and often.

As soon as I started my first job out of college, I started investing. It wasn't much at first, and I didn't know what I was doing. However, the important part was I had started and I was learning quickly. I would invest weekly by dollar-cost averaging into both individual growth stocks and index funds. I was off to a good start, but my career would soon take an unexpected turn.

Within a year and half of landing my first job, our nation faced the tragedy of 9/11. A massive recession followed, and I found myself facing an imminent layoff as our company unraveled. However, instead of remaining passive, I got resourceful. I left the company and started an IT consulting company with a couple of friends.

Business was slow at the start. We only had enough work to keep us busy half of the week. But we persisted and grew the company through word of mouth. Over the next ten years we were able to pick up some lucrative contracts, and even acquired a couple of smaller companies along the way.

When it came time to sell the business, I took my proceeds and reinvested them into additional equities and cash-flowing real estate. I worked for the acquiring company for a year and a half to help them transition and then I promptly retired from a traditional career path. I was 36 years old.

> Both the journey and the end goal of financial freedom often unlocks the best version of ourselves.

As I write this nearly ten years later, I am humbled by the many blessings I continue to experience. I have been able to be fully present for my family, and started up several side hustles and businesses. I also continue to invest in both equities and real estate. Most importantly, I get to work as much as I want, when I want. Financial freedom is truly as sweet as I imagined it would be.

Today, my passion is helping others accelerate their own path to financial freedom by passing along the advantages that I received. If I could follow my uncle's path, anyone can. But it takes a conscious decision and the right beliefs to invest in education, stocks, real estate, and/or businesses.

As an eternal optimist, I encourage anyone who desires more to take a leap of faith on themselves. Both the journey and the end goal of financial freedom often unlocks the best version of ourselves.

# I DON'T REALLY CARE ABOUT
# THE RE OF FIRE

### JEFF

*Leidschendam, Netherlands*

ONE OF THE things I find myself thinking about a lot (maybe too much) is the question: "And then what?"

What's life after becoming financially independent going to look like? What am I going to do then? And why am I not doing that now?

This intertwines with work decisions, and all the fun stuff I can, or cannot, do today. So, for me, these are big issues.

I don't want to end up sitting on a pile of money and regretting all the adventures I missed (especially the ones I may not be able to experience when I'm considerably older than today).

When I read about others who have achieved financial independence, many of them are now into making stuff, gardening, volunteer work. I admire this, and already do volunteer work, but they're not things I'm desperate to focus on when I've finished a demanding career. I get kind of depressed at the idea they might be my only options.

As a result, I don't expect the RE—or retire early—part of the FIRE equation to ever kick in for me. I am looking forward to not having to work for money, but I don't think I'll ever stop working until I'm physically or mentally no longer able to.

Instead, I want enough F-You Money to do what I want and to survive situations beyond my control. By prioritizing FI, I will ultimately have flexibility to shift priorities between enjoying life now and saving wealth for the future.

## A SECOND CAREER OF
## MY CHOOSING

### WOKE RETIREE

*Singapore*

I WAS BORN, RAISED, educated, and worked in Singapore. I retired there too—at 47.

I call myself a "Woke Retiree" not in the political sense, but because I vividly remember the moment I finally woke up and realized I had achieved FI.

I was working on my de-accumulation spreadsheet, stretching cash flows all the way out to age 90. Then I saw it had happened. I had finally reached the point at which I wouldn't run out of money.

A question suddenly occurred to me, and wouldn't stop flashing in my mind: "Why do I still need my day job?"

I enjoyed my role in consulting, but really didn't need it anymore—so I left.

The following year was spent under Covid lockdowns and travel restrictions, so I took a six-month course in elder care and aging. My original intention was to learn how to prepare for my own old age and to bump up my volunteer credentials. The course was amazing, though. It exposed me to new knowledge and experiences, with hands-on attachments at local nursing homes, dementia daycares and senior activity centers.

The opportunity to peek under the bonnet of these care establishments was priceless and gave me real insights into the industry. It also helped me formulate my own age care plans (very much in the same way I had planned my early retirement, I was now gathering data to plan for my old age).

In 2022, with borders finally opening but travel still a mess, I took up a part-time role as a caregiver at a dementia daycare. The experience has been richly rewarding. Pay in the elder care industry is worse than working in fast-food—the part-time pay rate is s$11/hr—but that's fine with me. I see it as part of my effort to give back. (For folks who need a job to pay bills, though, the care industry isn't paying a living wage—and I hope this changes with time.)

In many ways, my role is similar to that of my former consulting career. The job has a high degree of variability—so many situations crop up that require you to think on your feet to meet a senior's situation or limitations. It's a very people-focused role. Activities need to be tailored at the right level for each senior so that they feel a sense of achievement.

Each week I make personal observations around disease progression, fall-prevention risks, social/family support networks, finances and social assistance schemes. It's been a hugely rewarding experience—but also informative for my own expectations of old age. There's nothing like first-hand experience and data.

Financially, my spreadsheets have held up, and my portfolio has sustained my early retirement. I've also been able to refine my approach. I have three buckets:

1. Cash, for 18 months of spending.
2. Bonds—wholesale bonds, tiny bits of dividend-paying equity and bond funds, to generate current steady income (replicating a salary—no matter how hard I tried, I couldn't get comfortable with the 4% drawdown approach).
3. Long-term growth and legacy—indexed equities and a defined-contribution pension invested in a 50:50 equity/bond portfolio.

From 65, an additional monthly pension will kick in like an annuity. I'd like to make bucket number two run on autopilot, removing the need for me to monitor and make reinvestment decisions.

My plans are to travel once the pent-up demand has eased. I want to live borderlessly, making extended trips to different locations. Retired and in good health, the world is open for exploring.

## I DIDN'T KNOW I WOULD MAKE IT

### KDALE

*Brandywine Valley, Pennsylvania, USA*

I AM AT THE end of my career and preparing to step back from full-time work. My story is about how automating savings—of any amount—can play an important part in your future. But I really didn't know that until recently. That is the part that is surprising to me. I stumbled through my whole career hoping I'd be OK in retirement and not really knowing—until now.

My husband and I both had careers in nonprofits. My husband is five years older than I am, so when he was a few years shy of retirement we started to look into whether he and I could retire at some point, and how to plan for our income in retirement. We had taken advantage of our 403(b) options at work but honestly I just picked a percentage to set aside based on what I could afford. It was only 6% of my salary at first.

After the harrowing dotcom bubble of the early 2000s, and seeing my retirement balance decline so much, I had decided I was never going to look at my retirement funds again, and just accepted that I was likely never going to be able to retire. Kinda ostrich-head-in-the-sand.

Once my husband was close to stepping back from full-time work, it was clear we had to figure things out. At the time, conventional wisdom was to go see a financial planner to get some expert help. I spent time reading about how to select a planner, learning it was important to select someone that would work for a fee, not on commission.

We selected a local financial planner and had a free session, learning about their services, and the approximate cost to come up with a basic understanding of our long-term finances and retirement plan. But I was never comfortable with the idea of paying so much for someone else to give us what felt like generic advice. That, and the person hired to handle all of the investment accounts at this one firm was the owner's son, currently between careers. It opened up all sorts of concerns.

> I stumbled through my whole career hoping I'd be OK in retirement and not really knowing— until now.

I started looking for information myself. I remember wondering at the time why there wasn't an online social security tool I could use and not have to pay someone $250/hr?

That was when I discovered the FI community.

I was hooked on learning as much as I could about saving for financial independence and understanding how much you need to generate an income in retirement. I could never get an answer to that question until then.

Learning how others had done this, including what worked and did not work, helped me put things in perspective, as well as teaching what to apply to my situation.

Here is what I learned:

- I went from thinking you need a PhD in finance and math to retire to understanding that you don't even need a financial planner to implement your own financial independence.
- There are a lot of free online tools to teach you about social security, as well as ways to track your financial assets.
- Many default retirement scenarios make assumptions that the man in a relationship earns more than the woman, and that both spouses are the same age. This does not fit every

situation. There were no examples that explored our scenario until I did it myself with favorite FI bloggers' resources.

My dad was an economist, my nephew and brother-in-law are financial planners. Despite being surrounded by expertise, I never understood enough about retirement planning until I learned to do it for myself.

Thanks to the FI community, I now feel like I am in a position to help others learn from my mistakes, particularly folks at the start of their careers. I've taken to giving presentations to colleagues at work about how to aim for financial independence, plan for retirement, learn about the finance of work benefits and similar topics. My motivation is always to help people to be further ahead than I was in making these plans.

## KEEP WHAT YOU'VE GOT

TAYLOR LARIMORE

*USA*

*Founder of Bogleheads, a forum dedicated
to the teachings of Jack Bogle*

I WAS BORN IN 1924—the year the first mutual fund (Massachusetts Investment Trust) was also "born." My grandfather, Christopher Coombs, was one of three principals of The United Founders Corporation, the largest investment trust (now called mutual funds) in the Roaring Twenties. He was a multimillionaire owning three large homes located in New York,

Cape Cod, and Miami. He was invested almost entirely in stocks bought on margin.

My dad owned a restaurant near Boston. Few customers could afford to eat out during the Great Depression (1929–1939). The restaurant closed. This resulted in my father, mother, brother and I moving into my grandparent's Miami mansion in 1930 when I was six years old.

Subsequently, my grandfather became bankrupt and had a serious stroke. My immediate family was forced to move from the waterfront mansion to a three-story walk-up apartment.

The most important lesson I learned. When near or in retirement: **Keep what you've got**. Do not, under any circumstances, take unnecessary risks hoping to get more.

## IT HIT ME LIKE A HAMMER

### LEJERO

*Bavaria, Germany*

IT TOOK ME eight years to reach FI once I started. I finally got the guts to jump away from the corporate world in 2020, during the pandemic. I followed Warren Buffett's axiom of "be greedy when others are fearful," and secured a very good severance.

The transition to FI life took me by surprise. Here are the unexpected things I learned:

### 1. MONEY IS ACKNOWLEDGMENT

It hit me like a hammer in my first months after leaving the corporate world. I had some private projects—including founding a small company (just for fun)—but everything I did was unpaid. I received no money at all. And it's funny how much of an impact that has psychologically, even when you don't need the cash.

Of course, my wife praised me. She said she was proud. But I received no external or "objective" acknowledgment. I learned just how satisfying it can be to have someone pay you for what you're doing. It almost doesn't matter how much it is, just the fact that someone values your work so much that he is willing to pay you money for it.

I felt kind of stupid that I had not celebrated my monthly paycheck for the last two decades. "Hey, I am doing work so valuable for someone that he is willing to pay me money every single month for it!" That is something great. And I only recognized when I didn't have it any more.

## 2. HAVING TIME ALONE IS NO FUN

During my first 18 months of FI, I did a lot of things. I spent more time with my wife and children. I took interesting courses. I participated in sports. I went for many walks in the park—and even founded that new company. But most of my time was now spent alone.

And I discovered that was no fun for me. I wanted to spend my time with family, friends and business partners—not alone. So I increased my working time again. I started two more companies.

I still work less than before, but I really like what I am doing now because I do not *have* to do it; I can stop it anytime. My wife is still working, even though she does not have to do it for financial reasons. Our kids are still in school, so we cannot just travel the world. When my kids are older and my wife decides to stop working, we can look at it.

## 3. AFTER REACHING FI YOU ARE STILL THE SAME PERSON

This is the most important thing I learned. I always thought that when I reached FI, I would be enormously happy—and life would be wonderful. But now I can tell you: It is not. It is pretty much the same as before.

Agreed, some problems dissolve into dust. You have a lot more freedom. But you are still the same person. If you were unhappy before reaching FI, you will also be unhappy afterwards; if you were happy before, you will be happy afterwards.

On a happiness scale of 1–10, I was probably always a 6 or 7. Content most of the time; happy some of the time. Nothing has changed in that regard.

But here is why FI is such a good thing to strive for: I left the corporate world at 45, meaning I have 20+ years to work on what I want. And my main focus in that work doesn't need to be money: It can be my personal happiness and the happiness of my family.

I think everything I learned when reaching FI are the kinds of things you discover when you retire at a more traditional age. The difference with a standard retirement age is that you have a lot less time for improving yourself—and that is what really counts.

So do try as hard as you can to reach FI as soon as you can. It is not like entering paradise, but it is worth it. You will have the time and money to find out what is important for you and makes you happy, and then the time and money to acquire it.

I felt kind of stupid that I had not celebrated my monthly paycheck for the last two decades. "Hey, I am doing work so valuable for someone that he is willing to pay me money every single month for it!"

If you never reach FI ahead of traditional retirement, though: Do not worry. FI alone—without personal development—is only OKish. As long you find some time for your personal development during your journey to FI you can also climb the happiness scale, entirely without FI.

## USING LEAN FIRE TO LEAVE A TOXIC INDUSTRY

### MATT ALLAN

*Helsinki, Finland*

*www.zeromatters.com*

I'M AN ARTIST in the videogame industry. Weirdly, my career has a similar shelf life to a professional footballer. In fact it is often shorter, and pays a thousand times less. But it has still been possible for me to reach financial independence.

In 2016 (the same year I discovered FI), an IGDA survey revealed that two thirds of employees in the games industry were aged 20–34. Only 3.5% were in their 50s or over. Additionally, the average career length was only five years! After that, many either burn out, want more life balance, more stability, or better pay.

The games industry is a fast-moving place, with frequent periods of extreme overtime (known as "crunch") and job instability. In my experience, most successful people in the industry over the age of 40 have a glowing career on paper and remarkable talents, but behind the scenes there is often a different story: broken marriages, missed family events and milestones, a life of solitude, stress-induced health issues and even hospitalization.

This was not what I wanted for me or my family.

So it was time to build an escape plan. When I discovered FI, a lot of people in the community were engineers in Silicon Valley or finance people. Art salaries are usually far smaller than theirs. This made it hard to believe it was possible for me.

But after switching my pension into global index ETFs and putting in a little each month, I began to build stamina, as well as trust in the roller-coaster ride of investing.

I have always been a bit of a minimalist, only spending money on things that truly add value to my life. Once I was comfortable with ETFs, I maintained a high savings rate and maxed out my employee-match contributions. I also ensured life was still fun, interesting and inspiring—this was going to be a long journey, and I needed a life afterwards to escape to!

That first $100,000 seemed so far off, but I had found a community that had similar values and was keen to educate and share their experiences, so that kept me going.

I then moved to a better-paid job and was able to rapidly increase my monthly contributions. I felt very fortunate, but it also seemed true that when you start to focus on something and value it, you are more likely to find it in your life.

I was so glad that I had started with small monthly contributions and got used to the ups and downs, because when the Covid market crash came I could just keep going as usual. Even though I had far more invested than ever before!

> Weirdly, my career has a similar shelf life to a professional footballer. In fact it is often shorter, and pays a thousand times less. But it has still been possible for me to reach financial independence.

My mantra was: "Either the world is ending and money will be worthless, or we'll come back from this and build towards a brighter future." It paid off.

In the end, I did burn out in the industry. But I also FIRED, at age 37.

I only have enough for Lean FIRE, as the community calls it. But it means I have time to get better and focus on the meaningful relationships and routines in my life, before returning to work of some kind—if I want to.

I'm so thankful to the FI community. They introduced me to the parachute. I have pulled the rip-cord, and am now serenely floating down towards a more balanced and meaningful life, free to explore options for the future and reflect on the past.

The late ad executive Linds Redding once wrote a beautiful essay—"A Short Lesson in Perspective"—about wasting life on work, following a terminal cancer diagnosis. As he beautifully concluded:

"Do yourself a favor—power down, lock up, and go home and kiss your wife and kids."

# CONCLUSION

## THE LITTLE GIRL WHO WOULDN'T LISTEN

**A**ND SO WE *near the end of the journey of this book. But in many ways, this is where the story began.*

*We started by inviting you into a kind of roadside tavern beside The Simple Path. Picture the same tavern now. Beside the fire, there are three chairs: JL, the host of this book, has been joined by two guests.*

*The first is the person without whom none of this would have been created: his daughter, Jess.*

*The second is the superstar finance writer and podcaster Christine Benz.*

*They're here to discuss the unique origins of The Simple Path, and JL's and Jess's reflections on their own journeys—just like the other storytellers in this book...*

**Christine Benz:** I thought we could start by discussing the origin of the book, *The Simple Path to Wealth*, which has turned into a kind of bible for people who are pursuing financial independence.

JL, the genesis for that book was a series of letters from you to Jess. I'm wondering if you can discuss what you were trying to achieve with those letters?

**JL Collins:** I felt the need to write them because this stuff is so important, and getting it right can make a powerful difference in a person's life—but I had made the mistake of pushing way too hard, way too soon, and turning Jess off to all things financial.

Writing this stuff down was an act of desperation because I thought she might never be willing to hear this from me again, but maybe someday she'd be willing to read it. Then a friend of mine said it was pretty interesting and I should put it on a blog and share it with family and friends. I didn't mind sharing it—but it mainly seemed like a great way to archive the information.

**CB:** I'm curious, you said you had started too early in terms of trying to give Jess some financial education. How old were you, Jess? Do you remember the time and your reaction?

**Jess Collins:** [Laughs]

**JL:** That was pretty much her reaction right there.

**JC:** I think I had been home from the hospital maybe three days. OK, that's hyperbolic—but I really do have memories of being as young as four or five and trying to dive into VTSAX and dividends and saving your money and everything. So, yeah, too young means as early as you could possibly think.

**CB:** When your dad wrote those letters, did you end up reading them? What did you make of them at the time?

**JC:** What's funny is, I've actually never read the original raw letters—mainly because when he started writing them, I was still not interested. I was reluctant to absorb any of the information or have those kinds of conversations. By the time I was ready to really start thinking about it, the blog was up and running and had been for a while—and the book was out.

**CB:** JL, you quote Jess at the start of *The Simple Path to Wealth* as saying, "I know money is important. I just don't want to spend my life thinking about it," which I think sums up how a lot of people think about money matters. But that was a bit of a revelation to you when she said that. Why was that?

**JL**: That was an absolute epiphany for me because I had been pushing this stuff for a long time. One day she came home from college and I started in again, and that's when she said that. And it suddenly occurred to me that *I'm* the odd one out.

People like me—and, frankly, like you Christine—we're the odd ones out, the people who enjoy this stuff and like to talk about it all the time. Most normal people have better things to do with their time. They have bridges to build, factories to run, children to raise, and diseases to cure. And like Jess said, she knows that it's important, and that's the beauty of The Simple Path, that you don't have to think about this stuff all the time.

You just have to take it a little bit at a time, understand a few key basic things, put those basic things into motion and on autopilot, and then the less you think about it the better you will do. Because the less you think about your investments, the less likely you are to tinker with them. And of course, the more you tinker with them, the more likely you are to get subpar results.

So, my writing is specifically for Jessica, but by extension for all those people out there who feel the same way that she does. Yes, they know it's important—but they don't want to make it a full-time hobby. They just want to know what they need to know to make it work for them.

Now, of course, I also have readers who come to my book and blog because they are into this kind of thing, and they're the ones who are always saying, "JL, this is pretty good stuff, but if you tweaked it this way or that way..."—and I'd be willing to bet that my daughter who gets this set up and never does anything else will outperform people who are always tweaking over the next 20 years.

**CB**: Jess, I'm wondering if you can give us a little bit of background on your academic history and then what you do for your career. Has the advice in *SPW* achieved its goal of helping you get on with your life without really having to spend much time thinking about money?

**JC**: I've learned to appreciate my dad's advice. As you say, I don't really have an interest in this—so I've never gone looking for anything else. And it's *worked*, so I've never felt the desire to.

It's always been a constant in my life—a kind of security blanket that I've kept adding to. It has allowed me to live a life that I find incredible, and which makes me happy.

My career as a result has been a bit unconventional. I originally went to school to be a marine biologist, and then like lots of people switched majors a couple of times. I ended up graduating with a focus on international relations and French, did AmeriCorps and then Peace Corps. After the Peace Corp I traveled through Asia, making my way back to the US. Once home I began my business career, first selling events and then in tech sales into the human resource departments of client companies. I'm currently with Talent Neuron in this role.

Because I've had this constant security in my back pocket of knowing The Simple Path—and seeing it work—I have confidence in it and have been able to be adventurous with my career.

**CB**: JL, you talk about this concept of what you call F-You Money. Can you explain what that means and talk about how having it has helped you in your own life?

**JL**: I wish I could claim credit for the term. I'm not sure where it originates. It's been around for a long time. I first came across it in a novel by James Clavell called *Noble House*. He's written several novels; a great author. There was a character in that novel, a woman who stated her objective was to have F-You Money. It was the first time I heard the term and it absolutely crystalized what my objective was. I just had never had a name for it.

The way I think of it, F-You Money is the interim step between starting with nothing and being fully financially independent. It's not enough money to maybe never work again, but enough money that enables you to make much bolder decisions than you might've before.

**CB**: Jess, how about you? Have you had an opportunity to use the F-You Money concept in your own life?

**JC**: Not yet!

**CB**: Maybe that's a good thing.

**JC**: Yeah. I was trying to think about whether I should follow that up with, "Not yet but hopefully soon."

**JL**: It's still nice to know you have it in your back pocket.

**JC**: Exactly. It's nice to know I have it as ammunition, but no, I haven't used it yet.

**JL**: I would say—and correct me if I'm wrong—you're not financially independent at this point, but you do have F-You Money.

**JC**: Yes.

**JL**: By our definition.

**CB**: I'd like to talk about financial independence. JL, your pursuit of financial independence famously was never about retirement. How do you define FI—and what was it about for you instead?

**JL**: Well, in my mind financial independence is when you have enough money that your money is earning enough to pay for all of your expenses, so you no longer have to trade your time and energy for income. Your money is doing that for you.

And of course, that's a moving target. It all depends on how much any given person needs. And that'll change, and that will inform how much in turn you need to have to be financially independent.

For me, as you said, it was never about retiring. I think the FIRE acronym is a very clever one and I like it for that reason—but I almost never use it because the "retire early" gets a lot of people confused and some people upset, and it was just never my goal.

Having financial independence was—and that simply means you can choose to do whatever you want. You can choose to stop working. I know people who have done that and traveled the world, and I know other people have reached it and said, "I kind of like working and I'm going to keep doing it."

I think it's the fact that it gives you options that's the important thing.

**CB**: Jess, how do you think about financial independence?

**JC**: I've been in conversations where financial independence seems synonymous with retiring, but I'm still young and in the prime of my working years so I don't even think about retirement. And I am not sure that I would even want to retire early. I like working and I like being active, staying busy, and flexing on some skills.

So for me, financial independence is really just about having the power and the security to do what you want, when you want to do it.

You can like what you're doing right now and you like where you're living right now, but if tomorrow brings something that suddenly makes you incredibly unhappy, you can shift gears and look to something else and be flexible because you have that tool in your back pocket, even if it means that you can't necessarily never work again.

**CB**: Jess earlier referenced this idea of living within your means as a key virtue that you inculcated in her. So, JL, in that context, you often cite the parable or the monk and the minister and say that you're closer to the monk in your thinking. Can you talk about that parable and how you think of that as a spectrum of how people approach spending or not spending?

**JL**: It's a short parable—there are these two guys who were friends in their childhood, and as they grow up, they go off in different directions. One becomes a humble monk and the other becomes a very prominent minister to the King. Years later they meet on the road. They're catching up and the minister to the King looks at his friend, the monk, and sees him in his shabby robe and with his begging bowl, and he says, "You know, if you could learn to cater to the King, you wouldn't have to live on rice and beans." The monk replies, "If you could learn to live on rice and beans, you wouldn't have to cater to the King."

The spectrum is between those two extremes, if you will. We all get to choose where on that line we are. For me, I'm more comfortable closer to the monk in living a simpler life.

**CB**: Have you always been that way or has that changed over your life?

**JL**: I've kind of been hardwired that way. I've never particularly been enamored of material things. But I certainly haven't lived a monk-like existence. I've owned houses and cars, had great trips and what have you. I'm just not as extravagant as maybe the typical American would be with the kinds of resources that I've had over the years.

**CB**: Jess, I'm curious to get your perspective on that. If you think of this as a kind of gradation with the monk on the one side and the minister on the other side, where would you plot yourself? I'm also curious about the impact of social media which is so overt in trying to stoke our consumption habits. Can you talk about that?

**JC**: While my dad was explaining the spectrum, I was thinking, I wonder where I fit on that—especially in relation to my dad! I will say, I think I'm more on the monk side than the minister, but I don't think I am as far over as my dad is. I think I'm a little bit closer to the middle. He's a bit more extreme.

**JL**: Her robes are not as shabby as mine.

**JC**: Exactly. But the question about social media is a great one. My dad and I were recently talking about generational differences when it comes to financial independence and spending money. And I think social media is probably historically unique in its immediacy and prevalence—and the challenge that presents. My generation grew up on it and we live on it, and that's the way the world is right now. There's no turning back.

And now, not only do the Joneses have the car and the house to keep up with—but you see everything else they consume, too. People say, "Tik-Tok made me buy it" and "Instagram made me buy it and it made my life so much better." You get inundated every day with these things, telling you that this is what you need for your life to be great, for your life to be better. Or you deserve this because look how hard you work, look at all the stress you're under. Don't you deserve whatever is the shiny thing that's being pushed at you?

**CB**: It seems like a lot of social media is geared to urge us to make comparisons with other people and it doesn't seem to be making us happier. Is that your perception as well?

**JC**: I agree. And it markets products like they're a quick win to overcome this. "Get this and be happier." Whereas choosing to be very deliberate with your money, and *really* understand what you're trying to get out of it, is more demanding but ultimately more rewarding. I think defining your "Why?" helps you understand if you're making a purchase because it's something that will serve you, or just because Instagram told you it's what you need.

**CB**: JL, I'm curious to get your perspective on generational differences. You speak to a lot of FIRE proponents and younger folks who are on the road to financial independence, but you probably talk to plenty of older adults as well. I'm wondering if you've noticed any generational differences in how people approach their money and how they interpret The Simple Path?

**JL**: One of the great privileges of being in the FI community is that I now have friends of all ages—and I don't use the term "friend" lightly. The media presents a conflict between Millennials and Boomers, but what's striking to me is how similar the two generations are.

When I was a young Baby Boomer, all the negative things I now hear Baby Boomers say about Millennials are the same things the older generation said about us. We were lazy, we were entitled, we were privileged, we didn't understand what hard work looked like...

At the same time, if you came of working age (as I did) in the 1970s, it was in a very difficult economic moment—a time of high inflation and an underperforming economy, which came to be known as "stagflation." And of course Millennials have faced something very similar. The similarities are remarkable.

I think the most striking difference is that we Boomers didn't have college debt. It just wasn't widely available when I was going to college, and college was much less expensive because you couldn't finance it. It was also simpler. I lived in a much more basic dorm than the living arrangements available to my daughter when she went.

They figured out that they could get people to borrow money to go to college, and whenever you can borrow money for something it rachets up the price. I think it's a little criminal that these loans have been pushed on young people when they barely understand what a loan is, but I'll get off my soapbox on that.

**CB**: Jess, JL often talks about homeownership. He's not a big fan. I'm wondering if that has influenced how you think about settling down, being part of a community. Would you be similarly resistant to purchasing a home?

**JC**: I haven't really thought about it in those terms yet, but I do think I share some of the same sentiments. I think there's nothing wrong at all with wanting to own your own piece of property—as long as you understand the "why" behind it.

I've bounced around quite a bit in my adult life, and a lot of it is just curiosity—a sense of adventure. I have the energy to do it and I haven't found a place I want to settle in for a long period of time yet.

If I ever get to the point of settling down, I'd just want to make sure I'm clear on the why behind acquiring a property. It would have to be because I want to have a piece of land to call my own—not necessarily because I think it's a better financial move.

**CB**: JL, in case I mischaracterized, I'd be curious to get your perspective on homeownership, just so everyone is clear on your opinion on homes as a financial asset.

**JL**: Your characterization is understandable. When you write blog posts titled, "Why your house is a terrible investment," you tend to develop a reputation for being anti-house.

I don't see myself as being anti-house. I've owned houses for most of my adult life. What I'm against is this drumbeat from the industry that it is always or even commonly a good investment and it's something everybody should aspire to and do at the earliest opportunity. It's simply not.

In my view, homes are an expensive indulgence. Sometimes they work out financially if you happen to be lucky enough to buy in the right place. Sometimes if you buy in the wrong place, they turn out to be a disaster. I've never bought a house thinking it was going to be a great investment. I bought it because it was going to provide a lifestyle that I wanted at the time and that I could easily afford. I think that's the way to think about them.

I've also spent part of my adult life renting. After Jessica went off to college, I promptly sold the family home, and my wife and I rented for four years before we finally said, "You know what? These apartments are mostly expensive storage given how much we travel." So, we dumped the apartment and went nomadic.

**CB**: Jess, are there any key areas where you've taken a path that's consciously different than JL's Simple Path, and can you talk about how that decision has turned out so far?

**JC**: No, I haven't strayed from The Path at all.

**JL**: Well, not financially.

**JC**: Oh, yes. I'm assuming we're talking about The Simple Path to Wealth. If we're talking about life, that's a whole other story! But if we're talking purely just about money and The Simple Path to Wealth, no, I have not strayed from that Path at all. And honestly, that just comes down to the fact that this is still not something that really interests me. I'm still not somebody who geeks out about finance or investing.

It's also never seemed like something I've needed to do either— I've always been doing it, and it's always worked.

**CB**: It sounds like it's been a healthy journey. I wanted to talk about making mistakes though, because JL, you've written about how you constructed The Simple Path quite late on in your life after making all types of mistakes. The stories in *Pathfinders* show lots of people finding The Simple Path after they've taken detours and run into dead ends. Can you talk about examples from your own life where you've diverged from The Simple Path but made it back?

**JL**: I would say that once I figured it out, I haven't diverged from it. It just took me a long time to figure it out.

So, I started investing in 1975 and I probably didn't move on to index funds, which of course are the core of The Simple Path, until 2000. But once I made that move and began to think about it in these terms, if anything I became more and more focused on it.

For instance, when I first added index funds to the portfolio—and even as they became a major part of my holdings—I still had what I call "the disease." I was a stock picker. I was still analysing and picking stocks on the side. And I don't think I let that fall to the wayside until maybe 2013 or so. That was the last time I owned an individual stock.

Once I figured this out—which again took me an awfully long time, and that's the biggest mistake—it's been a matter of just narrowing the focus to what's really in the book, and what I've told Jess from the beginning.

The beauty of her journey on The Simple Path is that she started it so early and hasn't gone down any blind alleys and shows no inclination to do so. I've often thought to myself how much stronger my financial position would be if in 1975 I had been wise enough to embrace the world's first index fund—created that year by Jack Bogle at Vanguard. I didn't know about it for another ten years, and then it was another 15 before I was wise enough to embrace it. But Jessica has embraced it from the very beginning—a huge advantage.

**CB**: I'm curious if you have any advice for people going down The Path in tough times. The year 2022—when work on *Pathfinders* began—certainly featured all sorts of financial catastrophes, falling stock and bond prices, really high inflation. How about people who are questioning The Path when things are volatile and, in some respects, scary?

**JL**: My advice would be to stay the course. As Jack Bogle once famously said, "Don't just do something, stand there." The truth is that what's going on today is a bit different than what happened the last time the market crashed, which was Covid, which was a bit different than what happened the time before that. Whatever triggers these downturns is different, but they're all a natural part of the process. I think it's important for people to understand that.

We should expect these kinds of things. We're never going to know exactly what the trigger is going to be, but it should be no more of a surprise than blizzards in Chicago or hurricanes in Florida. They're intense, they're scary, they can be dangerous—but they shouldn't be a surprise. They're part of life.

If you're going to invest in the stock market, downturns, crashes, and corrections are a perfectly normal part of the process, and they never last forever. Just like blizzards and hurricanes don't.

**CB**: How about in good times? We've come through a period where there was a lot of euphoria in certain areas, in crypto and some technology stocks. Jess, it doesn't sound like you bit on any of those opportunities, but I'm wondering if either of you have any advice for keeping a cool head and staying on The Path when things are going really *well*?

**JL**: That's in some ways the more interesting question. In bad times, all I need to say is, "Stay the course." In good times, all these different things crop up to tempt you from the basic productive businesses represented by investing in a broad-based stock mutual fund.

Things like crypto and meme stocks are very seductive because you're suddenly reading stories in the media about somebody who took $10 and turned it into $10m dollars in ten days and you think, "Wow, why couldn't that be me?"

You have to realize that those sensational stories need to be taken with a grain of salt—even if they're true, they're sensational because they are so rare.

I'm not an investor in crypto, though interestingly the guy who does tech support on my blog is, and we have a couple of posts that he guest wrote as to why. To me, crypto is too volatile to actually operate as currency, so it's a speculative investment. It's something you buy hoping that at some point in the future somebody will pay more for it. You might be right; you might not be. In more recent history, you were less right than you were a little further back.

The same thing applies to gold and is why I don't own it either. Gold has no productive value; it's not out there earning money and creating cash flow. It's just something that you own and are hoping that at some point in the future somebody will pay you more for it.

That's speculation. And I'm not a speculator.

**JC:** I think sometimes when things are good, it might feel a little bit more tempting to skip—to not save one month or one year. And that soon adds up. Or perhaps to tweak somehow. I think the key, no matter what, in good times or bad, is to just keep doing what you've been doing.

Don't pause, don't tweak, just keep on The Path. If you do that, changes and fluctuations—positive or negative—don't matter as much.

**CB:** That wealth effect that you feel when you see your portfolio enlarged, it might prompt some people to spend more than they otherwise would—to take two big trips a year instead of just one, for instance. Have you felt any of that as you've been heading down The Simple Path with your index fund portfolio, watching it grow nicely over the years? Have you ever thought, "I guess I can spend more because I know that I have these investments that are doing really well for me?"

**JC:** I think sometimes when you are so disciplined—as my parents definitely are—it can require a mindset shift to remember that you're doing this for a reason. That's a conversation we've definitely had: Let's not forget the journey; let's enjoy life as well.

If you have all of your ducks in a row, you shouldn't be punishing yourself and not enjoying the journey along the way.

Have your habits, don't get in over your head by any means—but if you're not taking joy in life and doing things that make you happy then what is it all for? Is it worth it if we're just sitting at home twiddling our thumbs and feeling miserable?

**JL:** I think there are two conflicting ways to think about it. On the one hand, spending money is not a key to happiness. On the other hand, I'm famous for saving and investing 50% of my income and that's what people focus on. But the implication of that is that I was spending the other 50% of my income. And as my income rose, my spending rose with it.

So, when I was making $10,000 a year—as I was in my first professional job—I lived on $5,000 and invested $5,000; when I was making $50,000, it was $25,000/$25,000; when I was making $100,000, it was $50,000/$50,000; when I was making $200,000, it was $100,000/$100,000.

So, my lifestyle inflated but in a very controlled fashion. I didn't let it get in the way of my bigger objective of buying the thing that was most important to me, which was my freedom. But that didn't mean that I didn't spend more money as I had more resources.

**CB**: I want to switch over to discuss storytelling. JL, you were an English major at college and you've been praised for your use of storytelling to convey the principles of financial independence to a wide audience. *Pathfinders* is a collection of many stories. So, what is it about the power of story in particular that you think can help people reach financial independence?

**JL**: Well, let me tell you a story about that… [Laughter]

I think humans learn best around stories. Our recorded history is basically filled with stories. That's how we teach each other. All of the major religious books are filled with stories; all of the mythology from different cultures, those are all stories; fairy tales are all stories. It's how we teach and learn. So, I think it's a very powerful way for people to understand concepts.

The origin of this book, *Pathfinders*, comes out of my amazement at how my book, *The Simple Path to Wealth*, has been embraced and adapted by so many different kinds of people. I wrote that book for one person, my daughter who is at the beginning of her journey and who is an American. And yet people from all over the world have taken the basic concepts in it, and adapted it to their countries and the investment options available to them. People of all different ages have taken it and adapted it to where they are in their lives. They've shared these stories with me over the years and I find that endlessly fascinating.

Maybe because it was something that I never anticipated. I never anticipated that the book would be as successful as it's been, because I guess I never anticipated how creative people can be in reading something that has a very specific focus and saying, "I get it. I understand this story. I can adapt it to my own life in these ways."

That's what this new book is all about, sharing some of those stories of how people have done it.

**CB**: Jess, would you say you were surprised by your father's success with *SPW*, where he's going to conferences and he's kind of a big deal?

**JC**: Yes. I was so surprised!

**JL**: "Who would have thought my idiot father..."

**JC**: "People are reading this? What? They want you to give speeches? What?"

**JL**: This is from the girl who didn't want to listen to it, right?

**JC**: Yeah, where were all these people when I was four?

**JL**: I have kind of a funny story about that, seeing as we were talking about stories a moment ago. A number of years ago I was invited to come out to DreamWorks for a visit and to give a talk because there are a handful of people that work there who are interested in my work.

We were all traveling together, so we all went to DreamWorks. They were very nice. They gave us a tour of the facility, we had lunch, and then we went off to this little room where there were 25 or 30 people who showed up. The three of us are sitting at the front of the room fielding questions, most of which of course are coming to me, but at one point this woman in the group looks at Jessica and she says something along the lines of, "Jessica, it must've been wonderful growing up with this man as your father." And Jessica looks at this woman, she looks at me, and she looks back at this woman, and she says, "Not as much as you'd think."

So, I have long been put in my place by my daughter.

**JC**: It's important to stay humble.

**CB**: That's right. So, do you have any favorite stories in *Pathfinders*, JL?

**JL**: That's tough. I don't know I can single out my favorites, but there are two stories that are particularly striking.

We have a story from a guy in Ukraine who is talking about how he is staying the course and staying on The Simple Path to Wealth when his country has been invaded. That's an amazing story. We also have a story from a guy in Russia who is talking about how he is staying the course while living in a country that has become a pariah in the world, with all of the sanctions.

Of course, these guys don't know each other. It's just pure coincidence that we were fortunate enough that they chose to share their stories. But I find that incredibly fascinating, and obviously it's particularly timely in a tragic way at this moment.

**CB**: JL, you wrote in the intro to *The Simple Path to Wealth*, "My hope is that with it, her path will be smoother, her missteps fewer, and her own financial freedom will come sooner and with fewer tears." Jess, I'm curious, has that panned out so far?

**JC**: It sure has, yes. All of those boxes are checked. It's definitely been a lot smoother, especially knowing the stories that my dad has from his life. One-hundred per cent.

**JL**: I was about 50 years old when I figured this out. Jessica has accepted it from the very beginning. That's such a huge advantage and I envy her. I wish I'd written the book when I was in college.

**CB**: Is there anything you would have written differently than what you laid out in the letters and the eventual book?

**JL**: I think between the beginning of the blog in 2011—when I began taking the letter content and archiving it there—there were a few things that changed. For instance, I used to hold REITs as part of my portfolio, and I stepped away from those. But as of the book, *The Simple Path to Wealth*, which came out in 2016, there really isn't anything that I do differently or that I tell her to do differently.

**CB**: Well, congratulations. And Jess and JL, thank you so much for taking the time to chat today.

**JC**: Thank you for your time. Appreciate it.

**JL**: Yes, Christine, thanks for the great questions. This was a lot of fun.

**CB**: And thank you for listening and joining JL and the *Pathfinders*, and best of luck in your own travels on The Simple Path.

# ACKNOWLEDGMENTS

The other day I was talking to a friend I'd not spoken to in some time. He reminded me that back in 2021 I told him I was about to agree to do this book with Harriman House and how positive I was about the project. So, he wanted to know, how has it gone? Did they live up to expectations?

Exceeded them, I said.

Now I get to thank the people who made it happen.

### SALLY TICKNER

Sally Tickner is a publishing director at Harriman House (Hh). In the Fall of 2021, just as I was about to publish my second book, *How I Lost Money in Real Estate Before It Was Fashionable*, I received an email from her expressing interest in working on it with me. Since I was self-publishing that book, it was done, and I really had no interest in working with a publisher, I ignored it.

But then, a couple of weeks later with the new book out, I came across it again. On a bit of a whim, I decided to reply with an idea for a follow-up book to *The Simple Path to Wealth*. This was an idea I'd had since *SPW* came out in 2016 and for the five years since everyone I had showed it to said, "This is a terrible idea!" I figured Sally would say the same, if she bothered to reply at all, and that would be the end of it.

Reply she did and while she didn't rave about my idea, she did indicate it was something she and the Hh team could work with. In particular, Christopher Parker saw potential for something special there. That was the beginning of a series of conversations that both developed the idea into the book you have in your hands and led to the contract between Hh and myself to publish it.

It wouldn't have happened without Sally's outreach, insight, support, professionalism and enthusiasm.

## CHRISTOPHER PARKER

Christopher Parker is a commissioning editor and head of design at Harriman.

So impressed was I with his sharp intellect, enthusiasm for this project and ideas in fleshing it out, I insisted as part of my contract it be specified that Chris would be the guy working with me.

A bit embarrassingly (for me), a large part of the heavy lifting in creating this book has been done by Chris. He has made it infinitely better and my life infinitely easier through his hard work and dedication. Working with him is also just a blast. Chris is a brilliant editor, and that comes from a guy who loathes being edited.

At the risk of being redundant, this book wouldn't exist without his efforts.

Of course, creating a book is only the first step. Once it exists, it needs to be introduced to readers.

## LUCY VINCENT

Lucy is Hh's head of marketing and she has worked hard on the promotion of *Pathfinders*. If you are reading this there is a

ACKNOWLEDGMENTS

good chance it has been her efforts which have brought it to your attention.

## CHARLOTTE STALEY

If you are reading this in a language other than English and in your own country, you and I both owe this availability to Charlotte. She is Hh's head of international rights. Through her efforts, *Pathfinders* has been published in multiple languages and countries all around the world.

## TRACY BUNDEY & VICTORIA LAWSON-MCKITTRICK

I would also like to thank Tracy Bundey for her invaluable help with print runs and production, and Victoria Lawson-McKittrick for her help with proofreading.

My sincere thanks also to Kelly Younge and Kyle Landis-Marinello for all their comments and corrections.

## MY WIFE, JANE

Writing a book is hard work, and stressful. I've now done three and I am not always easy to be around while they are in progress.

Jane has been endlessly supportive of and patient with me. We've been married over 40 years now and I still marvel she hasn't stabbed me in my sleep.

Thank you, my love!

297

# CONTRIBUTORS

**THANK YOU TO EVERYONE
WHO SUBMITTED A STORY
TO *PATHFINDERS*.**

This book wouldn't exist without you, and I am deeply honored to know the many ways *The Simple Path to Wealth* helped you on your journey. Your stories here will inform, encourage and guide those who follow. You are very much appreciated!

JL COLLINS

Uncle Mike—Pacific Northwest, USA

Paul M.—Cologne, USA

George Choy—Tenterden, UK

Tiffany S.—Vermont, USA

J. Gonzalez—Washington, USA

Eric Reinholdt—Mount Desert Island, Maine, USA

Penny Price—Minnesota, USA

Outoftheboxtraveler—Canada

Gregory Edward Brenner—Houston, Texas, USA

Derek Singer—UK

Travis Daigle—USA

Michael D. Sutherlin—Madison, Wisconsin, USA

GrowingInFire1—Fishers, Indiana, USA

Anthony—Olathe, Kansas, USA

Jennifer C—Chicago, Illinois, USA

Steven—Waconia, Minnesota, USA

Andrew—Montana, USA

Joe Olson—Seattle, Washington, USA

Jen—Portland, Oregon, USA

Mark E—Mountain View, California, USA

CL Robinson—North Carolina, USA

Froogal Stoodent—Ohio, USA

Tina Plumley—Meridian, Idaho, USA

Michael He—Los Angeles, California, USA

Joana and Tony Carola (MeetCarolas)— Portugal

Braydon and Laura Larson—Kingman, Arizona, USA

Bruno Bontempi—Italy

Nomadicc—Mexico

John and Sara Grafton—Dayton, Ohio, USA

JSD (Just Some Dude)—USA

Laura Rojo-Eddy—Texas, USA

Mrs. Dink of Dinks on a Bus— Vermont, USA

Mark—Madison, Wisconsin, USA

CW—Chattanooga, Tennessee, USA

Lisa Schader—California, USA

ryquist—Minnesota, USA

Christina Connally Honkonen— Knoxville, USA

Brian Griesbach—Spanaway, Washington, USA

David W Bian—San Jose, California, USA

Liz, a professional married mother of two—Texas, outside a major metro area, USA

Jason—Austin, Texas, USA

Justin Hall—Arlington, Virginia, USA

Brian—Pennsylvania, USA

Nathan McBride—Utah, USA

Greg Windsor—Christchurch, New Zealand

Jason Martin—Maricopa, USA

Ben Shearon—Sendai, Japan

Rachel Hernandez—Texas, USA

Jen Hsin Chan—Taiwan

Kingsley Ezenwa—Calabar, Nigeria

Andy Lyon—England/UAE

MB (myFIcapsule)—Minnesota, USA

Swarnadip Chatterjee—Kolkata, India

Matt—USA

Alex—Sydney, Australia

Recent retiree—USA

Ryan J—New Jersey, USA

Danny—New York, USA

Laura C—London, UK

Chad, Florem and Triplets— California, USA

Mr. Newfarmer—Austria

William R—Minnesota, USA

Diandra & Brad—Wisconsin, USA

Hemani & Tanuj—London, UK

Roman Koshovskyi—Lviv region, Ukraine

Artem Voronov—Naberezhnye Chelny, Tatarstan, Russia

Edward Kim—Connecticut, USA

Tom—USA

Tom Benson—Houston, Texas, USA

Todd Havens—Los Angeles, California, USA

Tucker—Ottawa, Ontario, Canada

Teanna Keith—Bakersfield, California, USA

Florence Poirel—Thalwil, Switzerland

Paddy Tsigane—Montreal, Quebec, Canada

Christopher Johnson—North Salt Lake, USA

Lisa from Baltimore—Baltimore, Maryland, USA

Tim De Prijcker—Antwerp, Belgium

Ata Atanasov—North Bethesda, Maryland, USA

Anthony St. Clair—USA

Scott and Cindy—Los Angeles, California, USA

Michael Quan—San Diego, California, USA

Jeff—Leidschendam, Netherlands

Woke Retiree—Singapore

KDale—Brandywine Valley, Pennsylvania, USA

Taylor Larimore—USA

Lejero—Bavaria, Germany

Matt Allan—Helsinki, Finland

Aileen P. Kelly—Portsmouth, New Hampshire, USA

Alex—Germany

Anonymous—South Carolina, USA

A Purple Life—USA

BKS—Florida, USA

Cari Coff—Michigan, USA

Dave—UK

Gjef2871—Sydney, Australia

G10M—USA

Kris Crichton—Denver, Colorado, USA

Mahmoud Dahy—Atlanta,
  Georgia, USA

Rodion Mark—New York, USA

Samuel—Miami, Florida, USA

Toni Vitali—Gothenburg, Sweden

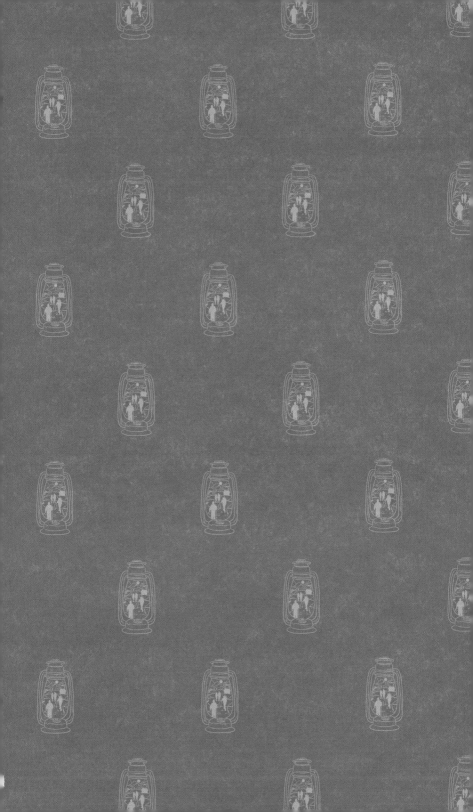

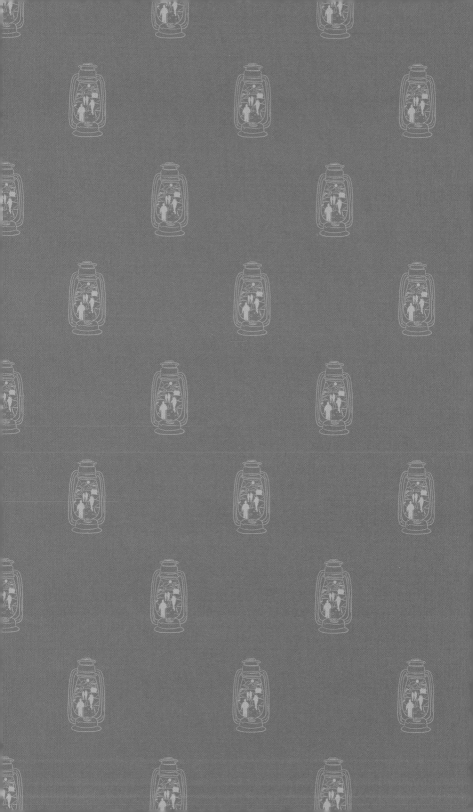